THE NEW CLIMATE ACTIVIS

NGO Authority and Participation in Climate Change Governance

At the 2019 UN Climate Change Conference, activists and delegates for groups representing Indigenous, youth, women's, and workers' rights were among those marching through the halls chanting "Climate Justice, People Power." In *The New Climate Activism*, Jen Iris Allan looks at why and how these social activists came to participate in climate change governance while others, such as those working on human rights and health, remain on the outside of climate activism.

Through case studies of women's rights, labour, alterglobalization, health, and human rights activism, Allan shows that some activists sought and successfully gained recognition as part of climate change governance, while others remained marginalized. While concepts key to some social activists, including gender mainstreaming, just transition, and climate justice are common terms, human rights and health remain fringe issues in climate change governance. *The New Climate Activism* explores why and how these activists brought their issues to climate change, and why some succeeded while others did not.

JEN IRIS ALLAN is a lecturer in the School of Law and Politics at Cardiff University.

The New Climate Activism

NGO Authority and Participation in Climate Change Governance

JEN IRIS ALLAN

UNIVERSITY OF TORONTO PRESS
Toronto Buffalo London

ISBN 978-1-4875-0838-8 (cloth)   ISBN 978-1-4875-3813-2 (EPUB)
ISBN 978-1-4875-2584-2 (paper)   ISBN 978-1-4875-3812-5 (PDF)

Library and Archives Canada Cataloguing in Publication

Title: The new climate activism : NGO authority and participation in climate
    change governance / Jen Iris Allan.
Names: Allan, Jen Iris, author.
Description: Includes bibliographical references and index.
Identifiers: Canadiana (print) 20200308386 | Canadiana (ebook) 20200308440 |
    ISBN 9781487525842 (softcover) | ISBN 9781487508388 (hardcover) |
    ISBN 9781487538132 (EPUB) | ISBN 9781487538125 (PDF)
Subjects: LCSH: Environmental policy – Citizen participation. |
    LCSH: Environmental justice. | LCSH: Environmentalism. |
    LCSH: Environmentalists.
Classification: LCC GE220 .A45 2020 | DDC 363.7/0525 – dc23

This book has been published with the help of a grant from the Federation
for the Humanities and Social Sciences, through the Awards to Scholarly
Publications Program, using funds provided by the Social Sciences and
Humanities Research Council of Canada.

University of Toronto Press acknowledges the financial assistance to its
publishing program of the Canada Council for the Arts and the Ontario Arts
Council, an agency of the Government of Ontario.

Canada Council   Conseil des Arts
for the Arts   du Canada

ONTARIO ARTS COUNCIL
CONSEIL DES ARTS DE L'ONTARIO
an Ontario government agency
un organisme du gouvernement de l'Ontario

Funded by the   Financé par le
Government   gouvernement
of Canada   du Canada

Canadä

Contents

Preface

This book is about the experiences of activists who brought social issues to global climate governance. Climate change was once viewed as an environmental issue with economic implications. This view of course still holds, and arguably still forms much of the political obstacles to climate action. But now climate change is also discussed as a bedrock problem that underlies our political, economic, and social orders. It's a gender, justice, rights, and intergenerational problem. The Pope has strong views. Grandmothers have been recently arrested for civil disobedience. Wide swaths of society see themselves as connected to – and impacted by – climate change. This mobilization has its roots in the work of activists working in the mid-2000s who first connected labour, gender, justice, rights, and other social issues to climate change.

As this book shows, it was not an easy process. Many potential social activists never participated in climate governance. Others attempted but were unable to gain a recognition in climate governance forums. New climate activists devoted considerable resources to learning about climate change, documenting links, and navigating the institutional and social terrain of UN climate meetings. Those embedded in climate change governance were not always welcoming to the newcomers. The successful new climate activists, I suggest, tended to be motivated by the need for a new issue in which to forward their claims. Other areas of global governance, notably trade, had reached a stalemate when many new climate activists pivoted toward climate change. That motivation was not enough. To successfully multiply their participation in a new area of global governance, activists needed to unite their group behind a new climate-friendly frame, find allies in climate governance, and leverage climate institutions to their benefit.

This book stems from a doctoral dissertation researched and written before the youth climate movement or Extinction Rebellion sharpened the attack on world leaders and corporations that are still slow to act in the face of the climate emergency. The roots of these movements – and their claims that climate change threatens the fabric and future of society – can be traced to these earlier new climate activists. This book was inspired by experiences at UN climate change conferences, where the climate movement had fractured into dozens of segments, each representing its own issue. Instead of statements about targets and timelines, emissions scenarios and impacts, I heard about the gendered, justice, and rights implications of climate change (a list that has continued to expand to include the rights of disabled peoples, LGBT communities, and others). Some of these new climate activists openly questioned the UN process and who it really served, raising important, although uncomfortable, questions about the future of climate change action. It is my hope that understanding the early efforts of new climate activists can help us engage in the much-needed social dialogue to achieve a sustainable, inclusive future.

I am grateful for the many institutions and individuals who supported me in this project. I remain indebted to the guidance and support of my committee members at the University of British Columbia: Peter Dauvergne, Katharina Coleman and Lisa Sundstrom. Funding from the Social Sciences and Humanities Research Grant facilitated the extensive fieldwork necessary for this book. The *Earth Negotiations Bulletin* team facilitated my participation in global environmental negotiations since 2011. Beyond such material support, my *ENB* teammates are also a remarkable group of environmental thinkers and doers that greatly enriched and challenged my understanding of global environmental governance.

This work also became stronger through feedback at the International Studies Association meetings and UBC colloquia. I am grateful to the many interlocutors that enhanced my work: Kate O'Neill, Craig Johnson, Jennifer Hadden, Matthew Hoffmann, Steven Bernstein, Tom Hale, Kate Neville, Yana Gorokhovskaia, Andrea Nuesser, Jon Gamu, Justin Alger, Charlie Roger, David Moscrop, Daniel Westlake, Deb Farias, Kate Harris, Beate Antonich, Elena Kosolapova, Mari Luomi, Rishikesh Ram Bhandary, Anna Schulz, Kati Kuvolesi, Kiara Worth, Katie Brown, Natalie Jones, Anju Sharma, Jessica Templeton, Melanie Ashton, Tallash Kantai, and Pia Kohler. Life does not stop during a PhD. It is difficult to envision how this project could have unfolded without my family's support, particularly my parents, Jean and Ralph Allan. Thank you for the encouragement to finish "my paper" and, with Russ, Sandy, Lonny, Shannon, Danny, Shelly, Yvonne, and Angie, the many nights of laughter under Northern BC's stars.

Acronyms

CJA	Climate Justice Action
CJN!	Climate Justice Now!
ETUC	European Trade Union Confederation
GCDCJ	Global Campaign to Demand Climate Justice
GCHA	Global Climate and Health Alliance
GGCA	Global Gender and Climate Alliance
IFMSA	International Federation of Medical Students Associations
ITUC	International Trade Union Confederation
IUCN	International Union for the Conservation of Nature
NDCs	nationally determined contributions
NGO	non-governmental organization
REDD+	reducing emissions from deforestation and degradation and the role of conservation, sustainable forest management, and enhancement of forest carbon stocks in developing countries
UNDP	UN Development Programme
UNEP	UN Environment Programme
UNFCCC	UN Framework Convention on Climate Change
WEDO	Women's Environment and Development Organization
WHO	World Health Organization
WTO	World Trade Organization
WWF	World Wildlife Federation

THE NEW CLIMATE ACTIVISM

NGO Authority and Participation in Climate Change Governance

1 Introduction

Climate change has a human face – a farmer facing worsening droughts, a mother walking farther for water, a worker retraining for a new job, to name a few. Connections between social issues and climate change are more common in climate discourse. The idea that a stable climate undergirds our economies and societies has largely achieved that elusive "taken for granted" quality. But ideas come from somewhere. The notion that climate change is a social issue is partly owed to the efforts of some rather unlikely actors.

Social movements and activists have reframed climate change as a social issue. Climate change was long conceived as an economic and environmental issue, a problem with effects that lay far in the future (Gupta, 2014). By 2009, at the UN Climate Change Conference in Copenhagen, the streets had filled with activists marching to demand action on climate change and on many other social issues including labour, Indigenous rights, faith, gender, youth, and global justice. Marches continued to grow, and civil disobedience entered the activists' toolkit, inspired by global justice activists who had been involved in the Battle in Seattle around the World Trade Organization meeting of 1999 (Hadden, 2015). As the push for climate action continued, joint letters signed by labour, environmental, development, and faith groups urged action. Veterans' associations and "queers for climate" joined climate marches in 2014 in New York, the latter explaining that "our communities faced near extinction throughout the early HIV/AIDS crisis. Today we are all facing the grave threat of an unstable climate" (Lowder, 2014). Greta Thunberg mobilized half a million people in the streets of Madrid in 2019, joined by angry protests by Indigenous rights, youth, and other activists inside the UN climate meeting's venue.

The Paris Agreement is the first environmental treaty to recognize human rights, as well as other social issues, and in doing so has broadened and solidified our understanding of climate change as a social concern. Negotiators debate and discuss gender and labour issues as part of standing programs within the central body for global climate change governance, the UN Framework Convention on Climate Change (UNFCCC). In the Local Communities and Indigenous Peoples' Platform, launched in 2015, Indigenous peoples and states now participate as equals. Years of campaigning by a wide cross-section of non-governmental organizations (NGOs) and social movements has contributed to changing minds and legal outcomes. This feat is particularly impressive considering most of these NGOs had not participated in a UN climate change meeting until the mid-2000s.

Though they started out lacking experience or allies in climate change governance and expertise on climate change, these social NGOs started to advance their issues and their authority in that context. Experience and expertise on a given issue are cornerstones of NGOs' authority, which they use to influence global governance (Avant, Finnemore, & Sell 2010; Stroup & Wong, 2017). But authority is a social relationship. Authority only works – that is, induces deference – if it is recognized (Avant, Finnemore, & Sell 2010). The audience matters. As newcomers to climate change, social NGOs faced a dilemma: How could their authority "travel" from their usual audiences into a wholly new context? Would they and their claims be recognized?

This book is about this new climate activism and social NGOs' search for recognition. The new climate activists linked social issues to climate change. That activism is more fragmented than ever before, comprising a wide range of voice and issues. As movements and NGOs new to climate politics started making claims that social issues mattered, civil society's voice on climate change diversified. Starting as outsiders, these social NGOs took on the climate cause, an issue on which they lacked expertise, experience, and recognition of their claims and authority. As I will show, these activists struggled and strategized to establish their authority amid a group that was sceptical of the merits of adding social issues to the climate agenda and reluctant to recognize the new activists as legitimate participants. Only some of the new climate activists succeeded in gaining such recognition; others remained outsiders. While justice and Indigenous rights groups protested in 2019, joined by many others, prominent civil society leaders walked past those holding banners that read "war causes climate change." Issues such as peace but also health and human rights have seen few activists in those arenas take up the climate cause. This book follows how some climate activists succeeded in inserting their issues, and their participation, into the arena of climate change governance. It also suggests why some activists and their issues remain marginalized.

An influx of new NGOs and movements is not unique to climate change. Indeed, for reasons discussed later in this introduction, climate change is only one among a number of other governance forums that confronted the arrival of many unlikely NGOs. Ten years before the Copenhagen climate march, a similarly diverse group, including "turtles and teamsters" (i.e., environmental NGOs and unions) had staged protests during the World Trade Organization (WTO) meetings in Seattle. NGOs were largely absent during the Uruguay Round of WTO negotiations. The subsequent Doha Round focused on development and trade issues and experienced a surge of NGO participation. These diverse groups, raising health, development, and environmental issues, all lobbied the WTO to minimize the adverse effects of trade on developing countries (Casula Vifell, 2010; Newell 2006, p. 117). Environmental NGOs campaigned for green development aid, targeting development banks as early as the 1980s. They worked to reduce the number of large-scale, environmentally destructive projects supported by the World Bank and other multilateral development banks (Keck & Sikkink, 1998; Khagram, Riker, & Sikkink, 2005).

NGOs spread their ideas to other forums besides trade and development. Women's rights became human rights after a concerted campaign by women's rights advocates to reframe violence against women using a human rights discourse and methodology (Keck & Sikkink, 1998; Joachim, 2007; Brown Thompson, 2002). Religious organizations, trade unions, and NGOs working on behalf of refugees and youth have been actively promoting their issues in the context of human rights (Gaer, 1995). The push by advocates to globally recognize the right to a healthy environment constitutes for Boyd (2011) a revolution in human rights discourse as much as a movement. To advance their issues, NGOs have become more mobile, nimbly crossing the traditional boundaries and issues of global governance.

It is clear, but underexplored, that NGOs and social movements can be migratory actors, traversing areas of global governance to lobby for their core areas of interest in various contexts. International regimes, often viewed as the "rules, norms, principles, and decision-making procedures around which actors' expectations converge in a given issue area" (Krasner, 1983, p. 4), are inward-looking, concerned with governing a given issue. International negotiations are focal points for contention among state, business, and civil society actors (Khagram, Riker, & Sikkink, 2002 Tarrow, 2001). Such negotiations become important political sites where actors communicate their ideas and assumptions about global governance and where shared ideas about standards of governance are constructed (Bäckstrand & Lövbrand, 2016). These forums become key targets for NGOs seeking to participate in and influence the politics of a new regime.

Recently, the climate change regime has been a prime target for NGOs and international organizations seeking to advance their issues and contribute to global efforts to address the climate crisis. As international organizations and civil society actors that traditionally have not worked on climate change continue to jump on the "climate bandwagon," there has been a proliferation of ways to view the climate crisis. This climate bandwagoning occurs as actors "discursively re-fram[e] issues in a way that foregrounds the climate benefits of the original/source issue," and, as Jinnah (2011, pp. 3–4) explains, it "involves the purposeful expansion of regime mission to include new climate-oriented goals that linking agents believe will further their own agendas, regardless of whether such linkages detract from the common good." Others have sought to explain the motivations of international organizations (Hall, 2015; Jinnah, 2011; 2014), and some have documented the fragmentation of the civil society presence (Muñoz Cabre, 2011; Orr, 2007; Unmüßig, 2011). Regarding civil society, however, the motivations have been left unexplored despite the considerable influx of religious groups, Indigenous peoples' advocates, labour unions, development NGOs, global justice activists, and many others into the climate change regime's central body, the UNFCCC.

The influx of these new climate activists has been significant: they are arriving in numbers sometimes nearly as high as those of their environmentalist counterparts – high enough to, at times, fracture the civil society presence. Figure 1.1 depicts NGO participation in UNFCCC meetings from 1995, when the first UNFCCC meeting was held, to 2015, when the Paris Agreement was adopted. In that figure, NGOs are categorized into broad groups.[1] The participation of social NGOs stands out: starting in 2007, their participation increased, at times rivalling that of the traditionally dominant environmental and business organizations. Social NGOs brought a range of social issues to climate change: labour, gender, Indigenous rights, justice, and intergenerational justice, among others. The civil society presence fragmented into a multitude of voices representing a wider range of issues.

Forum Multiplying

These new climate activists did not abandon their traditional causes or regimes; rather, they expanded their presence into additional forums to advance their causes. I call this strategy "forum multiplying." By this I mean the sustained mobilization of a group of NGOs in a new

Figure 1.1 NGO participation in the UNFCCC

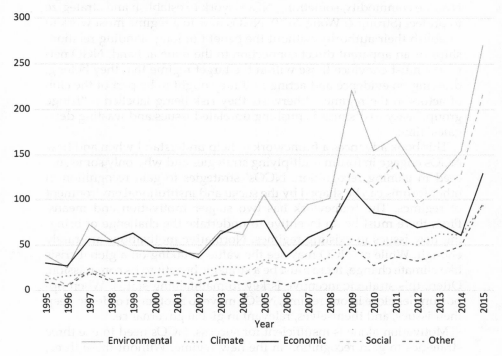

——— Environmental   ····· Climate   ——— Economic   - - - Social   - - - - Other

regime, facilitated by a discursive frame that links the NGO network's traditional issue to the issue governed by another forum. This strategy has become visible in global governance, with important implications for global governance, yet it remains unexplored.

Forum multiplying is neither simple nor cost-free. If NGOs want to acquire any degree of political leverage, they must do more than show up at an international negotiation. And it seems that influence is their aim. In a survey of civil society actors at the WTO and the UNFCCC, Hanegraaff (2015) found that those actors' principal motivation was to influence the negotiations. Influence requires recognition in the social environment integral to regimes (Levy, Young, & Zurn, 1995; Ruggie, 1993). In the climate change regime, often characterized by a "respectable" politics between states and NGOs (Gough & Shackley, 2001), many environmental NGOs draw upon their expertise – a valuable resource for those states that lack information (Chasek, 2001; Raustiala, 1997) – to become authorities. Others claim to represent a distinct public interest that is directly applicable to the issues under negotiation, thus situating themselves as authoritative members at the centre of world civic politics (Wapner, 1996). Even in their "home" regimes, authority is a rare commodity, something NGOs work to establish and strategize to protect (Stroup & Wong 2017). NGOs new to a regime must work to establish their authority without the benefit of long-standing relationships or an apparent direct connection to the issue at hand. NGO networks must convince those within the target regime that they belong, drawing on evidence and acting as if they ought to be part of the club of actors in the regime. Otherwise, they risk being labelled a "fringe group," easy to dismiss as pushing unrelated issues and wasting delegates' time.

This book advances a framework to help understand when and how NGOs engage in forum multiplying strategies and why only some succeed in gaining recognition. NGOs' strategies to gain recognition in other forums can be shaped by the social and institutional environment of regimes. The framework has two stages: motivation and means. First, there must be an incentive to undertake the challenge of bringing new issues to existing regimes. Normative motivations are rarely enough. While an NGO may see the value in taking on a global crisis like climate change, there must be a strategic benefit to its core mission. Often, this strategic incentive is key to maintaining status. When opportunities close in one regime, NGOs move to another in order to keep their issues, and themselves, relevant in global governance.

Motivation alone is insufficient for success. NGOs need to use three strategies to gain recognition in the new regime. Without these three, they may be marginalized, labelled as "fringe groups" raising niche, unrelated issues. First, NGOs working on similar issues need to rally around a discursive frame that links their issue to the issue governed by the target regime. Core members of the network, those with the ability to set or vet the agenda (Carpenter, 2011; 2014), are key to bringing unity among the group and defining the frame.

Second, incoming NGOs need allies in the target regime. These allies provide introductions and help orient newcomers to the social and institutional complexities of the regime. Less tangibly, allies can lend their authority, essentially saying "they're with me, therefore one of us." The allies are already known to the NGOs and are already embedded in the target regime. They are brokers, straddling both worlds, and are crucial to the success of NGOs' forum-multiplying efforts. Without brokers, these efforts fail.

The need for brokers becomes clear with regard to the third strategy, leveraging institutions. Institutions, here viewed as specific rules or norms, can shape actors' preferences and behaviour, facilitate alliances, and generate unintended outcomes (Hall & Taylor, 1996;

Thelen & Steinmo, 1992). The discursive link must be specific, and focused on a specific institution in the target regime. Such "discursive hooks" helps negotiators understand how the new issue is connected to their work and locate the new issue within the negotiations (Allan, 2018). General frames that are only broadly linked to the issue are less successful in the siloed world of global negotiations, where complex issues are broken into discrete negotiation settings. Rules related to process are equally important. Embracing the rules that govern how observers ought to behave can help NGOs gain visibility and access to delegates.

Rallying around a frame, finding allies, and leveraging institutions are difficult tasks for activists working in a foreign setting. A common thread running through all the cases explored in this book is the initial, steep learning curve. Each regime has its own rules and its own informal practices shaping how participants interact. Learning these formal and informal rules is necessary for activists who hope to truly be part of the social circle of governors in the regime.

What does it mean to join a regime? How do we know forum multiplying, and recognition, when we see it? At a minimum, one must accede to the shared rules, norms, principles, and decision-making procedures the regime's actors expect. An individual can do that in the privacy of their home, yet we do not necessarily consider that individual part of a regime. Generally, states join a regime when they sign a treaty. We have no equivalent metric to determine when a non-state actor is part of a regime. Non-state actors do not sign treaties or otherwise formally accede to multilateral law. Three aspects of a state's ascension to a treaty stand out as transferable to non-state actors: it is a public act, particularly speaking to others working toward the shared cause; it commits the actors to work with or leverage the institutions of the regime for change toward that shared goal; and it is recognized and accepted by those within the regime.

I suggest that these three aspects could signal when a non-state actor has joined a regime, and that together they serve as a qualitative measure of whether a non-state actor has successfully engaged in forum multiplying. Non-state actors broadly include international organizations, NGOs, private sector groups, and social movements. They must undertake a public discursive act linking their work to the issue area of the target regime, and that act must move beyond the regular circles of the actor to address governors within that regime. Simply issuing a press release, or giving a speech, declaring that a given issue is important, is a low bar. For example, James Orbinski of Médecins Sans Frontières stated to the Canadian Medical Association's General Council that climate change is a significant public health issue (Picard,

2016), yet the organization has no formal position on the issue and has never attended a UNFCCC meeting.[2] The act was public, but it was directed internally – toward other medical professionals – rather than toward climate change governors. A public discursive act is insufficient without engagement with actors in the target regime.

Second, the public act must include some commitment to the shared goals or institutions to which governors within the regime already ascribe. As chapter 2 points out, non-state actors must link their issue to the regime's institutions. Their discursive act is a frame that links these issues, often highlighting the issue of the target regime (Jinnah, 2011). Finding institutional entry points can help a non-state actor demonstrate that their issue can help address the problems the target regime is designed to govern. Demonstrating this connection to the regime's work helps position the non-state actor as a potential governor of the target regime – as belonging within the regime and worthy of participating in governance.

The final aspect of joining a regime is recognition, which is particularly difficult for non-state actors. Recognition involves the identification and acceptance of a given actor as a global governor for an issue area. Others recognize the authority of that actor and tacitly agree to abide by that authority. Recognition is part of states' sovereignty. Other states and non-state actors view states as primary actors in global governance, deferring to their authority to govern domestically and speak on behalf of their citizens internationally. Recognition, which for states is implicit, for non-state actors often becomes an explicit need. It is the difference between being a fringe actor and a new climate activist.

Because non-state actors' authority is so closely tied to the issue that they represent, recognizing a non-state actor as a member of a group of governors in a regime involves recognizing their issue as a legitimate inclusion in the regime. NGOs rest their authority on their ability to showcase their expertise and make principled claims for a cause (Avant, Finnemore, & Sell, 2010). NGOs cannot divorce themselves from their issue; it is the foundation of their authority. If the incoming NGO is to gain recognition, governors within the regime need to see the NGO's issues as connected with those of the regime. This underscores the need for NGOs undertaking forum-multiplying strategies to construct a convincing discursive frame connecting their issue as a cause, consequence, or potential solution to the regime's issue (more on this in chapter 2). Proponents cannot control whether a frame resonates, but they can take actions to increase the likelihood of its, and their, recognition. The empirical chapters in this book show the three strategies actors use to increase the likelihood they will be recognized:

leveraging institutions, finding allies, and, perhaps most importantly, constructing a frame that highlights their issue as a climate issue.

At its core, forum multiplying is about advancing NGOs' issues and, in turn, the NGOs' relevance and authority in global governance. To sustain the commitment, NGO networks continue their efforts to mobilize, bringing others to their cause in the context of their adopted governance area. In the case of climate change, forum-multiplying strategies ultimately led to the sustained rise in social NGOs and the diversification of the civil society presence at the UNFCCC.

Contributions

Questions of where and when NGOs seek to participate are theoretically interesting, for we lack an explanation of NGOs' migratory patterns across global governance forums. This book is meant to fill this broad gap in the literature by pursuing four core contributions to our current understanding of NGO politics and the politics characterizing sets of overlapping rules and norms of global governance, known as regime complexes (Orsini, Morin, & Young, 2013; Raustiala & Victor, 2004).

First, this book documents and explores forum multiplying, an evident yet untheorized strategy of international NGOs and social movements. This will contribute to our understanding of NGOs' *participation* in global governance (whereas scholarship tends to look at their *influence*). Numerous studies have brought to light NGO influence on global environmental outcomes, for issues including climate change (Betsill, 2002, 2008; Böhmelt, Koubi, & Bernauer, 2014; Ciplet, 2014; Downie, 2014; Lisowski, 2005), biosafety (Arts & Mack, 2003; Burgiel, 2008), forests (Humphreys, 2004; 2008), whaling (Andresen & Skodvin, 2008; Sakaguchi, 2013), and desertification (Corell, 2008). Outside the environmental sphere, human rights NGOs have proven adept at using tactics such as shaming to influence state behaviour (Murdie & Peksen, 2014; Murdie & Urpelainen, 2014).

Perhaps surprisingly, most scholarship on NGO participation is from the point of view of international organizations. Studying international organizations' openness to transnational actors across issues over a sixty-year period, Tallberg et al. (2013) argue that international organizations encourage NGO participation partly to strategically heighten their own legitimacy. Widening NGOs' participation can strengthen international organizations' agenda-setting and research activities as well as contribute to implementation (Bernauer & Gampfer, 2013; Hale, 2016; Steffek, 2010). There is growing understanding of international organizations' demands for NGO participation and the implications of increased openness (Jönsson & Tallberg, 2010).

This book is about the supply of NGOs as new participants; it demonstrates the political dynamics that drive NGOs' participation in a regime. Participation is a necessary precursor to influence. Answering the question "Who participates?" can provide first clues about who may influence global governance and the potential issue linkages that may emerge. By asking who participates, we can better understand NGOs' demands and how their ideas spread. In turn, we can develop a fuller picture of the dynamics of NGOs' contributions to accountability and legitimacy in global governance (Nasiritousi, Hjerpe, & Bäckstrand, 2015). Yet we lack an account of why the roster of participants expands or contracts, and why issues cross-fertilize among global governance forums.

Second, this book contributes to our understanding of the context-specific nature of authority, particularly the dynamics of establishing authority in new contexts. Authority is a social relationship deeply embedded in the context in which actors interact (Avant, Finnemore, & Sell, 2010, p. 7). NGOs seeking to use their authority must find recognition in their new social context. While Avant, Finnemore, and Sell (2010) consider the sources of authority and Stroup and Wong (2017) explore the limitations and consequences of having authority, this book explores how non-state actors strategize to become recognized as authorities. Recognition is an important precursor to authority. To be recognized as a member of the social group governing an issue, one must first be viewed as an authority on that issue. NGOs strategize to increase their likelihood of admittance, or recognition in the new social context. The politics of recognition are at the core of NGO forum-multiplying strategies. NGO networks strategize ways to use rules, relationships, and resources to improve their chances of recognition and, in turn, authority and influence in the new regime. Without authority, an NGO network cannot advance its cause in the new context. That new context is replete with institutions, forums, and regimes within which actors interact.

The third contribution this book makes is to add non-state actors to the emerging literature on regime complexes. Regime complexes are sets of interrelated, legally equal regimes with overlapping mandates and memberships (Raustiala & Victor, 2004; Keohane & Victor, 2011). Thus far, our understanding of how international actors move between international regimes is limited to accounts of states' strategies such as forum shopping (Busch, 2007; Hafner-Burton, 2009; Raustiala & Victor, 2004) or forum shifting (Helfer, 2004), as influenced by various attributes of the organization (Coleman, 2013) in the "chessboard politics" of regime complexes (Alter & Meunier, 2009). But this focus on public authority has come at the expense of how private actors operate within these complexes (Green, 2013).

Where the literature on regime complexes does acknowledge non-state actors, they are often viewed as cooperative actors, either linking regimes or otherwise seeking to facilitate cooperation in pursuit of their normative agendas or institutional mandates (Gómez-Mera, 2015; Orsini, 2013). In terms of non-state actors' participation across regimes, there are conflicting expectations. Multiplying the number of organizations could increase the number of opportunities for a non-state actor to influence policy (Alter & Meunier, 2009). That said, non-state actors may be less able to front the costs of participating in multiple forums (Drezner, 2009).

When non-state actors are neglected, important global governors are overlooked. The large literature on the many routes NGOs use to gain influence demonstrates the ability of non-state actors to engage in governance and shape policy outcomes. When regime complexity theory ignores those that hold power in global governance, it potentially underestimates some key sources of production, reproduction, or change in regime complexes. Some argue that states' interests and satisfaction with governance alone may drive change (Colgan, Keohane, & Van de Graaf, 2012). Non-state actors can use their influence to create ties between regimes, thus building or expanding regime complexes. In short, if we expect that non-state actors can influence one regime, we should anticipate that they can leverage the connections among regimes to exert a measure of influence in a regime complex. NGOs can influence specific rules. There is no reason to believe they cannot also influence the rules and norms shared among regimes in the complex. Or, by influencing one regime, NGOs could create new connections among regimes, thus contributing to regime complex expansion. NGOs' participation across regimes is as valid a route of inquiry as forum shopping and the shifting patterns of states, both of which have been extensively analysed by scholars.

The fourth contribution of this book is to contextualize our view of NGO networks by treating them as heterogeneous groups of actors confronted with unequal power relations. Scholarship tends to view NGO groups and transnational advocacy networks as was first proposed by Keck & Sikkink (1998) – that is, as a dense network of reciprocal relationships among actors. A growing body of work shows that some actors within the network matter more than others and that hierarchies exist even among the most principled actors in global governance. Carpenter (2007; 2010; 2014) argues that actors with many connections to other actors in the network can set, vet, or block the network's agenda. The number of ties confers advantages to some, as these "gatekeepers" can use their structural advantages to shape the advocacy agenda of the entire group (Carpenter, 2007; 2014). Furthermore, participation in multiple forums can help entrench the gatekeeper's centrality within the network (Orsini, 2013). Negotiations among individuals and organizations within a network can shape how the movement shapes its core demands and decides on its tactics (Hadden, 2015).

This book shares a view of NGO networks as heterogeneous entities, rife with internal politics. NGOs vary according to the strategies they adopt and their underlying views: some seek to work with states, others to fight against them; some would rather foster incremental change, others set out to upend the status quo. This sort of inter-NGO politics is largely discounted when the attention focuses on one cluster of NGOs working on a similar issue. Overstating the homogeneity of NGOs active in environmental regimes sacrifices an understanding of how the interplay among these networks, each striving to advance its own issues, may influence global governance outcomes.

The Book's Approach

This book adopts the point of view of the new climate activists and leverages literatures from various areas of international relations and comparative politics. Often, scholars privilege the structures of global governance over the agents that design, build, and link these structures (Dellas, Pattberg, & Betsill, 2011; Selin & VanDeveer, 2003). Here, I reverse the narrative, placing NGOs and the connections they form, use, and renegotiate at the heart of the investigation. Leveraging the insights made possible by comparing across social movements (see O'Neill, 2012) facilitates the contributions noted above and helps us understand how dynamics among NGOs can influence mobility across regimes and perhaps, in turn, global governance outcomes. Here, I explain some of the key choices made in conducting research using this agent-centred approach, fundamental definitions, and implications of these choices and definitions for the findings. I then briefly outline the approach to conducting the research.

Why Climate?

In this book, I explore NGO networks' efforts to join the climate change regime. There are many other documented cases of NGO networks targeting other regimes, including trade, human rights, and development.

In some ways, climate change is illustrative of the experiences in these other regimes, but as explored below, climate change may be a particularly tough case due to the timing of new climate activists' arrival.

Just as in the trade and human rights regimes, the new climate activists represent many different issues and arrived independently of one another, without coordinating their efforts. The diversity of new climate activists provides a valuable opportunity to study forum multiplying. The participation of these non-climate and non-environmental NGOs started at the same time. Muñoz Cabre (2011) documents NGOs' "climate bandwagoning," identifying twenty-two categories of NGOs accredited – that is, seeking permission to attend – since the first Conference of the Parties (COP 1) in 1995. My original database of NGO participation in UNFCCC meetings – which NGOs have attended, not just registered, over twenty years – further underscores the diversification of civil society engaged in climate change. The growth in social NGOs fragmented climate activism – a development driven mainly by groups representing gender, labour, justice, Indigenous rights, development, and youth.

Other NGOs that also work on social issues, however, did not participate. Muñoz Cabre (2011) suggests that human rights NGOs "woke up late" to climate change; my data, by contrast, show that they did the paperwork to become accredited but rarely actually attended climate meetings. Hanegraaf et al. (2019) use a smaller database to suggest that many NGOs showed up to one meeting only; my database indicates that this is perhaps a small overstatement – that said, several NGOs only attended a few times. For example, Amnesty International attended two meetings, in 2009 and 2015, for reasons explored in chapter 7. The climate change regime offers the opportunity to explore and compare how several different networks of NGOs engaged in forum-multiplying strategies to the same target regime.

As with other instances of forum multiplying, climate change was high on the international agenda when new NGOs began participating. The trade regime at the beginning of the Doha Round on development drew environmental and other NGOs (Casula Vifell, 2010). The climate change regime in the late 2000s attracted considerable attention. UN Secretary General Ban Ki-moon made climate change a signature issue for his office in 2007, launching the Caring for Climate Initiative, and later hosting summits, including in the months before the UN climate conference that adopted the Paris Agreement. New NGOs moved toward regimes governing salient issues. While further work is required to determine whether this is a consistent trend, it does seem indicative of how NGOs may select a given regime.

At the time that NGOs rapidly increased their numbers, in 2008 and 2009, the climate change regime was engaged in a new round of negotiations that were expected to strike a new legally binding agreement in 2009. This mirrors the experience of the WTO: several new NGOs joined the regime when the Doha Round on development talks launched. Negotiations for new treaties or other types of agreements are an opportune time for NGOs to advance their interests. If they can set the agenda and manage to embed their issues in a regime's institutions, their influence and their issues can remain entrenched in the regime.

Yet the timing is not as analogous as it seems, and this represents the first reason climate change can be a relatively tough test of NGO forum multiplying. Early social NGOs moving to climate change arrived either before or just on the cusp of the new round of negotiations. They were both too early to influence the negotiations and too late to set the agenda. Many of the early new climate activists started participating between 2005 and 2007. The agenda for the new treaty was broadly discussed in 2006 and agreed in 2007. Being new, these activists lacked key information and connections to influence the discussions. While the momentum generated by high-profile negotiations helped mobilize support (as this book's empirical chapters show), many social NGOs started participating in climate change for reasons unrelated to the state of the climate change regime.

Another key area of difference is the regime's record of success. The human rights regime had a record of successful treaty adoption and expansions of rights through the various "generations" of human rights. The WTO completed the Uruguay Round successfully before embarking on the Doha Round. Yet when many of the early NGO network members expended scarce resources to participate, the climate change regime was stagnant. Grounded in the UNFCCC, the climate change regime was in a state of "arrested development" (Young, 2010) or even "collapse" (Victor, 2001; 2011), before the adoption of the Paris Agreement in 2015. Yet social NGOs started participating during the period of stagnation. They remained, even after the talks collapsed in 2009 and were not restarted until 2011.

The final difference was that there was not a "natural" connection, either institutional or scientific, between climate change and social issues when the influx of new climate activists occurred. The WTO had an explicit mandate to address agriculture and other issues with clear environmental links, yet neither the Framework Convention nor the Kyoto Protocol are equipped to address social issues. Neither mentions people, communities, populations, women, gender, or Indigenous peoples, and as a consequence, social NGOs struggled to link their issues to climate change, given how little institutional affiliation or substantive connection already existed in the UNFCCC. Climate change became a social issue, as we now understand it, in part due to the efforts of activists to reframe climate change in social terms.

Scientific understanding also cannot explain the connections between disparate issues and the involvement of NGOs across areas of global governance. For example, *The Lancet* (Costello et al., 2009; Watts et al., 2015) and the Intergovernmental Panel on Climate Change (IPCC) (IPCC, 2007a; 2007b; IPCC 2014) identified numerous ways in which climate change will threaten public health, through changing geographic patterns of vector-borne disease, worsening cardiovascular health, and rising mortality from heat-related events. According to my database of NGO participation (1992–2015), few health organizations participated. Similarly, no human rights NGOs routinely participated, and only one refugee NGO has attended the UNFCCC conferences since 2009, despite links between climate change and migration and human rights. A seemingly natural or scientifically grounded affiliation between the network's issue and climate change cannot explain the influx of NGO networks. Indeed, our understanding of the links between climate change and social justice issues may be the result of the efforts of social NGOs and social movements since the mid-2000s. What is now seen as a natural connection between climate change and social issues may have begun as a carefully constructed discursive frame designed as a means for social NGOs to enter the climate change regime.

The diversification of civil society within the climate change regime offers an opportunity to explore the dynamics within and among networks as they encounter the same sets of institutions and actors. The cases[3] are NGO networks that are traditionally devoted to social issues but also engaged in climate change activism. They became participants in the climate change regime late in the regime's development (or, in the null cases, they chose or failed to become participants at a later stage).

In essence, I "bounce" the networks off the same sets of rules and norms and examine the differing strategies and effects.[4] This strategy enables a close understanding of the approaches adopted by networks and their effects on forum-multiplying efforts. It is a strong approach to examine the agency and interplay of networks within the opportunities and constraints posed by institutions.

Controlling for several aspects of the regime can limit the inferences this study can make, which I believe to be navigable. One may argue that there is something unique about climate change that causes NGO networks to multiply into the regime. For example, networks flocked to climate change when it rose to prominence on the international agenda.[5]

Relatedly, one could argue that there are other "pull" factors attracting networks, such as a new round of negotiations. In 2007, delegates in the climate change regime agreed to the agenda for the negotiations for a new, legally binding treaty. Given that the agenda-setting stage can be particularly amenable to NGO influence (Betsill & Corell, 2008), NGOs may have sought out this opportunity.

Yet some networks were not motivated, or, if they *were* motivated, they found themselves unable to achieve recognition in the climate change regime. Given this variation, such pull factors focusing on the regime are insufficient to explain the NGO forum-multiplying patterns. While my research cannot directly dispute regime-centric claims because it lacks a comparative assessment of networks' forum-multiplying efforts vi-à-vis other regimes, it offers considerable insight into the full range of NGO forum-multiplying behaviour. As previously stated, there are many cases of NGO forum multiplying, and the phenomenon is not unique to climate change. My research aims to provide fresh insight into why the relationships among actors within networks can influence decision-making and the ability of NGO networks to multiply within other regimes.

Why NGO Networks?

Much of the scholarship considers transnational advocacy networks (for a few examples of this scholarship, see Carpenter 2007; Keck & Sikkink, 1998; Price, 2003). Transnational advocacy networks include a wide range of actors, such as NGOs, international organizations, grass-roots community organizations, and individual activists. I focus on the NGOs in these networks because they share broadly similar incentives and constraints.

The ties among actors form networks, constituting a layer between individual agency and macro-level social structures and processes (Diani & McAdam, 2003, p. 284). The links among actors can take many forms, from personal relationships to information flows, which for Keck and Sikkink (1998, p. 27) are the "most valuable currency" of advocacy networks. For Price (2003), networks are an imagined community of actors all viewing themselves as part of a shared cause. There is power conferred by relationships among actors rather than on the attributes of individual actors. Both aspects of networks – sharing a cause and information – are important ties weaving NGOs into advocacy networks.

For the study of collective behaviour, such as multiple NGOs collectively mobilizing in a new forum of global governance, networks are a more appropriate unit of analysis than individual organizations (della Porta & Tarrow, 2005, p. 240). The structure of the network – for example, whether it is highly centralized or decentralized – reflects how information flows from actor to actor. Examining networks helps elucidate who has information and who shares it with whom. A focus on the relational ties that enable some NGOs to select and mobilize in the new regime is better suited than a sole focus on the attributes of individual organizations. So this research first considers which actors in the network have structural advantages and then explores their actions in the context of the incentives and constraints brought forth by the internal dynamics within the network.

Methodological Approach

Above I outlined the general approach to studying the labour, gender, justice, health, and human rights networks seeking entry into the climate change regime. These five cases represent significant variation. While labour, gender, and justice all managed to forum-multiply, the health and human rights networks did not. This approach helps correct for the selection bias noted in scholarship on transnational advocacy networks, where work tends to focus on successful cases (Price, 2003), and on international organizations, where work tends to overestimate the participatory norm in international organizations (Tallberg et al., 2013). Each network differs in structure, size, and degree of centralization. Importantly, only those cases where brokers were present and well-connected NGOs were motivated to forum-multiply were successful. Health and human rights networks lacked such motivated "lead NGOs" and brokers. The institutional rules serving as potential entry points facilitated labour and gender and, to a lesser extent, justice, while constraining the efforts of others.

The following table outlines how aspects of the theory correlate with the successful, or unsuccessful, forum multiplying strategies of the NGO networks, prefacing the theoretical framework elaborated on in chapter 2 and in the subsequent empirical chapters. The framework underscores the importance of allies and institutional access for building a network's case for recognition. Without major NGOs in the network speaking on behalf of the cause, or a broker willing to provide introductions within the target regime, NGOs struggle to find a place in the institution's social environment. In terms of the rules, securing constituency status and linking the network's issues to the target regime's institutions are key strategies for showing that the network's claims are relevant and worth hearing.

NETWORK	Network structure	Allies	Institutional access points	Forum-multiply?
Labour	Centralized	Broker	Yes	Yes
Gender	Decentralized	Broker	Yes	Yes
Justice	Decentralized	Broker	Yes	Yes
Human rights	Centralized	None	No	No
Health	Centralized	None	No	No

What is less clear in the table is how network structure can matter. As Paterson (2019) observes, social network analysis is a useful broad brush for studying networks in global environmental governance, but it can overlook key interpersonal processes. Process tracing is a useful tool for uncovering mechanisms that may be less apparent when considering the correlations among variables alone (Brady & Collier, 2004). At first look, there seems to be little relevance to the network structure; centralized networks were both successful and unsuccessful in forum multiplying, as were decentralized networks. Yet, as the empirical chapters show, co-operation among the lead NGOs in the various groups helped overcome the divisions in the network, leading to successful forum multiplying. It is the network's overall cohesion, and the ability of central NGOs in the network to build and maintain that cohesion, that mattered. Where the lead NGOs were unable to cooperate, parts of the network advanced differing claims and competed for already scant attention in the target regime, ultimately undermining the overall effort.

To explore these cases, I engaged in participant observation in the UNFCCC negotiations, conducted interviews, and completed social network analyses. As a participant in the UNFCCC, I attended twelve of the fifteen meetings of the UNFCCC from June 2012 to December 2015 (the period of negotiations for the Paris Agreement). I participated in my capacity as a writer with the *Earth Negotiations Bulletin* for the International Institute for Sustainable Development.[6] This role provided unique access to the negotiations as well as an institutional role that was helpful for working with negotiators. I was embedded in the process. I clearly remember, thanks to detailed notes, being a newcomer to climate change negotiations: learning the informal practices and routines, as well as the norms of interaction, occasionally by inadvertently violating them. Like some new climate activists, I became socialized into the climate change regime. Working with the *Bulletin* meant developing a detailed knowledge of the rules of climate governance and witnessing how NGOs attempted to influence those rules over several years.

The seventy-two semi-structured interviews conducted with NGOs, UNFCCC Secretariat members, other international organizations' representatives, and state delegates helped me triangulate claims (see the Appendix for more information on qualitative methods). Such triangulation is particularly important when studying NGOs or social movements, because activist groups have incentives to overstate their influence and level of recognition while state representatives are reticent to admit that a non-elected interest group may have influenced their ideas (Betsill & Corell, 2008). Within the NGO community, I interviewed representatives from organizations situated in various places in the network, from those on the fringes to the powerful NGOs at the centre of the network. Within the organizations, I interviewed board members, policy officers, and other activists holding various positions within NGOs and, as a result, different views on their organization's strategy and motivations. I also conducted key informant interviews with the pivotal NGO delegates working to bring their issues to climate change in the mid-2000s. In total, I interviewed respondents from 57.1 per cent of the "new climate activist" organizations in the case study networks, (i.e., organizations that were new to climate change and that participated in the UNFCCC) in addition to traditional climate change actors and some organizations in the networks that did not participate in the UNFCCC but were identified using the social network analysis.

I chose interviews for three reasons. First, as Gamson and Meyer (1996) observe, opportunities to influence politics or mobilize a movement are shaped as much by the perceptions of actors as by the objective realities. Interviews provided a window into the views of NGO delegates as to what constituted a viable opening in the climate change regime, or closing doors in their traditional, "home" regime. Second, delegates were more likely to speak about internal rifts and negotiations within the network if they could do so in private. Such information would not be publicly available. Third, because the network itself is a form of imagined community, who is in or out of the network reflects what is in effect a political process for controlling the scope of the agenda (Schattschneider, 1960). Interviews also helped confirm the findings and explore the quality of ties among actors identified by the social network analyses.

Information flows are central to advocacy networks, and I use a quantitative social network analysis to uncover the flows of information and the overall network structure for the NGO networks (see the Appendix for a detailed explanation of social network analysis methods). The networks here are labour–climate, gender–climate, justice–climate, and health–climate. For reasons related to data availability that are outlined in the Appendix, it was not possible to map the entire network of a given case as it exists in its home regime. Instead, the social network analysis shows which NGOs participated in climate change and their connections inside and outside the climate change regime. The "nodes" are organizations, and the connections between the nodes are measured in two ways. The "starting points" for the network analysis – in other words, the first organizations from which connections are subsequently traced – are the NGOs in a network that attended a UNFCCC COP (listed in the Appendix).

From those starting points, the two types of connections among organizations were traced. First, common membership in a climate-related coalition was considered a tie. This helped measure the cohesion of the networks as they engaged in climate change–related campaigns and strategies. Given the resources and mechanisms developed for coalition memberships to communicate among one another, it is reasonable to assume that organizations in the same coalition are aware of one another's membership and have access to and share common information. That is, they are connected in ways that allow them to exchange information.

Second, I used the *Yearbook of International Organizations* for all the organizations that were starting points. The Yearbook asks organizations to list other organizations they consider partners. This measure is useful for uncovering an organization's links to others in its home regime and in the climate change regime. This is an accurate measure of which organizations share information because the NGOs themselves identify their key partners and collaborators.

Social network analysis is useful for identifying important organizations in the network. Degree centrality, the number of connections an actor has, is an indication of importance. The more connections, the more central an actor is in that network. Both measures for the links between actors also helped me identify potential allies, inside and outside the climate change regime – identification that was subsequently vetted through interviews and document analysis. For example, Greenpeace and other environmental organizations show up in the health–climate network, but these organizations only collaborated on other environmental health issues, not on climate change. One benefit of the mixed-method approach employed in this research is that it allows one to use qualitative and quantitative insights to improve the robustness and depth of analysis of the overall project.

This approach to social network analysis usefully embeds those engaging in forum multiplying in the network of their home regime and shows which actors in the home network did not participate in forum multiplying. It also reveals their connections within climate change as reported over time. That is, the methods used help us understand the hybrid nature of networks as they engage in forum-multiplying strategies and try to build connections in their target regime while attempting to mobilize actors from their traditional regime. Changes over time can be difficult to research when one has only a static snapshot of the network. To overcome this challenge, I used data from two time periods to create two views of the network, one from 2005 to 2008 and the other from 2009 to 2015. The first snapshot corresponds to the network's early efforts to forum-multiply; the second captures the ensuing and sustained mobilization efforts within the climate change regime. Particularly when coupled with the interview data, this approach helped identify and confirm the arrival of new actors, the recruitment of allies within the climate change regime, and the increasing centrality of lead NGOs over time.

Chapter Overview

To explore NGO forum-multiplying strategies as they related to the climate change regime, I begin by putting forward a framework to help understand forum-multiplying patterns in general terms in chapter 2. Chapter 3 provides a brief history of institutional change in the UN-FCCC, with a focus on how climate change was framed, the rules developed in response to new frames, and the rules governing observers' access and behaviour. Chapters 4 through 6 present the cases of labour, gender, justice, and human rights and health. In chapter 4, I introduce the successful cooperators, namely, the gender and labour movements. These two movements had ample motivation to take up the climate cause, and both had to overcome divisions within the network to craft a discursive frame linking gender and labour, respectively, to climate change. They leveraged the rules of the game and existing relationships in the UNFCCC and aligned with the norms of non-state actors' behaviour. They walked the walk and talked the talk of climate delegates. Conversely, the global justice movement, sometimes called the alter-globalization movement, sought to upset the status quo, as explored in chapter 5. Looking for a new cause for their claims, the movement became a founding part of the climate justice movement and decried many existing climate institutions as "false solutions." Despite leveraging some rules and forging new alliances, the climate justice movement lost control of its central frame, largely turning toward protest and national movement-building for climate justice. Chapter 6 explores the null cases of the human rights and health NGO networks. Human rights NGOs were not motivated to undertake climate change work, preferring to apply their influence in the human rights regime. Health also struggled to motivate much of the network, leaving some environmental health NGOs to try to advance various frames linking health to climate change. Ultimately, they proved unable to find institutions or allies within the climate change regime to help forward their cause. Chapter 7 considers the implications of the findings for future climate activism, and the expansion of the regime complex for climate change and for climate action under the Paris Agreement more broadly.

2 Forum Multiplying to New Regimes

NGOs participate in multiple regimes, including some that govern issues far outside their traditional areas of authority and influence. To successfully do this, the NGOs have something of a chameleon act to play. They must show they belong in the regime in the hope that governors in their target regime will view them as "one of us" and as an authoritative voice worth heeding. As chapter 1 highlighted, scholars have identified several instances in which NGOs have done this effectively and gained acceptance in regimes outside those in which they would typically operate. NGOs' mobility has spread ideas and shaped how we understand global issues – environmental problems are development issues, women's rights are human rights, and, more recently, climate change is a social justice issue.

Despite considerable mobility, we do not see all NGO networks migrating freely among regimes, and we do not see all regimes inundated with new NGOs. Several networks either chose not to, or were unable to, participate in the climate change regime, such as those advocating for health, human rights, refugees, peace, human security, and safe waste or chemicals management. NGO forum multiplying entails selecting a new regime, gaining entry to it, and mobilizing within it. Even if network members have a motivation to forum-multiply, they may still fail in their efforts to participate and mobilize in the new regime. The channels of migration reflect the uneven patterns of NGO forum multiplying. Clearly, NGO networks are limited in their ability to identify, enter, and mobilize within a target regime.

This chapter puts forward a framework to explain these uneven patterns of forum multiplying. I outline a two-step process. First, key NGOs in the network must have political, normative, or, to a lesser extent, financial motivations to participate in a new area of global governance. For reasons explored below, relevance, not funding, is often the dominant currency for NGOs engaged in forum multiplying. Yet as many social movement scholars point out, grievance is insufficient for a movement to occur (Tarrow, 1998; Tarrow & McAdam, 2005). Second, NGOs in the network must collectively find the means to gain recognition in the new regime. They need coherence in the network, allies in the target regime, and rules they can leverage to show their claims have merit. In the difficult process of forum multiplying, all three are necessary. The two stages together underscore the barriers to NGO mobility across regimes and the reasons why NGOs are not as free to participate across areas of global governance as one might assume.

Forum Multiplying

Forum multiplying involves NGOs identifying and mobilizing in a new regime to advance their traditional interests. It is the sustained mobilization of a group of NGOs in a new regime, enabled by a discursive frame linking the NGO network's traditional issue to the issue governed by the target regime. When participating in a new forum, NGO networks do not entirely leave their home regime, within which they have accrued considerable authority. Instead, they multiply into new forums. NGOs in this way expand their political terrain, multiplying the forums in which their central issue is considered. This behaviour is like that of domestic interest groups that "spend considerable amounts of time venue shopping, looking for institutional access where they might have a competitive advantage. They often launch offenses in several venues and defend their interests in several venues simultaneously" (Weible, 2007, p. 101; see also Baumgartner & Jones, 1991; 1993). Moving to different regimes opens multiple fronts for networks to advance their issues. It also raises the costs of participating in global governance.

Forum multiplying is a form of mobilization meant to advance interests. The engagement of NGO networks cannot be a brief affair. The time scale is years, not single meetings or brief campaigns. Signing onto a single joint statement with a few other NGOs representing other issue areas does not constitute NGO forum multiplying, which, rather, involves a network of NGOs collaborating and individually accepting considerable investment and effort over the medium to long term. This effort involves mobilizing around, and seeking to disseminate, a shared discursive frame.

Finally, the discursive frame is the proverbial key to the gates of the regime. The frame highlights the network's issue in the context of the regime issue. It is at the heart of issue linkage and the politics of bandwagoning to a new cause (Jinnah, 2011). The network's frame can claim political space or belonging within the target regime if it demonstrates a connection to the institutions of the target regime. Making claims is central to contentious politics, as actors make "claims that bear on someone else's interests," which "almost always involve at least one subject reaching visibly toward at least one object" (Tilly & Tarrow, 2015, pp. 7–8).

Frames are a popular concept in the social sciences; in particular, they are used to explain the success of activists (see, for example, Keck & Sikkink, 1998). Frames are viewed broadly as representations of events or issues that enable actors to understand what is happening and what aspects of the issue are salient (Goffman, 1974, p. 21; Snow & Benford, 1988). Frames are constructed to highlight some aspects of a situation over others, or they are "the conscious strategic efforts by groups of people to fashion shared understandings of the world and of themselves that legitimate and motivate collective action" (McAdam et al., 1996, p. 6). By highlighting some issues over others, frames serve as powerful tools for conveying meaning and shaping understanding.

Frames help attract attention and recognition by positioning one issue as a cause or a solution to a given problem. They have diagnostic, prognostic, and mobilization aspects (Benford & Snow, 2000). Diagnostic aspects of frames highlight the causes of a problem. When forum multiplying, network members could highlight their issue as a cause of the target regime's issue, underscoring the need for their issue to be recognized as a "root cause" of the problem faced by the regime. Or frames can have prognostic elements, suggesting solutions to the problem. NGO networks can highlight their issue as a novel solution to the target regime's problem, positioning the members as actors ready to help solve problems and reach common goals. Finally, frames serve to mobilize actors. This aspect is particularly useful in bringing network members to the new forum. Frames can also help build relationships with key actors in the regime (Allan & Hadden, 2017). The motivational aspect of the frame is helpful when recruiting new allies, while proposing either a new solution or cause can help show the NGO network's commitment to the regime's shared cause and underscore that including the network will bring added value to governance efforts. As Kapstein and Busby (2013) note, a central challenge for a transnational social movement is to unite different types of appeals, moral or practical, focused on causes or solutions, into a single demand. Frames therefore do much to explain why a network of NGOs attempt, and perhaps succeed, in gaining recognition of their asks, and themselves, in another regime.

We can identify and measure forum-multiplying strategies, and their success, qualitatively, using three yardsticks.[1] Joining a regime requires a public act directed at those within the target regime, commitment to the institutions of the regime, and recognition by others within the regime. These aspects of joining a regime can be used to spot forum multiplying when it occurs. First, the public act directed at governors of the target regime is evident in the continued participation in a forum in the regime. Participation is more than showing up at a conference: people rarely attend a meeting and speak to no one. Participating actors engage with governors in the target regime, exchanging views and information. It is a public act that is decidedly outward-looking, designed to engage governors in the target regime rather than to send a message to those within the network.

The second aspect, commitment to work with, or leverage, the institutions of the regime for change, is evident in the discursive frame that explicitly highlights the benefits of the network's issue for the target regime's issue. The frame is fundamental to forum multiplying; it serves as the claim for belonging in the target regime by making the case that the network's issue is related to the institutions of the target regime. Furthermore, the frame positions network members as integral to achieving the regime's ultimate goals.

The third aspect, recognition, is something of a Holy Grail, the ultimate ambition of forum multiplying, and it is often beyond the control of NGO network's members. They cannot control whether governors within the climate change regime will accept them. But network members *can* position themselves as integral actors to the work of the regime and build new alliances in the process. Being accepted into coalitions of other actors and having those within the target regime use the network's frame are signals that the network has achieved recognition and found new allies in the target regime. Together, these three measures (participation, frame construction, and recognition) can show when NGOs are using forum multiplying and when it is successful.

NGO Forum-Multiplying Framework

Multiplying the number of regimes in which an NGO network participates requires considerable resources. NGOs must ask their staff to conduct research, mobilize supporters, or engage new stakeholders – actions that will take longer when experts in one issue are asked to work on an entirely new issue. More fundamentally, it means finding ways to convince a new audience of one's authority. Success is not guaranteed. As figure 2.1 shows, several factors must be present for NGO forum multiplying to succeed.

Figure 2.1 Forum-multiplying framework

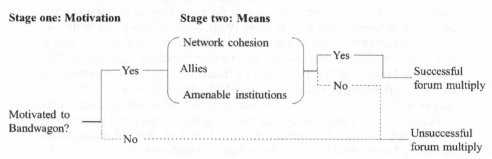

Here, I first outline the motivations for NGOs' decisions to employ such a costly strategy, with a focus on the lead NGOs in the network, given their disproportionate influence on advocacy networks' issue selection. Getting these NGO heavyweights on board is vital; without them, forum multiplying cannot take place. Second, I look at three further factors that explain why some NGO networks succeed while others do not: a cohesive network, an entry point in the rules, and a group of allies in the target regime.

Motivation

NGOs are often viewed as moral pillars of the international community, working to correct the wrongs of corporations and shame states into doing the right thing. Yet resources and political clout are required to achieve these goals. Maintaining relevance on the global stage is a key political motivation that can help keep a cause alive, while also maintaining the lead NGOs' authority, which, as Stroup and Wong (2017) show, is a rare commodity.

Among NGOs, the motives of centrally connected leaders in the network are particularly relevant. Such leaders are uniquely able to exert their preferences among their peers. Lead NGOs have many connections to others in the network, and those others look to them to signal which issues are important for the network (Carpenter, 2014). While they face limits to their ability to unilaterally set the network agenda, these NGOs are motivated to bring their resources and activate their connections to engage in a new area of global governance – all of which is vital to forum multiplying. Without a motivated and well-connected NGO, or multiple such NGOs, forum multiplying does not occur. They are not all-powerful, but they are necessary.

What motivates such NGO heavyweights is subject to ongoing debate. Some view principled motivations as a defining feature of transnational advocacy networks (Keck & Sikkink, 1998), while others point to the political acumen of movement leaders and their professional self-interest as key to determining which issues are selected for campaigns (Bob, 2005; Cooley & James, 2002). Operating in a fiscally insecure environment can foster competition in the course of which donor demands ultimately shape NGO strategies (Cooley & James, 2002). Sundstrom (2005; 2006) offers a more nuanced view, demonstrating that frames and material resources interact to influence the strategies and success of movements. Similarly, I argue that funding alone is an insufficient motivation when it comes to decisions to engage in forum multiplying.

Funding might appear to be an enticing explanation, but it ultimately falls short. Forum multiplying *could* enable NGOs to capitalize on new sources of funding or to manoeuvre around changing donor priorities, but this is unlikely in practice. These NGOs will be new to the regime, lacking information and the credibility to convince donors to give them funds instead of supporting established actors. Donors are responsible for the funds they distribute and are under pressure to show that their investments realized their goals. Donors are more likely to support trusted NGOs to deliver results on the issues central to the regime over a new NGO that lacks experience on the issues. It makes sense to support the WWF, an environmental NGO, to work on climate change. A donor may be less likely to fund a trade union to deliver climate projects. Major NGOs evaluate their opportunities carefully; they may hope for funding, as always, but it is not a sole or primary motivation because they understand that they are unlikely to win competitive grants in a new regime, and likely lack information on what opportunities exist.

By contrast, political motivations are highly relevant. As Schattschneider (1960) explains, weaker actors try to expand the scope of an issue to put themselves on the agenda, making themselves relevant in different political arenas. Controlling the agenda can limit who participates and, ultimately, the outcome. Powerful actors want to limit the scope of the conflict, while the weak want expansion to help build alliances and find new homes for their issues.

The logic is the same for forum multiplying. By moving to new regimes, NGOs can expand the scope of their conflict, thus fulfilling their role as counter-hegemonic forces, balancing the power and overrepresentation of states and business interests in global governance (Cox & Schechter, 2002), and targeting states or corporations (Wapner, 2002). They can find new allies and stay relevant in global governance by advancing their issue across different regimes.

NGOs can also use forum multiplying to outmanoeuvre opponents who block their issues in their traditional regime or to avoid becoming embroiled in stalemates and ineffectual regimes. Stalled negotiations are problematic for NGOs because they are unable to advance their issues, and also because they no longer have ongoing conflict to generate media interest or galvanize supporters. These are important metrics of authority and worth defending (Stroup & Wong, 2017). In stalemated regimes, there are no targets for their contention and no ways to advance their issues – only routine, circular discussions. Forum multiplying is a means for NGO networks to keep their movements advancing by remobilizing across areas of global governance.

The second relevant motivation is normative. Wanting to contribute toward a new cause, however, is not enough to motivate forum multiplying. Individual activists can identify many issues where they would prefer to see change, yet they will not view all of these issues as something that they could work on. For a normative motivation to propel forum multiplying, activists must internalize the link between the issues and the notion that continuing to advance their traditional cause legitimately entails tackling the new issue in its regime. Members of the network may seek to help solve the issue addressed by the target regime in order to be part of the solution.

These three motivations – political, material, and normative – can be all be present, although the political and normative motives tend to crop up more frequently in the first stage, when central NGOs in the network are deciding whether to migrate to a new regime. The motives of key NGOs are not enough. The means to achieve recognition – cohesion, allies, and rules – are all required for even the most motivated lead NGOs.

Means

While many NGOs may share these motivations, only some networks succeed in mobilizing and gaining recognition within their chosen regime. There are three useful resources for networks seeking recognition in a new regime: a mobilized, cohesive group; some well-connected allies; and an institution in the regime that serves as an entry point.

RALLYING NETWORK MEMBERS

A single consistent message from the group can help new climate activists amplify their claims for recognition. Speaking with one voice makes it possible to avoid mixed messages and increases the chances that a consistent message – crucially, the discursive frame linking the issues – will be broadcast to a wider audience. The frame linking the network's traditional issue to the target regime's issue ultimately serves two purposes. First, as discussed above, the frame has an external-facing role. It is a public discursive act that tries to demonstrate why some issues are connected and why new NGOs belong in each governance space. NGOs use the frame to secure recognition for their cause as well as for their authority.

The second, internal function of the discursive frame is to get all the members of the network on board in supporting the frame. Developing cohesion within the movement regarding shared goals and demands is often vital to its success (Tarrow, 2005). A collective frame, that is, a frame that all members support, is often more important than individual frames advanced by members within a group (Junk & Rasmussen, 2019). The frame is a product of negotiations among network members. This negotiation process is vital to achieving solidarity among members and bringing everyone to the same message.

The network's support in developing, disseminating, and (when necessary) defending the frame is vital for two reasons. First, negotiations to achieve solidarity around the frame reduce the proliferation of rival claims. Competition among frames linking the network's issue to the target regime's issue leads to mixed messages that can be confusing for those within the target regime. When subsets of the network vie for attention and influence, the overall message fragments into rival frames. Such frame competition enables actors within the target regime to select their preferred option, dismissing claims made by portions of a divided network and perhaps undermining the chances of recognition.

Second, disseminating the frame in a new regime requires a group effort. A single NGO, even one with a known brand and a sizeable budget, cannot interact with all the key actors and potential allies. The frame cannot be espoused by one NGO. Dissemination requires a group of NGOs speaking as one. A handful of major NGOs can pool their list of contacts to expand the number of delegates able to disseminate the frame. A sizeable network can amplify the frame to a still broader audience. Solidarity within the NGO network can bolster the strength and distribution of the message. It can also help the network defend the message from new interlocutors seeking to co-opt or add new dimensions to the frame.

Such cohesion can be difficult to achieve. The need for cohesion, perhaps even consensus, among network members can mean negotiation within the network on how to frame its issues in the context of the new regime. During negotiations, there are incentives to defect. Members may want individual recognition and will have their own ideological stances. Supporters will likely keep a "rebel" NGO in check, constraining how far it can stray from its long-held ideology. To achieve cohesion, negotiations will have to take seriously the ideologies of those in the network. In this context, the central, well-connected NGO, or NGOs, must be able to convene and coordinate discussions to develop the frame.

Some NGOs' many connections within the network can facilitate cohesion. Ideally, their centrality should enable them to set, vet, or block the network's agenda, and others will take up their signals and act accordingly (Bob, 2005; Carpenter, 2007; 2014; Lake & Wong, 2009). In practice, particularly in more extreme cases of forum multiplying, even the most influential NGOs face limits. Unilateral dissemination is not always possible. Central NGOs use their connections in other ways, to convene negotiations and to collaborate with other similarly powerful organizations in the network.

In more centralized networks, there is one well-connected NGO. It can create, or itself serve as, a forum for negotiations. Its many connections can bring the network members together to discuss and decide on a frame. After convening negotiations to arrive at a consensus on the frame, the organization can disseminate the frame back to network members. Unilateral decisions are risky and have the potential to alienate members of the network who might prefer a different way of framing the issues. By leveraging its connections, the NGO can bring members together.

Less centralized networks require coordination, often among multiple organizations. In such cases, the network is often divided into different factions, united by their own identities and ideologies. Each faction will likely have its own leader, an organization well connected among members of that group and viewed by members as able to speak on their behalf. For the network to rally around the same frame, these NGOs will need to coordinate. Among these NGO heavyweights, cooperation is difficult because of ideational differences and the temptation to capture attention and resources. Equipped as they are with their own separate followings and resources, they may be greatly tempted to "go it alone." Without coordination, the network risks fracturing into rival groups, each espousing a different frame.

Consistency and cohesion deliver. Speaking with one voice makes the frame more credible, but this requires intra-network cooperation. These negotiations can lead to broad frames, serving as umbrellas that include everyone's views. This is not necessarily a problem, particularly if the broad frame mobilizes new allies to help NGOs navigate the target regime.

USING ALLIES

A newcomer can find it surprisingly difficult to demonstrate that it belongs in a new social and institutional context. Political sensitivities, unwritten codes of behaviour, and subtle interpretations of the rules take time to learn and master. It helps – indeed, it is necessary – to have an insider who is willing to show new activists the ropes and provide introductions to key actors. Such a broker, as an actor connected to both the NGO network and the target regime, can choose, introduce, and diffuse new ideas, and this makes brokers important norm entrepreneurs (Burt, 2004; Goddard, 2009; Granovetter, 1973).[2] Brokers can reduce the costs of participation by providing or facilitating access to resources such as funding for participation or research. They can also use their status within the target regime to facilitate accreditation and secure badges for incoming NGOs to participate in the forum.

Less tangibly, but importantly for recognition, brokers can lend their authority. By associating itself with the incoming network and its frame, the broker can provide a powerful introduction to the target regime. Essentially, the broker shows "they're with me, and therefore one of us." If the broker has authority within the target regime, if it is viewed as a trusted expert, moral leader, or competent actor, it can amplify the discursive frame beyond what an outsider could articulate on its own.

Because regimes are social environments, NGOs that are new to a regime require these introductions and this information. Substantial information is available to outsiders about the rules and procedures of a regime. One can look up the text of a treaty, or the procedures to participate. But once at a meeting, and trying to sway the discourse, newcomers often find themselves lost in the social norms around how participants behave toward one another. The orientation provided by the broker is therefore essential. Such information helps the network members to climb the substantial learning curve, to quickly behave like others in the target regime. Without a broker, forum multiplying cannot take place.

LEVERAGING INSTITUTIONS

Transnational social movements face a dilemma that their domestic counterparts do not. While domestic movements and NGOs can use hierarchical rules and offices, such as constitutions and ministerial departments or courts, to advance their claims, transnational movements lack such structures to "latch" onto (Kapstein & Busby, 2013). The concept of political opportunity structures is generally applied when referring to informal or formal institutional conditions that provide openings for social movements to form and be heard (Tarrow, 2005; McAdam et al.,

1996). In chapter 3, I identify the frames informing how actors viewed climate change and the rules of observers' participation as key parts of the political opportunity structure of the UNFCCC. These formed background conditions against which NGOs could make their claims, but their success in gaining recognition for those claims rested on their ability to align themselves with specific rules and norms in the climate change regime.

Strategically aligning claims with policy-makers' views can occur through grafting (Price, 2003), congruence (Acharya, 2004), or fit (Kingdon, 1984). It is a common and effective strategy for non-state actors to gain influence in an institutional context. Incoming NGOs do this in two ways. They use substantive rules as discursive hooks for their claims, and they leverage procedural rules as footholds to increase their visibility and their access to negotiations. Both these strategies show that the NGOs are like those in the regime and should be recognized.

The substantive rules are those rules and norms that prescribe behaviour directly related to the issue at hand. For example, in the endangered species regime, substantive rules are those related to reducing poaching or banning the import of ivory. These rules are at the heart of the regime members' efforts to address the problem they face. Therefore, NGOs construct a frame that foregrounds the substantive connections, discursively hooking their issue onto the institutions of the target regime. The substantive connections can be forged by proposing that the incoming issue is either a cause of (diagnostic framing) or a solution to (prognostic framing) the target regime's problem or can motivate others to work toward the target regime's goals (motivational framing).

The diagnostic and prognostic elements of the frame are linked most directly to the substantive rules and norms of the target regime. By identifying root causes or proposing solutions, these elements highlight how the network's issue causes or helps solve the problem addressed by the target regime and can directly link to an institution in that regime. For example, framing species extinction as a matter of habitat loss implicates forests – and those working on forest conservation – in the biodiversity regime. Or, proposing that policies to protect species will be less effective if they ignore Indigenous knowledge and land tenure rights positions Indigenous peoples as central actors. By reframing the problem and its solution, the network can position itself as integral to the regime's efforts, bolstering its claim for acceptance in the target regime.

In many ways, it is advantageous to leverage the prognostic elements of the frame to a specific institution. First, institutions generally exist to identify, support, and implement solutions to the problem, in this way serving as hooks for the network's claims. Rules often specify ways of reducing the magnitude of a problem, or eradicating it: they are solutions. Norms can also be solutions, in the form of socially acceptable standards of behaviour. By focusing on solutions, network members have a ready entry point to leverage and link to in a way that foregrounds their issue. Leveraging these institutions shows that the NGOs are "here to help" by providing new solutions or new ways to make old solutions work.

Second, proposing additional solutions shows tacit if not explicit acceptance of the regime's definition of the problem and its solutions. Governors share frames of the problem. If they view a new network of actors as also sharing that framing, then governors may be more willing to accept a new network. After all, this new network aims to support, not overturn, the regime's efforts. By focusing on the diagnostic element of the frame, NGOs in the network position themselves as integral to the solutions, but also as like the governors of the regime and worthy of acceptance.

The procedural rules and norms offer equally valuable opportunities for incoming NGOs. These institutions govern the "how" of international negotiations and implementation, including matters related to non-state actors, such as their access to negotiation sessions, allowed activities and forms of protest, and opportunities to attend special sessions with limited participation. Within the climate change negotiations, security concerns have had consequences for civil society's tactics and agency (Hadden, 2015; Orr, 2016). Also, the consequences for breaking these rules are set out in procedural rules and can include permanent exclusion from the forum.

Learning and leveraging the regime's procedural rules can signal that the newcomers belong and should be recognized as members of the regime. Some political systems are more open than others to claimants (Eisinger, 1973; Kitschelt, 1986; Tarrow, 1998; Tilly, 1978). Such "political openness" is not uniformly distributed among claimants, and although these differences may be poorly understood (Meyer, 2004), it seems that marginalized groups can use institutions as footholds to mobilize their movement (Tilly, 1978). There is a selection effect where governors within the target regime may be reluctant to admit or recognize new claimants that seem too unlike those already within the target regime.

An important example of procedural rules that benefit some observer groups over others is rules related to how observers are organized. International organizations and negotiation forums have categories that delineate observer groups (often called "constituencies") – for example, business NGOs or environmental NGOs. These vary by organization and by negotiation forum. There are many benefits to constituency status. The Secretariat offers constituencies speaking time in negotiations, invitations to workshops and other events with limited participation, advance information about negotiations, and briefings with officials.

Because constituencies are broad categories, they can open opportunities to claim belonging to one. One option is to try to create a new category, a new constituency. If a group has constituency status in a related forum, the observer group can make the case for status in the target regime as well. This strategy is only useful for groups that are recognized in forums that address similar issues or have similar mandates. Actors in the target regime would need to see the other forum as a precedent. Another option is to claim to belong within an existing constituency; however, this would threaten to take space and benefits from the NGOs already occupying that constituency. This is likely to lead to conflict, since existing constituency members will want to safeguard their benefits and will likely view the incoming group as too dissimilar to themselves. And when it succeeds, this strategy can create fractures within the constituency.

Other rules and norms will favour some newcomers over others, related to how NGOs "ought" to behave. NGOs that are more likely to abide by rather than challenge the edicts will benefit from their aptitude and desire to play by the rules. Tarrow (2005) and Smith (2008) identify divides between reform-oriented and justice-oriented "activist solitudes." Reformers tend to use insider strategies such as lobbying, whereas justice-oriented activists lean toward outsider strategies, such as protests and boycotts (Alcock, 2009; Keck & Sikkink, 1998; Orr, 2006; 2007; Ciplet, 2014). For Newell (2006), justice-based NGOs and social movements are often "outsider-outsiders" with little access to international negotiations; they operate outside the institutionalized process, using tactics such as civil disobedience and protest marches to argue that the market is the cause of environmental problems. Social and environmental NGOs are increasingly playing the role of activists in climate change negotiations, mobilizing grassroots climate campaigns (Betsill, 2015; Fisher & Galli, 2015). Such nonconformists will find it difficult to mobilize within the target regime because of the norms of how observers ought to behave. Non-compliant, even antisocial behaviour can marginalize a network and undermine its acceptance within the regime, which operates according to pre-established norms.

Their reform-oriented counterparts will likely encounter fewer difficulties. Many of these NGOs, particularly the most authoritative, have moderated their claims as well as their means of contention (Dauvergne & LeBaron, 2014; Stroup & Wong, 2017). Such NGOs often provide expertise and lobby delegates in the hallways through socially acceptable means, often taking on the role of diplomat, seeking to work with countries (Betsill, 2015). In Newell's (2006) schema, these "insider-insider" NGOs enjoy preferential access to delegates and take a benign view of the market, whereas "insider-outsiders," have access but are on the periphery of civil society and the negotiations, in part due to their critical view of markets. Repertoires of action are deeply engrained in a movement: they speak to the core of its identity and are unlikely to change. Networks can, however, try to claim belonging and to fit within other procedural institutions.

Leveraging the existing rules takes considerable skill. NGOs learn about substantive rules that can serve as discursive hooks and find ways to use procedural rules to their advantage. While some regimes may be inherently more open that others to some claimants, there is still ample space for the creativity and agency of NGOs to strategize how to be most effective within these rules. The innovative capacity of many new climate activists is a common thread throughout the empirical chapters that follow.

Conclusion

Two important questions guided the discussion in this chapter: Why would NGOs – at their own cost – engage in a new area of global governance? And why do some succeed while others fail? There is motivation to expand the scope of contention and attract new audiences to advance an NGO network's issue. Until recently, many lamented the multilateral gridlock that beset several issues, including trade and climate change (see, for example, Hale, Held, & Young, 2013). So one may expect to see a high degree of NGO mobility as NGOs migrate from a gridlocked regime for material, political, or normative reasons. Yet NGO mobility is not as free or common as this logic may imply. Only some are recognized in the new regime – those able to rally supporters, find allies, and leverage institutions.

The empirical chapters later in this book trace motivations and mobilization as they relate to various NGOs' success, partial success, or failure in their efforts to engage in the climate change regime. Before outlining these cases, however, a brief primer on the climate change regime, and particularly its central forum, the UNFCCC, is necessary.

3 Understanding and Governing Climate Change

Climate change was once understood solely as an environmental issue, a matter of reducing greenhouse gas emissions in the present to protect the atmosphere in the future. We now view climate change as an issue intimately connected to our present-day economic, political, and social systems. Examples of this shift abound, from analyses of how climate change could raise coffee prices, to debates on whether climate change contributed to the Syrian civil war, and even the development of floating islands to house climate refugees. That changes to our climate will have a disproportionate impact across countries, and across peoples within countries, is now a commonplace assertion, a social fact. Climate is no longer an abstract environmental issue; indeed, a stable climate is seen today as fundamental to economic, political, and social life.

This paradigm shift in our understanding is the result of several smaller changes in how climate change is understood and governed. This chapter broadly outlines how institutions have shifted, thus opening new opportunities for NGOs to participate in the UNFCCC and link their issues to climate change. These formal and informal openings for NGOs and social movements to participate in and influence the process (i.e., political opportunity structures [Tarrow, 2005]) form the broad background to understanding how new climate activists identified an opportunity to link their social issues to climate change and how they strategized the means for gaining recognition. As chapter 2 outlined, and as the empirical chapters that follow will show, advocates' ability to link their claims to specific rules proved important to their success.

This chapter traces the broad shifts in the climate change regime's institutions. One aspect I do *not* focus on is the various waves of negotiations, such as those for the Kyoto Protocol (1995–98), the Copenhagen Accord (2007–09), and the Paris Agreement (2012–15). While the time periods here are bookmarked by major events, the dominant views of the issue and the rules changed incrementally over time (Allan, 2019) and did not correlate with the influx of activists. New climate activists mobilized in the lead-up to the 2009 conference in Copenhagen, when a new, legally binding treaty was expected to be adopted. The diversity of NGOs widened considerably during this time, but similar expansions did not occur in the lead-up to the negotiations for the Kyoto Protocol or the Paris Agreement. As shown below, the same NGOs attended, in similar numbers, but without further diversification through new participants arriving. Largely, this recent stability is due to the stability in the institutions: there have been few new rules or norms for potential newcomers to use as discursive hooks for their claims.

This account of the history of the climate change regime focuses on the substantive institutions, dominant understandings, and rules governing observer participation. Over time the institutions have expanded, transforming the climate change regime from one that focuses on mitigation only to one that now includes adaptation, finance, and loss and damage, among other issues. Most of this expansion occurred before 2009; few new issues were added afterwards. Also important to consider, but rarely traced, are the shifting norms and rules as they relate to observers, which expanded over time to admit new categories of observers but also contracted to limit how observers could engage with the UNFCCC negotiations. This is a unique view of the climate change regime's history. It serves as a backdrop for the subsequent chapters, which focus on how NGOs sought to gain recognition in this institutional context.

I divide the history of the climate change regime into three periods. The first period begins with the start of negotiations for a climate change agreement between 1990 and 2005, when the Kyoto Protocol came into force. The second period, 2006 to 2009, encompasses the intense negotiations for an agreement to replace the Kyoto Protocol. During this period, the climate change regime took what many call the "adaptation turn." Countries and civil society actors within the regime experienced the effects of climate change, and this prompted calls to build resilience and reduce climate vulnerability. The final period, 2010 to 2015, traces the resurrection of the climate change regime from failure in 2009 in Copenhagen through to the Paris Agreement. Others have divided the history of the regime in ways best suited to their inquiries (see Busby & Hadden, 2014; Gupta, 2014; Hadden, 2015). Here, I highlight shifts in the accepted frames and institutions of the regime, using major historical milestones to bookend each period. Primarily, I follow the history and political opportunities of the UNFCCC. The climate change regime is undergoing a period of fragmentation, with more international organizations and other transnational actors governing climate change and climate-related issues; even so, the UNFCCC remains a focal point for this expanding regime complex (Biermann et al., 2009; Hoffman, 2006, Zelli, 2011; Zelli & Van Asselt, 2013).

In the first period, the dominant framing offered a narrow view of climate change as an economic and environmental issue, and the burgeoning regime remained open to observers' participation and influence. Together, these factors created fertile ground for a few types of NGOs representing environmental and economic issues to participate in and influence the regime. In the second period, a new frame began to gain widespread acceptance with the adaptation turn and, relatedly, more organizations from other regimes started to participate in the UNFCCC. In the third and most recent period, the discursive environment continued to expand, albeit at a slower pace, with loss and damage – a contested frame focused on the irreversible effects of climate change – entering the climate vernacular. Some rules related to observers narrowed access in several subtle but important respects. As a consequence, fewer new groups of NGOs forum-multiplied to the climate change regime, and some of those that had been present earlier on found the constraints imposed too burdensome and left the hallways of the UNFCCC to pursue other strategies for influencing climate politics. As this chapter shows, there are close connections between the participation of NGOs and the rules and frames related to the issue at hand and observer engagement.

Political Opportunity Structure, 1992–2005

The first years were marked by hopeful enthusiasm that countries would be able to address climate change just as they had ozone-depleting chemicals. During this period, there was a rapid development of international climate law. But after these initial successes, the regime languished waiting for the Kyoto Protocol to enter into force. Climate change was an environmental issue with economic consequences, and it drew a limited range of non-state actors, mostly businesses and environmental groups. These two types of observers alone constituted nearly all NGOs attending the UNFCCC during this time: 34 per cent and 48.5 per cent of NGOs respectively.[1] Excluding universities and think tanks, all other NGOs comprised just 1.6 per cent.[2] These observers conformed to, and largely shaped, the nascent norms regarding how NGOs should participate, and they aligned with the narrow scope within which actors discussed and understood climate change.

The negotiations for the UNFCCC began in 1990 and culminated in 1992 at the Rio Earth Summit, where state leaders signed the Convention text. By March 1994 the Convention was in force.[3] Shortly afterwards, in 1995 in Berlin, parties concurred that the Convention was inadequate to meet its objective, which is to avoid causing anthropogenic damage to the world's climate. The resulting Berlin Mandate launched a process for strengthening developed countries' commitments through a protocol or another legal instrument, which parties achieved in 1997 when they adopted the Kyoto Protocol. In only eight years, states had agreed to undertake multilateral cooperation and negotiated two legally binding agreements, one of which entered into force. Then, after this rapid start in global efforts to address climate change, the pace slowed.

The world's largest emitter at the time, the United States, walked away when the rules strengthened. President George W. Bush rebuked the Protocol in one of his first political announcements. The main reason offered was that it threatened the United States' economic competitiveness against major economies that did not have targets under the Protocol. The Americans' climate abstinence created a transatlantic "climate divide," as the United States and the European Union took opposite approaches to the issue (Busby & Ochs, 2004; Schreurs, Selin, & VanDeveer, 2009).

The focus shifted to the "Gang of Four" – Canada, Russia, Australia, and Japan – which, along with the EU, could tally enough emissions representing a sufficient share of global emissions for the Protocol to enter into force.[4] These four countries were necessary to tip the balance and make the Protocol a legal reality. To bring the Gang of Four on board, the negotiations over the rulebook of the Kyoto Protocol (later known as the Marrakesh Accords) included compromises on forest sinks, particularly, although not exclusively, designed to appease Russia.[5] The generous rules for credits from forest sinks led some NGOs to refer to the Kyoto Protocol after the 2001 Marrakesh meeting as "Kyoto Lite."[6] These concessions worked. With Canada's, Japan's, and finally Russia's ratification, the Protocol entered into force on 16 February 2005.

With the entry into force of the Kyoto Protocol and domestic action sprouting in some states, climate change action seemed poised to become real on the ground. European legislation was in place, including the European Emissions Trading Scheme, which began on 1 January 2005. Carbon markets were a significant part of the cautious optimism, as the International Emissions Trading Association and the World Bank wrote in the *State and Trends of the Carbon Market, 2005*:

> The regulatory framework of the carbon market has solidified considerably in the past 12 months, with the start of operations of EU ETS on January 1, 2005 and the entry into force of the Kyoto Protocol on February

16, 2005. While regulatory uncertainty continues, notably for the regis-
tration of Clean Development Mechanism (CDM) projects by the CDM
Executive Board, the approval of climate mitigation plans in Japan and
Canada, or the allocation plans under the EU ETS for the 2008–2012 period, the very existence of policies constraining greenhouse gas emissions
up to 2012 is no longer in doubt. (Lecocq & Capoor 2005, 3)

After years of inaction, there was hope for change. Change was meant
primarily to address a single question: how to reduce emissions while
minimizing the economic costs. The focus on "flexibility mechanisms,"
such as markets and forests, reflected attempts to address this question
directly. Markets were a way to create cost-effective incentives for mitigation, and forests could absorb carbon without changing the status
quo of economies run on fossil fuels.

Climate as an Environmental and Economic Issue

All these negotiations took place with the understanding that climate
change is an abstract environmental issue that carries potential consequences for some economic sectors. As such, those within the climate
change regime discussed its effects as temporally distant and as possible to mitigate by reducing emissions early. The Declaration from the
Conference on a Changing Atmosphere in 1988 warned that "if rapid
action is not taken now by the countries of the world, these problems
will become progressively more serious, more difficult to reverse, and
more costly to address."[7] Environmental NGOs supported the view
that climate change could be mitigated (Betsill, 2008). Mitigation, not
adaptation or building resilience to climatic effects, was what most climate change actors understood to be the appropriate response to the
issue.

In the effort to mitigate, actors identified two sources of climate
change: the overuse and inefficient use of fossil fuels, and overpopulation. At the Rio Earth Summit in 1992, many speeches by heads of state
mentioned overpopulation, particularly in the Global South. Yet the
UNFCCC does not mention overpopulation. As Rahman and Roncerel
(1994, pp. 244–247) explain, NGOs based in the Global South ultimately
convinced NGOs in the Global North to abandon their proposals to
address population growth in developing countries and to appreciate
Southern NGOs' calls for per capita emissions entitlement. Southern
NGOs schooled northern NGOs in the realities of development, arguing that the right to development included access to energy and
urging a stronger focus on consumption. In this way, Southern NGOs

"emphasized that the debate must go beyond just the discussions of climate change as a scientific issue" (Rahman & Roncerel, 1994, p. 246). In part based on these normative calls, rather than scientific appeals, the dominant frame focused primarily on the energy sectors.

Climate change was also understood as an economic issue. The decision that the UN General Assembly, and not the UN Environment Programme (UNEP) or the World Meteorological Organization, would oversee the negotiations on climate change highlights how it was set apart from other environmental issues. Brazil, India, and other developing countries argued that climate change is inherently tied to modes of production. Countries did not make a similar case for the other "Rio Conventions" under negotiation at the time under the auspices of UNEP.

The treaties reflect worries that efforts to address climate change would have economic consequences. The market mechanisms and flexibility options were intended to ease the economic burden of mitigation for developed countries. When the Kyoto Protocol entered into force, then UNFCCC Executive Secretary Michael Zammit Cutajar informed UN Secretary General Kofi Annan that the world had forged one of the most significant economic treaties in recent history.[8] The narrow scope of climate change as it was then understood and the focus on mitigation led the regime to connect to only a few sectors, and this ultimately limited the types of claims that non-state actors could make. Others involved in the global governance of social issues had no opening to link their issues and claim a place within the regime.

Relationship with Environmental NGOs and Business Groups

During the formative years of the climate change regime, the rules and norms of observer participation involved rather *ad hoc* arrangements, which were later concretized into a more formal system. Few types of NGOs participated, principally environmental NGOs and business and industry NGOs (BINGOs), in line with the environmental and economic frames of climate change that were dominant at the time. Toward the end of this period, other groups sought entry to the climate change regime.

During this period, parties established the rules governing non-state actors' access to the climate change regime and their relationship with the Secretariat. According to Article 7.6 of the Convention, NGOs and other observers "which [are] qualified in matters covered by the Convention, and which [have] informed the Secretariat of [their] wish to be represented at a session of the Conference of the Parties as an observer, may be so admitted unless at least one third of the Parties present object" (UNFCCC, 1992). The Conference of the Parties (COP) approves these applications annually, to take effect the following year. With accreditation, observers can access plenary and contact group meetings, unless one third of the parties object.[9]

Constituencies are broad groups of non-state actors that choose a focal point for communicating between the group and the Secretariat. The constituency arrangements in the climate change regime started to form before Agenda 21 established "Major Groups" at the Rio Earth Summit in 1992. Other Rio Conventions use the Agenda 21 Major Groups; the UNFCCC has a slightly different set of categories, which have developed over time.[10] During the negotiations for the Convention, environmental NGOs and BINGOs formed loose groupings to coordinate among themselves and with the Secretariat. Later, these groups concretized into constituencies. Parties approved additional constituencies for local government and municipal authorities in 1995, Indigenous peoples in 2001, and research and independent NGOs in 2003.

Constituencies confer benefits for those NGOs participating in the group. The Secretariat furnishes constituencies with information before and during a meeting; time to speak to the plenary when all states are present; and invitations to ministerial receptions, technical workshops, bilateral meetings with officials, and regular meetings with the Executive Secretary of the Convention and co-chairs of key negotiating groups. In the early years of the regime, particularly open relationships with NGOs complemented the constituency arrangements.

During this time, NGOs capitalized on the opportunities presented by the norms of political openness. The intergovernmental negotiating committee established a uniquely open working arrangement with NGOs, in part because the complexity of issues led many negotiators to seek out NGOs' opinions and to use NGOs to test out ideas. As Rahman and Roncerel (1994, p. 250) observe, "the most controversial issues were not even brought to the main forum of negotiations until after consultations between the delegates and NGOs." Negotiations were usually conducted in the open, as "closed negotiation sessions [were] historically the exception rather than the rule in the UNFCCC" (Climate Action Network, 2006). Environmental NGOs could use their technical expertise, and their access, to inform the debates surrounding several contentious issues, particularly carbon trading and sinks (Betsill, 2002).

The early years of the climate change regime established open rules and norms of NGO participation. Among the five established constituencies, environmental NGOs and BINGOs outnumbered the rest in terms of delegation size and influence. These two dominant constitu-encies aligned with the two understandings of climate change – as an environmental issue and as an economic one. The paucity of evident links to other areas limited the participation of other actors in the re-gime. However, the frames used for thinking about climate change, and consequently the institutions to govern the issue, were set to expand rapidly with the negotiations for an agreement to replace the Kyoto Protocol, from 2006 to 2009.

Political Opportunity Structure, 2006–2009

Facing a stillborn Kyoto Protocol without the United States, parties sought to reinvigorate global cooperative efforts on climate change. Negotiations to extend the Kyoto Protocol and to replace it with a new, legally binding agreement began, and this raised new issues that ulti-mately became integral to how we understand climate change. More than ever, actors discussed climate change in terms of its consequences, and linked forests in developing countries to mitigation. The adapta-tion turn had begun.

New climate activists capitalized on the opportunities presented by the new round of negotiations, particularly by introducing adaptation as a new frame. The impact of the influx of new climate activists on NGO participation during this time was dramatic. New constituencies were established, and non-environmental NGOs' participation rose, from 1.6 per cent between 1995 and 2004 to 27.2 per cent of all NGOs between 2006 and 2009; social NGOs alone accounted for much of this increase, accounting for 22 per cent of all NGOs. Social NGOs were on par with BINGOs, comprising 22.1 per cent of NGOs, but were still well behind environmental NGOs, which accounted for 50.6 per cent.[11] When the new climate activists arrived, they found a regime in flux as actors underwent dramatic changes to their understanding of climate change.

Sharing views and information was part of this change. At the 2005 meeting in Montreal, the parties agreed to convene a two-year series of round tables called the "Dialogue on Long-Term Cooperative Ac-tion to Address Climate Change by Enhancing Implementation of the Convention," commonly referred to as the Convention Dialogue. The Convention Dialogue round tables discussed four issues: sustainable development, adaptation, technology, and market mechanisms.

The first three of these issues were central for developing countries, particularly because they opened negotiation space for developing countries to raise their key issues. Adaptation was the newest to the agenda, less well understood and discussed than sustainable development or technology. It was also viewed as a developing country issue, despite the need for all countries to undertake adaptation efforts (Schipper, 2006). For civil society actors, adaptation was increasingly discussed in side events, far more than in the previous years, and by a broader range of NGOs, including by NGOs linking adaptation to social issues (Hjerpe & Buhr, 2014).

The fourth issue, markets, was a chance to showcase how central these had become to countries' climate efforts. The Clean Development Mechanism was increasingly popular; 62 projects were registered in 2005 compared to 427 and 433 in 2007 and 2008, respectively.[12] Countries proposed new markets, including for reducing emissions from deforestation in developing countries. The idea of reducing emissions from deforestation and degradation (REDD+)[13] garnered significant political attention, yet countries disagreed over the use of markets (Allan & Dauvergne, 2013).

The Dialogue concluded in 2007, before the conference in Bali. As one observer points out, anyone following the Convention Dialogue would have foreseen the key elements of the Bali Action Plan.[14] It generated the negotiating agenda for the legally binding agreement set to be concluded in Copenhagen in 2009. The Plan had four pillars that organized the subsequent negotiations: mitigation, adaptation, technology, and finance. Among mitigation issues, REDD+ had a dedicated space on the agenda. The negotiations for the new agreement were conducted at a feverish pace over the next two years. Parties met four times a year (twice as often as usual practice) leading up to the 2009 Copenhagen conference.

The Copenhagen conference – called "Hopenhagen" by some – disappointed very high expectations. Developing countries and civil society derided the Danish hosts for the lack of transparency of the negotiations, which included closed-door negotiations among a handful of heads of state, as well as draft texts that were leaked to the media before being distributed to delegates. Negotiators walked into the meeting with a roughly 200-page negotiation text, and left having taken note of a five-page political agreement called the Copenhagen Accord.[15] Under the Accord, each country was to put forward its pledge to reduce emissions. Even REDD+, which in the view of some was the most advanced text of the agenda items laid out by the Bali Action Plan, possibly even ripe for completion,[16] received only a brief paragraph with little substance.

Participants, NGOs, and the media widely considered the Copenhagen conference a failure of multilateralism. But the debacle did not roll back any of the agenda-setting gains of developing countries. Adaptation, REDD+, technology, and finance remained important in the subsequent discussions of how to move forward after multilateral failure.

The Adaptation Turn

Climate change had previously been framed as an environmental issue with effects that would only manifest themselves in the distant future. In the mid-2000s, this view began to change. The effects of climate change were becoming impossible to ignore and were particularly felt by those in developing countries. It became necessary to speak not just about the effects of climate policy, but about climate change itself.

This "adaptation turn" constituted a new frame for the climate change negotiations and was espoused most strongly by developing countries. These countries were, and are, on the front lines of climate change. Adaptation also represented a new source of political leverage in the negotiations, because it underscored the need for developed countries to assume their past responsibility for climate change, as well as the need for increased support to build resilience to climate change. This leverage has yet to be fully realized. Adaptation remains a "poor cousin" of mitigation, receiving far less funding and political attention. During the Paris Agreement negotiations (and since), nearly a decade after the adaptation turn, there were still calls for a balanced treatment of adaptation and mitigation by developing countries and the EU.

While adaptation issues struggle to get the attention they deserve in material terms, the reframing of the issue in the mid-2000s was significant. The adaptation turn necessitated new discussions on the effects of climate change and the consequences of ineffective (or non-existent) climate policy. It put climate change in the present tense – no longer a long-term issue with distant effects, it became a problem for current generations. This placed new pressure on the UN process to address the "climate crisis." The discursive move toward deliberating on climate impacts also opened doors for social NGOs and movements to highlight how their work related to climate change.

New climate activists now used the adaptation turn to link their issues. Adaptation allowed those advocating for issues related to developing countries (poverty, for example) or social issues (such as gender inequality) to envision a role for themselves in the climate change regime. A former Secretariat member recalls that "the politics of international development arrived in the climate change arena, including the associated NGOs and international organizations [IOs]. Suddenly, development and other NGOs and IOs arrived, telling us that we weren't discussing an environmental issue anymore."[17] The adaptation turn opened discursive space for new NGOs to link their issues to climate change, which helped spur the rapid rise in the diversity of NGOs outlined in this book.

The adaptation turn was contested. A strong core of state delegates and NGOs was still invested in framing climate change in strictly environmental, mitigation-centric terms. Some environmental NGOs worried that discussing adaptation could divert attention from the need to reduce emissions, as Saleemul Huq, an early adaptation campaigner, recalls:

> CAN [Climate Action Network] didn't want to talk about it – they worried that if we talk about adaptation we are giving up on mitigation. I had trouble explaining to them that there isn't choice. For the poor it's not mitigation, it's dealing with impacts. Adaptation matters to a vast swath of the world for whom emissions are not a problem. Emissions are confined to those who are emitting, not to those who are feeling the impacts. These are different groups of people. Reducing emissions was the first, and for a long time the only framing, where people thought climate was A. environmental B. global and C. a faraway problem.[18]

The Bali Action Plan brought adaptation to the centre of climate change discourse, bolstered by the findings of the IPCC. The IPCC's Fourth Assessment Report highlighted the impacts of climate change more than ever before, providing evidence of the emerging effects on natural and human environments, such as agriculture and forest management, human health, and Arctic activities like hunting and travel over sea ice (IPCC, 2007a). While adaptation had been mentioned in the past, the 2007 Bali Conference was the watershed, bringing the issue to the fore. It was the first time that adaptation was major area of negotiations, that it was given roughly the same weight as adaptation and appeared in a key decision that laid the foundation for the post-Kyoto regime. Some cited it as a key "win" for the IPCC.[19]

While all countries need to take adaptation measures as seas rise, agricultural patterns change, and droughts and fires increase in frequency and severity, actors in the climate change regime discussed adaptation as a developing country issue. During a high-level event convened by the UN Secretary-General, several states highlighted, or expressed solidarity with, small-island developing states and least developed states as those bearing the brunt of climate change even while contributing the least to the problem; indeed, one developing country delegate underscored that "development and adaptation efforts go hand-in-hand"

(UNSG 2007). The climate frame expanded to discuss the effects of climate change in developing countries side by side with the environmental impetus to reduce emissions.

Relationship with a Broader Group of Observers

The influx of new climate activists led to the establishment of new constituencies, albeit through different procedures than those used for previous constituencies. While the formal rules of the climate change regime remained largely unchanged during this period, some informal practices started to shift, presenting subtle challenges to new civil society actors and setting the stage for diminishing openness to observers in the future.

New climate activists used old norms from Agenda 21 to secure the benefits of constituencies in the UNFCCC. Using their status as Major Groups, labour unions, women's and gender organizations, youth groups, and farming organizations argued that they too should have constituency status in the slightly different system of the UNFCCC. Gaining this status, leveraging the Major Group system, would not prove as easy or straightforward as it had for constituencies established during the early days of the UNFCCC. These groups faced more hurdles than local governments or other constituencies established before 2006.

The Secretariat established a provisional process for the new groups to accede to constituency status. Under the system, the group first had to apply for two-year provisional status as a constituency. The group could then submit another application for full constituency status. This second application was, according to several respondents,[20] detailed and lengthy; it included a summary of all the activities undertaken by the group over the two-year period, a list of the organizations and individuals in the proposed constituency, and a nominated organization, and an individual within that organization, to serve as the focal point.

Most constituencies cleared these hurdles. The Trade Union NGOs became an official constituency in 2008. The Youth and Women and Gender constituencies had their status approved in 2009. The Farmers constituency had only provisional status for many years because of the group's decentralized nature, and that the focal points were individuals (not organizations) with fewer resources for coordinating group activities to prove their active role in the UNFCCC.[21]

With these additional constituencies, there are now nine, which more closely mirror the Major Groups established by Agenda 21. The Climate Justice Now! (CJN!) network took a different approach by declaring itself an environmental group, it succeeded in negotiating an arrangement to split the environmental NGO constituency with Climate Action Network in 2009. CJN! and Climate Action Network both communicate with the Secretariat through their respective focal points, share invitations to events, and use one minute each of the two-minute speaking time in plenary. This arrangement was meant to be temporary but remains in place today.[22]

Largely due to CJN!, protest and civil disobedience tactics became more common in the climate change regime (see Hadden, 2015). The mass mobilization at the 2009 Copenhagen conference, and the continuing rise of civil disobedience and protest strategies, sparked new, informal arrangements and tighter security at climate negotiations. The unprecedented mobilization in Copenhagen exceeded the capacity of the conference centre. In response, the Danish hosts significantly curtailed civil society's access to the negotiations. The merging of movements and poor planning by the hosts contributed to the disenfranchisement of civil society (Fisher, 2010). In response, efforts were made to limit the number of observers allowed to participate in the annual UNFCCC meetings, and to constrain their behaviour at the conferences.

Political Opportunity Structures, 2010–2015

During this period, the climate change regime rebuilt itself, ultimately leading to the Paris Agreement. The failure in Copenhagen was a blow to the UNFCCC's legitimacy. Many were angered at the lack of transparency in Copenhagen and openly questioned the UNFCCC's ability to deliver a global treaty on climate change. During this resurrection, very little changed in how actors understood climate change. Few new types of NGOs participated, in part because the issues stayed the same. Despite subtle changes making the regime less open to observers, participation increased, particularly among the new climate activists. Environmental NGOs represented 39 per cent, business and industry NGOs 19.2 per cent, and social NGOs 41.8 per cent of the total number of NGOs attending UNFCCC meetings between 2010 and 2015.[23] During the negotiations for the Paris Agreement, social NGOs – and the social issues for which they advocated – were well represented to lobby states to include their issues.

The 2010 Cancun Agreements started the resurrection of the regime through an agreement that advanced issues including REDD+ and climate finance. Left outstanding was the expiry of the Kyoto Protocol's first commitment period in 2012; there was no agreement in place to replace or extend it. In 2011, countries agreed to establish a second commitment period, the details of which were settled through agreements in 2012. The 2011 decision in Durban included an agreement to "develop a protocol, another legal instrument or an agreed outcome with legal force under the Convention applicable to all Parties," to be completed by 2015 and to enter into force in 2020.

The negotiations for the new agreement proceeded throughout 2012 to 2015. For the first two years, the parties again initiated informal discussions. This process tabled several proposals and produced the concept of intended nationally determined contributions, a new version of the pledge system established by the Copenhagen Accord. These contributions would constitute the backbone of the Paris Agreement on Climate Change adopted in 2015.

The Paris Agreement on climate change sets its sights on holding "the increase in the global average temperature to well below 2 C above pre-industrial levels and pursuing efforts to limit the temperature increase to 1.5 C" (UNFCCC, 2015). It does so by creating a machine propelled by two gears: contributions and transparency. Every five or ten years (currently under negotiation), parties are to submit a nationally determined contribution that is more ambitious than the last.[24] This is a legally binding obligation to submit a more ambitious contribution every five years; however, the content of that contribution is not legally binding. Countries can choose what to put in the contributions without international oversight. The second provision, and the only other legally binding one, is related to transparency. All parties will report – using a common framework but with certain flexibilities for developing countries – on their progress in meeting their contributions. The Agreement aims to achieves a balance between mitigation and adaptation in terms of its political importance, including by setting a long-term global goal for adaptation. The enthusiasm was palpable after ten years of negotiations. In 2016, the Paris Agreement became the fastest treaty to enter into force after enough ratifications were deposited by countries.

The fervour was short-lived. US President Donald Trump pulled out of the Paris Agreement, repeating the past. Parties could update their pledges in 2020, when the Paris Agreement took effect. Few did. Fresh questions about the ability of the UNFCCC to address climate change now take the place of the enthusiasm of 2015.

Expanding to Loss and Damage

After the frame competition of the mid-2000s, actors' understandings of climate change largely stabilized. Both mitigation and adaptation came to be accepted as parts of the climate issue. One newcomer emerged, prompting its own debates: "loss and damage." This issue further underscored that the failure to act in the past had created a new set of challenges in a warmer world. Loss and damage as a concept refers to the irrevocable effects of slow- and rapid-onset events caused by climate change (e.g., prolonged drought, intensified natural disasters, sea level rise), although conceptual differences in how actors understand loss and damage remain (see Huq, Roberts, & Fenton, 2013).

Countries debated whether loss and damage was a new issue or a subset of adaptation. Developing countries argued that loss and damage occurs when both mitigation and adaptation prove insufficient, so it must be treated separately. For developed countries, loss and damage is a symptom of low resilience and is, therefore, an extreme among issues related to adaptation. In a compromise reached in 2013, the Warsaw International Mechanism for Loss and Damage Associated with Climate Change was established – a win for developing countries, which had tried for years to address the issue – but it resides under the Cancun Adaptation Framework, as demanded by developed countries. Addressing loss and damage separate from adaptation remained a central demand of developing countries throughout the negotiations for the Paris Agreement, right up until the final days before adoption.[25] Much of the debate revolved around compensating developing countries to enable them to cope with both the slow and rapid changes wrought by climate change.[26] Actors discussed climate change in roughly the same terms, albeit acknowledging the grim reality of irrevocable damage; meanwhile, the regime's relationship with observers was shifting in subtle ways.

Relationship with Increasingly Disobedient Observers

After the mass protests in Copenhagen, and die-ins in Cancun, the Secretariat made several changes to NGO access. The Secretariat now allots a set number of badges, with input from observer organizations. In 2015, some NGO representatives suggested that the organizations were receiving about 20 per cent of the badges they had requested.[27]

Meanwhile, security around UNFCCC meetings increased, particularly in relation to protests. Since 2010, NGOs have had to register their demonstrations and get the approval of Security. Failure to secure approval can have consequences, including being "debadged," which means being asked to leave the conference and not being allowed back inside.[28] At times, for particularly disruptive protests, the individuals deemed responsible have lost their badges permanently.[29]

The introduction of new forms of protest – particularly non-violent civil disobedience outside the venue – highlighted and questioned the

norm of how NGOs ought to engage in the climate process. The outsider tactics used by some movements, NGOs, and individual activists
have not been well received by many within the climate change regime.
While many NGOs supported a civil society walkout of the negotiations in 2013, the CAN could not participate because some of its members disagreed with that action. Some CAN members even complained
to the heads of some of the organizations planning the walkout, trying
to stop it.[30] The norm that NGOs in the UNFCCC should provide information about protests and engage in more muted forms of it inside the
venue suited the strategies of some groups but constrained the organizing efforts of others.

Conclusion

Climate change is a dynamic natural phenomenon, with feedback loops
and non-linear changes. Our understanding of the issue has similarly
undergone shifts and turns, adding new issues and refining old ones.
These changes within the regime, especially those in the mid-2000s,
provided opportunities for the new climate activists to claim political
space in the climate change regime. Once open to civil society, the process has become more closed over time, in part as a response to the
rapid growth and diversification of civil society. In the chapters that
follow, I consider the experiences of some new climate activists: the
successful reformers; labour unions and gender NGOs; the partly successful revisionists, the climate justice movement; and those who could
not, or did not want to, find recognition in the UNFCCC: health and
human rights NGOs.

4 The Reformers: Labour Unions and Gender NGOs

The experiences of the global labour and women's rights movements illustrate why and how activists navigate the challenges of forum multiplying. There are many similarities between these two networks' experiences. Both began participating in the UNFCCC in the mid-2000s, although some forerunners attended earlier on. The pivot to climate change was prompted by a decline in work in other arenas, such as the International Standards Organization (for labour unions), the Convention on Biological Diversity and global women's conferences (for women's rights organizations), and the WTO (for both movements). Once motivated, both movements benefited from international organizations that served as allies brokering their entrance into the UNFCCC and from their status as constituencies under the Agenda 21 system, which, they successfully argued, meant they deserved similar recognition as UNFCCC constituencies. While labour sought to link to mitigation rules, and women's rights organizations to adaptation rules, both cultivated strong discursive frames linking their issue to climate change. True to their reformist roots, these claims to belonging were not designed to overturn the status quo, but rather to identify new ways to understand climate change and build political coalitions for addressing the crisis.

Where these groups differ is in their network structure. This difference offers insights into how internal dynamics can influence how new activists develop their ideas and the likelihood those ideas will resonate within their chosen forum. The labour movement is highly centralized around the International Trade Union Confederation (ITUC). The ITUC was able to use its place as a centrally positioned organization to bring the labour movement together to call for ambitious climate mitigation, notwithstanding disagreements among unions. Some unions represented workers in sectors in which green jobs could grow, while others represented workers in fossil fuel industries, who viewed climate change policy as a threat to their jobs.

By contrast, the women's rights network was split between those focusing on women's rights and the environment, who tended to take more reformist stances to work within the UN system, and those who saw themselves as environmental NGOs using a gender lens and were more comfortable making more radical claims. These two factions cooperated to develop and advance a frame linking what they could agree on, excluding reproductive and population issues and NGOs from the network.

With that cooperative effort, women's rights organizations, like the labour movement, ultimately became new climate activists, accepted by climate actors in the climate change regime. Both networks meet the three criteria for successful forum multiplying: participation; a discursive frame; and recognition by others. Labour unionists increased their participation by 84 per cent, from 3 organizations with 31 delegates in 2006 to 12 organizations with 195 delegates in 2015, all extolling the need for a "just transition" to a low-carbon economy. The just transition frame underscores a deep commitment to supporting action on climate change, because, as goes a common slogan in the labour movement, "there are no jobs on a dead planet." Despite initial opposition – some climate NGOs and delegates worried that unionists would be an obstructionist force – the labour movement became part of the UNFCCC social community. States accepted the labour movement's just transition frame and in 2010 created space in the response measures forum for a just transition of the workforce and the creation of decent work and quality jobs. The ITUC became a key member of the Climate-7, or C-7, an informal coalition of high-profile NGOs from the development, faith, environment, and labour sectors campaigning on climate change. In 2015, C-7 with the B Team and We Mean Business signed a declaration titled "Call for Dialogue: Climate Action Requires Just Transition."

Women's rights organizations similarly met all three qualitative metrics and were more successful than the labour movement in terms of influencing states to adopt decisions related to gender and climate change. The lift-off in terms of participation came in 2007, when women's rights NGOs launched the Global Gender and Climate Alliance (GGCA). The presence of gender NGOs rose from 3 organizations and 23 delegates in 2005 to 16 organizations bringing 183 delegates in 2009, and 18 organizations with 99 delegates in 2015. These delegates and organizations overcame internal differences to develop a two-part frame that highlighted the disproportionate impact of climate change on women and positioned women as committed agents for climate solutions who need to be included in decision-making.

Clearly, the UNFCCC now recognizes the gender frame and gender NGOs. Recognition is a precursor to influence, and the gender network proved remarkably influential. CAN, the largest umbrella organization of environmental NGOs in the UNFCCC, welcomed several gender NGOs into its network, viewing them as fellow actors working to address climate change rather than gender issues more narrowly.[1] Nearly twenty decisions in the UNFCCC refer to gender, and the Lima Work Programme on Gender and Climate Change established in 2014 proved an important victory for advocates after years of effort. At first, some delegates openly questioned the value of bringing a social issue such as gender in the UNFCCC negotiations; today, however, gender is being discussed as a regular item on the agenda of the Subsidiary Body for Implementation.

This chapter introduces these networks and then outlines the history of their engagement, the reasons they multiplied their presence to climate change, and the means they drew upon to do so. This first empirical chapter demonstrates the value of the theoretical framework, showing the similarities in these movements' trajectories toward becoming new climate activists.

Moving to the Climate Change Regime

The labour movement and the women's rights movement joined and mobilized within the climate change regime in similar ways. Both had a few members participating in the early years of the regime, massively increased their participation in the mid-2000s, continued to participate after multilateral failure in 2009, and joined mainstream climate NGOs in their actions and demands in the lead-up to the Paris Agreement. Figures 4.1 and 4.2 show how many organizations and individuals from these movements attended UNFCCC meetings. Both figures reveal that these very different movements had a similar pattern of participation: minimal attendance followed by a rapid mobilization.

As these figures show, there were a few delegates representing labour unions and gender NGOs in 2005. These early delegates explored ways to make their issues heard, and they came to understand the need for a large-scale presence. They found themselves isolated and somewhat bewildered by the process. The International Confederation of Free Trade Unions (ICFTU), a key international labour federation at the time and precursor to the ITUC, "sent one person [to the Montreal meeting in 2005] who was well informed on the content but not keyed up on the process. He meandered around the first meeting wondering what to do with this paper [an early report on green jobs]."[2] Labour advocates felt like outliers, and some wondered why they had come, for they were unable to find an opening to approach delegates or navigate the process. Early delegates from gender NGOs

Figure 4.1 Gender NGOs' participation in the UNFCCC

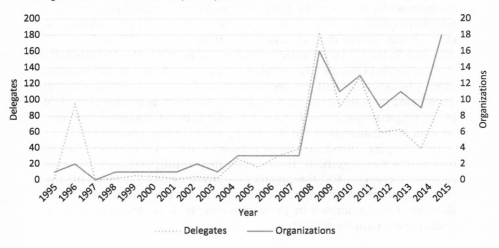

Figure 4.2 Labour unions' participation in the UNFCCC

felt similarly small in the context of a broad and complicated negotiation process. Some members of the women's ecology movement, an
outgrowth of women's opposition to nuclear politics, had participated
since COP 1, but they lacked the capacity and presence to influence
policy-making (Hemmati, 2005, 21). The increasing participation that
would follow would lead these activists to celebrate that "after almost ten years of discontinuous and uncoordinated participation by

women's organizations, the path from COP1[3] was finally picked up again" (Hemmati & Röhr, 2009, p. 24).

The Bali Conference in 2007 was significant for both movements. Gender NGOs launched two separate coalitions devoted to the links between gender and climate change: the GGCA and Gender CC – women for climate justice. Gender CC was founded by the NGOs that had previously been involved in the UNFCCC. Behind the GGCA were powerful, well-known NGOs, including the Women's Environment and Development Organization (WEDO) and the International Union for the Conservation of Nature (IUCN), as well as UNEP and the UN Development Programme (UNDP). These two groups were separate, with their own ideologies and connections, but together they spurred a rapid increase in the participation of gender NGOs in the UNFCCC.

Labour unions also sent a large delegation to the UNFCCC in Bali. Most of the delegates were from national unions around the world and were attending under the banner and accreditation of the ITUC. In total, ninety-one people from twenty-three countries were part of the ITUC delegation (ITUC, 2007). The labour movement was not wholly united, and disagreements sometimes erupted in public.[4] Not all unions at the time were in favour of climate advocacy, and the ITUC's climate-related activities caught their attention, as "information started oozing out among the affiliates, getting the attention of the coal unions in the US who at the time really objected to this work. This woke everyone up, creating a critical mass."[5] While the ITUC accounts for most of the labour presence, the rift between American unions in the fossil fuel sector and other unions would persist for years to come.

Many in unions and gender NGOs left this initial experience in the UNFCCC both impressed and confused by the complexity of the process. They understood that a learning curve loomed ahead, to learn the issue of climate change and the array of formal and informal rules governing it. Labour union delegates at Bali were "overwhelmed by the apparent complexity of the discussions," and this led to an agreement among ITUC affiliates to establish a working group on climate change to coordinate their engagement, set priorities, and spread information among affiliates.[6] Gender NGOs were already organized into two coalitions, and the newcomers in the GGCA experienced difficulties in applying their experience in other environmental governance forums, such as the Convention on Biological Diversity. The informal rules of engagement were very different. One key organizer, Cate Owren, calls their early years "comical. We made a lot of mistakes trying to introduce gender issues from the floor, and to set up allied governments to introduce language. This all backfired. We had a big argument with the

UNFCCC Secretariat. We were in the wrong places, making everyone's job harder."[7]

Labour unions and gender NGOs had much to learn, but they continued to engage. Both groups faced questions about their involvement and the value it would bring to the UNFCCC. Commonly, they would be asked, "You don't work on climate, why are you here?"[8] or, more positively, "Wow, why are you interested in this?"[9] There was little space for them to make their case in the early days because "climate change for decades was thought of as a science or business issue. There was no room to open the dialogue, no comprehensive conversation."[10] Some climate actors' responses went beyond apathy or silent neglect.

Some climate NGOs and officials worried that engaging gender or labour issues would be detrimental to the climate negotiations. In response to a question about the inclusion of gender and other social issues in the expected new agreement, then Executive Secretary Yvo de Boer suggested that addressing gender issues could impede the negotiations.[11] Social issues such as labour and women's rights were seen as distractions from negotiations for an environmental treaty. Unions faced more overt opposition. Environmental NGOs especially worried that unions would obstruct progress in the negotiations and heighten climate denial.[12] It became clear to many in the labour movement that the perception that UNFCCC actors had of union involvement was "very far from what we thought we were bringing."[13] Many of the labour movement's early efforts would involve overcoming perceptions of the "jobs versus environment" dilemma (Räthzel and Uzzell, 2011). The two groups would employ similar strategies to show delegates that labour and gender issues were climate issues and that including these issues could help bring about global climate action.

Labour unions and gender NGOs aimed to get the word out that their issues were both relevant and necessary to address climate change. Members of each group organized multiple side events, presentations held on the margins of the negotiations, at every conference, as a way to showcase the links between their issues and climate change to delegates.[14] Gender NGOs organized meetings to inform delegates about the links between gender and the issues under negotiation (informally known among gender NGO representatives as "training of delegates" meetings or "TODs"). These meetings proved useful for the organizers to forge relationships with state delegates.[15] Labour unions drew on their existing connections with government ministries to build their relationships with delegations at the UNFCCC to organize briefings on the labour implications of various issues (ITUC, 2007; 2008; 2009).

The mobilization and lobbying efforts were all geared toward the 2009 Copenhagen Conference. Unions and gender NGOs sent their largest delegations to date. The streets filled with demonstrators marching peacefully (for the most part) for climate action. The labour movement marched under the banner "Unions Have Solutions," and members of Gender CC carried signs declaring "No Climate Justice Without Gender Justice." Unions convened the inaugural "Work for Work (WOW) Pavilion," which included twenty-eight workshops and attracted more than one thousand participants to help inform those within and outside the labour movement of the connections between climate action and employment (ITUC 2009a).

Union and gender NGO delegates expected to witness the adoption of a climate treaty that included language on a just transition and gender. There were references in the draft negotiation text to gender considerations related to adaptation; there were also references to a just transition in the context of shifting investment patterns and financial support as well as to workforce development and vocational training in the section on technology transfer.[16] In light of the failure of the negotiations, each group had to decide how to respond and continue its engagement.

Their responses and future efforts would reveal fissures in the movements, both old and new. For the labour movement, there remained a divide between progressive unions seeking strong climate action and American unions representing workers in the fossil fuel sector. After the failure in Copenhagen, the American Federation of Labour and Congress of Industrial Organizations (AFL-CIO), the largest union in the United States, questioned the value and legitimacy of the UN process going forward.[17] Several American unions were satisfied that developed countries had stood firm and did not accept emissions targets without other major economies doing the same. The ITUC, however, had a different response. It expressed disappointment that developed countries were not assuming responsibility, contending that this failure "reinforced an environment of mistrust and conservatism on the part of the emerging economies" (ITUC, 2010).

Gender NGOs, already facing their own internal disagreements between the GGCA and Gender CC, encountered a new group with seemingly controversial views. The Population and Climate Change Alliance had formed to advocate linking reproductive health to climate change, aiming "to influence the climate change agenda, in particular around the 2009 Copenhagen Climate Change Summit."[18] A key founding member of this alliance was Population Action International, which had secured funding and early successes that documented the links among reproductive rights, health, and climate change.[19] The new group sought to coordinate with the GGCA and Gender CC, yet several Gender CC members and other gender NGOs expressed little interest.[20] Despite these internal fissures, and multilateral failure in Copenhagen, both the labour unions and the gender NGOs continued their advocacy.

Labour and gender advocates justified their continued engagement on similar grounds. Both realized that their movements were growing in the climate change regime, bolstered by allies within their networks and the regime. Participation continued to grow, and both movements were joined by local unions or women's organizations, especially in 2010, 2011, and 2014, when COPs were held in the Global South.[21] Other civil society members started to accept and collaborate with labour unions and gender NGOs. CAN welcomed working with gender NGOs, viewing these organizations as "committed to addressing climate change, and willing to sign onto statements, even if there isn't a mention of gender."[22] The ITUC reported that its growing connections among state and non-state delegates meant it was now recognized as a "legitimate player" (ITUC, 2010).

The "Warsaw Walkout" epitomizes the integration of gender and labour organizations with the broader climate activism community. Under the slogan "While They Talk, We Walk," many NGOs walked out of the National Stadium, the conference venue. As part of the C-7 alliance of NGOs, the ITUC was integral to this walkout. The WWF had arrived at the Warsaw conference with a mandate to undertake an action such as a walkout, but only if other organizations agreed to participate, particularly the ITUC as a large, membership-based organization that would require approval.[23] Walking out was a more radical action for gender and labour groups. Labour had never left an international negotiation before, and gender NGO members discussed the walkout as an unprecedented action that was, however, necessary.[24] Neither group was used to challenging the legitimacy of an international organization. But they were frustrated with the slow pace of negotiations despite the many new institutions established on labour and gender and climate change, respectively.[25]

Before the Paris Agreement, both movements secured gains in the negotiations. In the Cancun Agreement in 2010, parties established a forum on the impact of the implementation of response measures for climate change.[26] One issue addressed in this forum is a just transition of the workforce and the creation of decent work and quality jobs. This forum provides a regular and institutionalized opportunity for the ITUC to present its views directly to parties. While some delegates involved in the negotiations still viewed the response measures forum as a "negative space with some baggage,"[27] the labour movement used the space provided and in 2015 argued for an institutionalized process for using the information shared in the forum to inform decisions taken by the UNFCCC.[28]

To date, there have been more than twenty UNFCCC decisions that reference gender. Seven are devoted solely to establishing mechanisms for discussing and advancing gender equality or gender responsiveness in the UNFCCC. These decisions sparked controversy. The 2012 decision calling for gender balance was spearheaded by UNFCCC Executive Secretary Christiana Figueres and Mary Robinson, the former Irish prime minister and founder of the Mary Robinson Foundation for Climate Justice, with sporadic collaboration with the Women and Gender constituency.[29] Some constituency members were not satisfied with a decision that focused merely on "counting women" and that excluded deeper understandings of gender.[30] Some in the constituency considered speaking out against the decision. Others in the constituency urged unity, ultimately quieting those critical of the minimal decision and how it had been developed.[31]

Intense negotiations underpinned the Lima Work Programme on Gender and Climate Change.[32] Saudi Arabia opposed references to gender equality and strongly preferred phrases such as gender balance (IISD, 2014a).[33] In response, some male delegates from Muslim developing countries participated in the gender negotiations to send the message that Muslim countries supported a progressive work program on gender and climate change.[34] Mexico sought clarification that gender-equal did not mean a 50/50 male-to-female ratio on delegations, because Mexico had more women than men on its delegation (IISD, 2014a). As a developed country delegate recalls, the gender NGOs "really had to teach us what these words – equality, balance, sensitive – meant and that they held different implications. This was all a new language for us."[35]

The labour and gender movements continued to work within these institutions and with civil society and state partners to argue for their issues to be included in the Paris Agreement. While there is only one reference in the Paris Agreement to a just transition, union delegates viewed this as a foundation to build upon when operationalizing the Agreement; however, the ITUC underscored that the agreement only "takes us part of the way" to addressing the climate crisis (ITUC, 2015). Traditionally more successful in terms of influencing UNFCCC decisions, gender NGOs were disappointed that there was only one reference to gender in the preamble. In one version of the draft agreement, there had been references to gender in five places: preamble, mitigation, adaptation, finance, and technology.[36] Both movements sent their largest delegations ever: 100 delegates from gender NGOs and 197 delegates from unions. They participated as equals with other climate activists, a far cry from the earlier days of their involvement, and successfully had their issues recognized in the most significant climate change treaty adopted to date.

Labour–Climate and Gender–Climate Networks

Social network analysis confirms the above narrative as well as the changes wrought in the labour and gender networks as a result of their engagement with the UNFCCC. There are many similarities between the labour movement's and women's rights movement's experiences in the UNFCCC, even though their networks are structured very differently.

Both networks grew considerably, gaining new allies within the climate change regime and bringing traditional labour and women's rights organizations to climate change. The number of organizations in the labour–climate network grew from 481 to 593. The increase for the gender–climate network was more pronounced: it started with 366 between 2005 and 2008, but by 2015 there were 888 organizations directly or indirectly involved in gender–climate linkages.

There is one key difference. The labour movement is highly centralized around the ITUC while the gender network has two centrally positioned NGOs: the GGCA and Gender CC. The ITUC clearly had more connections in both periods, 114 and 120 respectively, nearly quadruple the number of connections of the next highest organization. Figures 4.3 and 4.4 show how important the ITUC is within the network as well as the central, convening role it is well positioned to fulfil. These figures also show how little the network changed over time.

The transnational labour movement has long been centralized. The ITUC is comprised of trade and labour unions in a hierarchical relationship: local chapters are part of national unions, and national unions in turn are affiliates of international federations. The international federations liaise through the Council of Global Unions. Formed through a merger of the International Confederation of Free Trade Unions and the World Confederation of Labour, the ITUC has 340 affiliates, making it the world's largest trade union confederation. As the largest, and well-connected, union confederation, the ITUC can serve as a global hub for unions.

The ITUC's position as a central association for labour facilitates the mobilization of workers. Unions keen to engage in the UNFCCC do not

Figure 4.3 Labour–climate network, 2005–2008

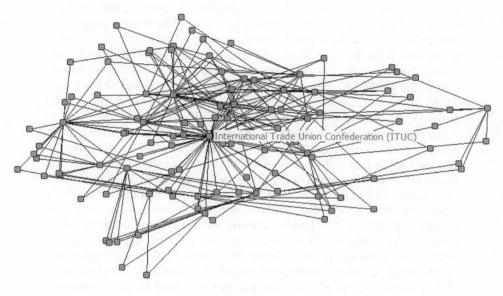

Figure 4.4 Labour–climate network, 2009–2015

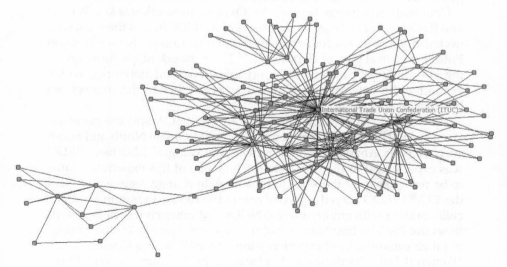

need to seek their own accreditation or devote resources to learning the procedural or substantive rules of engagement. Instead, they can use the knowledge base and resources of the ITUC. The central position of the ITUC eliminated the need for a new alliance or Secretariat devoted to the link between climate change and labour. The ITUC could coordinate the network and establish the trade union NGO constituency within the UNFCCC without creating a new organization or loose network. These benefits are not as easily available to those in the gender network, divided as they are between two alliances.

For the gender–climate network, there are multiple central organizations, and the network maps point to internal contention. Gender CC and the GGCA had different ideological starting points. Figures 4.5 and 4.6 show the two principal clusters that reflect the two parts of the overall network and identify the lead NGOs. The second map, for 2009–15, shows the emergence of a third cluster, the Population and Climate Change Alliance in 2009 (shown around the International Planned Parenthood Federation).[37] The Population and Climate Change Alliance worked to advance the links between climate change and reproductive health and rights. Strongly opposed by Gender CC, and by some GGCA members, the alliance was ultimately vetted from the network. The internal cooperation between the GGCA and Gender CC led to a shared frame around gender and climate change, one that excluded reproductive rights issues (see below).

Cooperation between the main NGOs in the network was key. WEDO and IUCN were key founding partners of the GGCA, and the most connected organizations, followed by Women in Europe for a Common Future, a central part of Gender CC.[38] The network maps show growing coordination between these organizations and networks, which expanded the network overall and also strengthened the connections between its members.

WEDO and IUCN were important to the GGCA and the network. Founded in 1991 by key feminist figures in the Global North and South such as Bella Abzug, Vandana Shiva, and Wangari Maathai, WEDO was experienced in the UN system. The value of this experience came to be recognized by those within the climate change regime and Gender CC.[39] WEDO played a pivotal role in the Rio Earth Summit in 1992, collaborating with environmental NGOs and other civil society groups to secure the identification of major groups in Agenda 21, then bringing their organizational experience into the 1995 Beijing Conference on Women (Clark, Friedman, & Hochstetler, 1998). Later on, WEDO became the convener of the Women's Major Group in the Commission for Sustainable Development and organized the women's caucus at the

Figure 4.5 Gender–climate network, 2005–2008

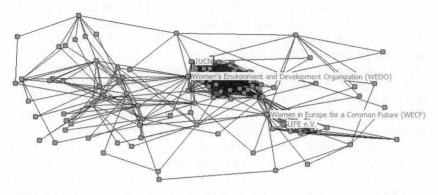

Figure 4.6 Gender–climate network, 2009–2015

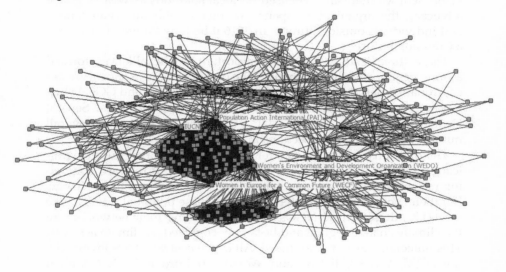

UN Conference on Population and Development in Cairo. From these beginnings, WEDO continued to lobby within UN meetings, including those on the UN Convention on Biological Diversity, the UN Convention to Combat Desertification, and the Beijing Conference on Women's Rights. As a UN veteran, WEDO held several advantages when starting its work within the UNFCCC.

IUCN is unique in the network. Technically an NGO, it has status as an intergovernmental organization in the UNFCCC because its national chapters give it a quasi-governmental character. With a dedicated Global Gender Office since 1998, it provides expertise and support to all arms of IUCN, including its programs, commissions, and national-level organizations. It also supports IUCN's network of regional gender focal points. IUCN is a large environmental NGO with substantial experience in gender issues as well as connections with other NGOs and intergovernmental organizations. With WEDO, UNEP, and UNDP, IUCN formed the GGCA.

Women in Europe for a Common Future was a key actor in the other gender–climate alliance, Gender CC. Formed by European women active at the Rio Earth Summit, the organization had connections with the women's ecology movement in Europe, which had its roots in the anti-nuclear movement.[40] Its engagement in climate change, before WEDO or IUCN participated, was prompted by suggestions that nuclear energy could become an approved activity under the Clean Development Mechanism.[41] Focused on local solutions as well as global advocacy, the organization opened its membership to organizations and individuals outside Europe. In 2016 it became Women Engage for a Common Future.

These three lead NGOs were important in the alliances formed around gender and climate change. The network analysis shows greater coordination between the two groups. The Gender CC and GGCA clusters both grew and increased their connections with each other. Several Gender CC members became GGCA members, increasing the overall number of actors and connections in the network.

The divisions within the gender network could have caused significant problems had the GGCA and Gender CC put forward competing visions of how to address gender in the context of climate change. But their cooperation ultimately mitigated these potential pitfalls. Like the ITUC, these central NGOs managed to bring their networks into the climate change regime and became recognized as climate activists. This outcome was not guaranteed. All of the central NGOs involved – the ITUC, WEDO, IUCN, and Women in Europe for a Common Future – faced several hurdles to their participation but continued to strive to expand their political influence in global governance.

Motivation

Why did these key organizations engage in the climate change regime? Especially in the early years, labour and gender delegates faced pushback from climate change actors, who questioned their motives and their relevance to the regime. They were marginalized and even accused of impeding efforts to achieve a global climate treaty by trying to add new issues to the agenda. Even so, these organizations mobilized hundreds of supporters to attend key UNFCCC meetings and patiently built relationships with civil society and state delegates in the climate change regime. The mobilization began with a few dedicated people within key organizations that were normatively committed to addressing climate change. Later, they were able to convince others to take up climate change as an issue, not out of normative convictions, but rather from the motivation to maintain and even expand their political relevance in global governance into new regimes.

Funding, however, was of only fleeting relevance to the labour movement, and meanwhile, some gender NGOs enjoyed considerable support for their work on climate change. Gender-related work in developing countries is often funded by development donors whose priorities "run in fads, as funding streams shift, and NGOs need to adapt. It's an ebb and flow not a clean answer. Donors became interested in the intersections between gender and climate change."[42] The larger organizations, such as WEDO and IUCN, have long been able to find "niches" in donor funding and have excelled in the competitive funding environment, while others, such as the smaller organizations in Gender CC, have at times struggled to find support for their climate work.[43] True to form, WEDO and IUCN secured funding early on for the GGCA from development donors, including Scandinavian countries that are traditionally supportive of gender-based analysis, in order to ensure their participation in the Bali conference and beyond.[44] GGCA members proved effective fundraisers – of all of the cases explored in this book, only the GGCA secured significant and sustained funding for its activities. The labour case is more typical – a small investment was made, then abandoned.

Labour's capacity to tap membership dues lessened the sting of weak financial support and meant that money was less of a motivation to undertake climate-related advocacy. UNEP provided $500,000 to SustainLabour for a three-year project on Strengthening Union Participation in International Environmental Processes (SustainLabour, 2010). SustainLabour then confronted a 20 per cent reduction in grants in 2010 and 2011 before closing in 2016 (SustainLabour, 2010; 2011.). Even the ITUC finds it difficult to access climate funding. Despite its efforts, donors have not supported unions in their climate-related work.[45] Using internal funds allows for independence from the demands of donors, particularly in terms of results-based management. Internal funding based on membership dues provides the continuity required for the "generational struggle" the climate crisis requires.[46]

This belief that climate change is a generational struggle is what propelled a few people in the labour movement and within the gender network to start advocating for their organizations to tackle climate change. Individuals within both groups saw environmental causes as part of their work. For those working on health and safety, the labour movement is also an environmental movement,[47] which means that a significant group of labour activists are willing to work on climate change for normative reasons. Many members of Gender CC and the GGCA, including WEDO and Women in Europe for a Common Future, had their roots in the Rio Earth Summit held in 1992.

These small groups in both movements drew lessons and motivation from the IPCC. The IPCC's Fourth Assessment Report (AR4) was a turning point for awareness of climate change and its impacts on workers and women; it also catalysed engagement on climate change issues. In its AR4, the IPCC declared that a warming climate was an "unequivocal" fact and provided the strongest evidence to date that climate change was already affecting ecosystems on every continent (IPCC, 2007b). Its evidence for climate impacts was based on observation, not modelling, and demonstrated how climate change was manifesting itself in women's daily lives. This sparked interest among some NGOs to participate in climate change work.[48] All of this led to "murmuring in the network" that climate change might be reversing the gains that had so far been made in women's rights and development.[49] For unions the IPCC provided a scientific clarion call that helped spur members to join the mobilization within climate change through educational programs and presentations, which were provided to any interested union. One of these unions put it this way: "When you know the science, how can you be silent?"[50] Normatively committed individuals would use this scientific base to help make the case that their organizations, and indeed movements, engage in climate change.

There were other, more pressing reasons. Both movements were facing declining prospects to influence other regimes to adopt new rules or norms related to their issues. Also, members of each movement were pushing their central organizations to start work on climate change. Unions found themselves on the back foot when faced with growing questions about where they stood on climate change. Gender NGOs heard from their supporters in the Global South that climate change was already influencing their advocacy efforts and projects. Politically, climate change had become an issue both too big to keep ignoring as well as fertile new ground for advancing labour and gender concerns at a time of narrowing opportunities elsewhere in global governance.

Before engaging in climate change, the agendas of both movements were very full as they worked across a range of regimes.[51] This constrained the resources and attention that organizations could steer toward climate change, even if they were normatively motivated (which some unions were not). Unions were engaged at the international level in helping develop new standards for social responsibility, and several in the movement thought this threatened to undercut occupational health and safety standards.[52] By the mid-2000s, it had been agreed that the social responsibility standard would serve as a set of guiding principles only, and an agreement was reached between the ILO and the International Standardization Organization that recognized the ILO's competence over labour standards. While labour unions still watch the ISO's work closely,[53] much of the labour-related work in that forum had started to wind down toward the end of the 2000s.

In addition, unions were engaged in the WTO as part of the "teamsters and turtles" protest coalition. While it didn't immediately occur to many in the labour movement that the international trade negotiations would impact them nationally, they came to realize the importance of engagement. In this regard, the "Union Activist's Guide" lays out several concerns, including threats to workers in developed and developing countries as transnational corporations relocate to reduce production costs, and how the removal of non-tariff barriers could lead the WTO to rule against labour standards and health and safety rules (Labor Notes, 2000).

These international battles came at the same time unions were feeling "under attack" in several countries, which occupied the agenda of the ICFTU. These fronts took up much of the time of the occupational health and safety committee, which is the group that would have addressed climate change, had there been time:

> It was a movement that wasn't terribly open to the topic [climate change] and had a lot of other fish to fry. Attacks on trade unions by national governments became a huge preoccupation. Then, in addition, [there] were emerging trade issues, debates about the WTO, ISO standards. At least 85 per cent of energy of the [health and safety] Committee was devoted to OHS [occupational health and safety] despite the fact that we had a mandate to work on the environment.[54]

Many showed little interest, save those few normatively motivated individuals, and unionists felt that a number of other areas more directly impacted their work. The labour movement stood alongside WEDO and other women's rights organizations at the WTO. Women's rights organizations were fighting against structural adjustment programs and trying to mainstream gender-based analyses into the WTO's decisions and decision-making process (Moghadam, 2005). In the 2000s, these women's rights organizations were also trying to mainstream gender into the land and biodiversity regimes, mainly because of how these related to the UN Sustainable Development process, which most of the gender and environment NGOs followed after the 1992 Rio Conference.[55]

The Convention on Biological Diversity (CBD) and the UN Convention to Combat Desertification (UNCCD) both include principles recognizing gender and/or women in their respective convention texts. There were entry points for gender advocates to advocate for operationalizing this language throughout implementation and policy decisions and (in the case of the biodiversity) in the subsequent protocols. In the early and mid-2000s, these processes were following divergent paths, neither of which proved conducive to sustaining advocacy on gender issues.

The desertification regime focused narrowly on implementation while the biodiversity regime grew through negotiations for new treaties. The UNCCD parties established a a ten-year strategic framework to enhance implementation in 2007, but it does not include a reference to gender.[56] The CBD, by contrast, had embarked on a process to negotiate a new protocol on Access to Biological Services in 2001. These biodiversity agreements continued to reflect gender even if sometimes the references were slow to emerge.

In part, such successes closed the doors to gender NGOs seeking greater influence. Both regimes included principles related to gender equality and the participation of women. There was a sense that gender NGOs had achieved all they could in these regimes.[57] Several NGOs increasingly questioned the value of continuing to participate and arguing for more relevant forums to be identified.[58] Meanwhile, "climate change was something of a black hole, one that was becoming increasingly too hard to ignore."[59]

Moreover, the members of organizations within both movements were increasingly unable to ignore climate change, and this created further political motivations to engage on the issue. Movements seek to mobilize support, which means listening to their members and responding to them. In the case of climate change, labour unions increasingly pulled other unions into the issue, while women's rights organizations provided an extra push for central organizations to work on climate change. For many in the gender network, climate change seemed a "natural" extension of the work several were already doing on land and water, particularly in developing countries. Through this work, WEDO and others became more aware that climate change was already affecting their projects and women's ability to manage and access resources in sustainable ways. As Cate Owren puts it, there was a "murmuring" from the networks in the Global South as "partners would say in meetings that something [is] happening and we don't know what to do – water supplies changing, crop calendars changing. We've always focused on intersections, so our work on climate change seemed a natural evolution."[60] The effects of climate change, which were accelerating in many regions in developing countries, pushed WEDO and other central gender organizations to start the GGCA at the behest of their partners. For labour, it was even more purely political, in that unions faced the political reality that climate policies were inevitable.

The entry into force of the Kyoto Protocol and signals that several major economies seemed poised to pass climate legislation placed many unions in a reactionary position. By around 2005 the media and policy-makers were asking unions what their positions were on various climate policies, the Kyoto Protocol, and emerging efforts to negotiate a new treaty. They didn't have answers, and ICFTU members agreed to start developing positions on climate change and submitting their views to the UNFCCC.[61] In the scramble to formulate policy (these internal negotiations are detailed below), some unions, particularly in the United States, echoed the positions of their national governments, while others appeared to borrow their positions from environmental groups.[62] With the Bush years ending in the late 2000s, many union members anticipated that a Democratic government would be more open to forging a new climate policy.[63]

For American unions, the election of Barack Obama as president in 2008 further signalled that climate policy was on its way. Unions on both sides of the climate issue would now have to respond.[64] President Obama, who had made climate change a prominent part of his campaign, spoke of a "Green New Deal" with other world leaders.[65] Under the George W. Bush administration, American unions had been conflicted about their overall stance; the "miners were the tail that was wagging the dog," and many powerful American unions took a very "anti-Kyoto, anti-climate" stance.[66] Within the large federations, such as the AFL-CIO, views conflicted: some members wanted to fight environmental regulation, notwithstanding the presence of some progressives in their ranks.[67] President Obama's election made it clear to some unions that the United States was going to change its trajectory on climate change, and this created optimism among unions that favoured climate policy that such policies were on the way.[68] Others observed that "aside from Obama being more ready to engage with the climate issue, the ending of the Bush era gave unions more room to move with their own constituency and with less fear of being attacked by business."[69] Those who were normatively committed to addressing the climate crisis had more political space, and those who were unconvinced had a political need to address the issue or at least respond to it.

Labour unions and gender NGOs sought to protect workers' and women's rights. In each movement, some had been drawn to climate change out of a normative conviction that a globally salient and increasingly pressing crisis needed to be addressed. These individuals were unable to get others on board until other pressing issues either had been resolved or had become unviable for advancing their issues. Those without normative motivations found political motivations to engage in climate change, to advance their issues within a regime that was increasingly impacting their advocacy efforts. After these political motivations emerged, the GGCA and SustainLabour were founded using resources from donors.

Of course, the funding helped, but it was not the overriding motivation for either movement. Funding is allocated to specific organizations working on their own or in partnerships with other organizations. For these organizations, financial contributions can help support engagement with an issue or regime, but it can't support a movement. Without normative or political motivations – that is, the belief that they ought to engage in order to advance its social issues – the funding would have little influence on a movement's overall mobilization. Smaller organizations without funding would not engage. Those with funding may have left once the support ran out (as, for labour, it did). Yet both labour and gender organizations sustained movements working on labour–climate and gender–climate connections, regardless of the material support for their causes. The need to continue to engage in global governance and to respond to demands of their members proved decisive in the labour and gender movements' decisions to undertake climate change advocacy. Next, I turn to the second stage of the forum-multiplying framework – means – to explore how these movements succeeded in gaining recognition as new climate activists.

Means

Major unions and women's rights NGOs found themselves drawn into climate change governance through questions raised by their members and by the need to represent and defend their interests. From this motivation, practical questions arose. Simply showing up at a UNFCCC meeting was not enough, as the labour movement had learned with their one delegate and his report in 2005. Climate change actors had to be convinced to consider labour and gender issues and to recognize those representing those issues. Both movements adroitly found the network cohesion, allies, and rules to leverage in order to prove they were "like" those in the climate change regime.

Building Cohesion

Both movements overcame considerable internal debates and divisions to construct a frame linking labour or gender to climate change that everyone could support. The labour movement marginalized some unions that held fast to climate-denying views, and the gender NGOs vetted the coalition working on reproductive rights. The frames the two networks arrived at were similar in several ways.

The just transition concept was not invented by the labour movement specifically for climate change; rather, it borrowed from other work linking jobs and the environment. Initially, it was used in the context of protecting workers from exposure to organochlorines and justifying legal action against employers' "pollution abuses" (Kohler, 1998; Snell and Fairbrother, 2012;). Its use increased in connection to climate change, coinciding with the labour movement's growing participation in the UNFCCC in 2007 (Hampton, 2015, p. 70). A just transition has several components, including the creation of green jobs, retraining opportunities, social protection for those left behind (e.g., early retirement), and ongoing dialogue between governments and unions (ITUC, 2010). At its heart, the frame links key labour concerns, such as employment and worker's rights, to the need to reduce emissions and transition to a low-carbon economy.

Stating that climate change is a gender issue oversimplifies the frame constructed and disseminated by gender NGOs. Their frame highlights two ways in which gender matters when discussing climate change: first, women are the disproportionate *victims* of climate change; and second, women are *agents* of positive change.[70] Not included in the frame are key gender issues, such as freedom from violence[71] and access to maternal health and reproductive health. The gender NGOs that engaged in the UNFCCC framed gender broadly, in a way that positioned women's role in relation to climate change – as affected but also influential. NGOs used this frame to inform their positions on several discrete issues, originally adaptation and later REDD+, mitigation, and finance.

True to their reformist roots, both frames linking climate change to labour and gender focus on how considering workers' and women's rights can help solve the climate crisis, offering solutions rather than new problems. Neither group questioned the status quo of the negotiations or climate actors' conceptions of the issues at hand. Yet the networks achieved coherence among their members around these frames in very different ways, owing to the different structures of their networks. The labour movement was able to hash out its disagreements at the ITUC and then use the regular meetings and forum provided by the ITUC to develop the just transition frame; gender NGOs negotiated largely in the UNFCCC context, which served as essentially neutral ground between the ideologically divided GGCA and Gender CC.

For labour, the divisions were immediately apparent, and perhaps inherent because of the nature of the climate issue and the diversity of workers' experiences. Climate policy, such as reducing greenhouse emissions, represented an opportunity for some unions but a threat for others. Climate policy could create jobs in the public service and renewable energy sectors but perhaps jeopardize jobs in the automobile and fossil fuel industries. These two camps held widely divergent views as unions wrestled with their stance on climate change issues, particularly mitigation (Sweeney, 2014). To bring these camps together, the ITUC convened negotiations using its own mechanisms.

The ITUC could convene negotiations because of its standing as a peak association for labour with a large and global membership. It served as a coordinator, using its regular World Congress meetings to debate positions and working group meetings to operationalize those decisions. Roughly half the ITUC affiliates have nominated a member to work on the climate change working group, which has almost equal representation from developed and developing countries.[72] This group debates, drafts, and approves policy statements before the UNFCCC meetings, and those statements both inform and constrain ITUC delegates' actions at those meetings.[73] It was through these forums, the working group and the Congress, that climate policies developed over time, with the result that the question of what mitigation targets to support was eventually set aside and a broader just transition frame was developed.

In the lead-up to the Copenhagen conference, unions felt considerable pressure to present a united front. Many recognized the need to find a "form of words" that everyone could support.[74] Continuing fractures, especially public ones, would destabilize any trust labour actors had started to build with climate actors, who would be wary of any (further) climate denial from unions. There was a recognized need to position unions as a

legitimate actor in the climate discussion. That we stood on the right side of history. We could not allow roaming speeches happening all over the place. The media is fantastic for noticing any differences or problems. They look to the unions for opposition to climate change and are uninterested when we're for climate action.[75]

The unified position shifted toward the broader idea of a just transition. This culminated at the ITUC's Second World Congress in June 2010, where climate change was a central issue. In a resolution on "combating climate change through sustainable development and a just transition," the Congress called for "promoting an integrated approach to sustainable development through a just transition where social progress, environmental protection and economic needs are brought into a framework of democratic governance, where labour and other human rights are respected, and gender equality achieved" (ITUC, 2010). The ITUC reiterated its support for limiting global temperature increase to two degrees, reducing global emissions to 85 per cent by the year 2050, and setting out interim targets, including a target for developed countries to reduce emissions by 25 to 40 per cent by 2020 relative to 1990 emissions (ITUC, 2010). The decisions were carefully crafted to reflect the concerns of most unions, which led to acquiescence by other unions, including the AFL-CIO.

As Rosemberg (2013) stresses, the discussions were transparent, not "hidden negotiations among a few high-powered unions." References to democracy and human rights in the definition of a just transition were inserted by unions from developing countries.[76] The Congress resolution also included language related to increasing adaptation efforts in developing countries and supporting the UNFCCC's principle of common but differentiated responsibilities (ITUC, 2010). These insertions were important to secure the support of unions from developing countries, particularly those from emerging economies, which tended to follow their national government's positions on climate change.[77] Emerging economies' positions in the UNFCCC from 2007 through to the Paris Agreement's adoption in 2015 moved incrementally toward accepting a greater role in reducing emissions. Even so, they firmly supported the principle of common but differentiated responsibilities, arguing that the principle meant that their actions were to be voluntary, as in the Kyoto Protocol, and nationally determined, as in the Paris Agreement, and that developed countries should bear most of the burden for addressing the climate crisis. Following this position, unions from emerging economies pushed strongly for including a reference to the idea of differentiation between developed and developing countries, even though it meant that their American counterparts could face greater job insecurity resulting from stronger climate action.

With these countries' support, a critical mass developed in favour of the resolution. Several expected the AFL-CIO to object, yet it remained silent. Agreeing to the consensus was a strategic decision, not a drastic change in policy positioning. Voting against the resolution would have brought "unwanted attention" to the AFL-CIO.[78] The organization viewed the potential backlash from fellow unions and perhaps the media as costlier than acquiescing to the climate resolution.

This perhaps was not a difficult decision. The ITUC has no authority over its members. It could not force the AFL-CIO to domestically advocate for the IPCC target or for a just transition. As one union delegate noted, several American unions continued to lobby the Environmental Protection Agency to dismantle its carbon regulations. The AFL-CIO averted reputational damage while continuing business as usual on the ground.[79]

The ITUC too had a reputational stake in achieving a consensus resolution on climate change. It somehow had to maintain its position as a central hub in the movement, particularly because the ITUC had only existed for three years at that point. As one American delegate recalls, "the ITUC would have lost all legitimacy with unions in the South if the resolution had failed."[80] With the Congress resolution adopted, the ITUC could go to the UNFCCC meetings armed with several concrete calls stemming from the just transition frame. In time, the frame overtook the more concrete policy proposals, which is perhaps not surprising. Other labour confederations also found it easier to find agreement on general political messages rather than on concrete proposals owing to the different effects of climate policy on unions.[81] The frame had broad (enough) support and could accommodate several messages on how unions could support efforts to transition to a low-carbon economy.

The ITUC could use its own forums to bring together the movement and paper over the tensions with the just transition frame because the frame accommodates nearly all unions' views. Gender NGOs faced divisions as well, given that the GGCA and Gender CC started from different ideological points regarding how to address climate change. Because there was no central organization to bring the two groups together, the UNFCCC ultimately, and inadvertently, served as the forum for their collaboration. In establishing the Women and Gender Constituency (explained further below), the two coalitions had to find consensus on their statements and positions. The GGCA and Gender CC pursued the constituency together, and it became an effective meeting space to improve cohesion among gender NGOs and coordinate with others.

While anyone could attend a meeting of the Women and Gender constituency, NGOs in the constituency were responsible for reaching agreement on all statements.[82] The constituency proved a useful civil society space that afforded political freedom from the more conservative stances of the international organizations that were part of the GGCA. The constituency became a new outlet for positions, such as stronger calls for mitigation targets, than was possible from within the GGCA."[83]

The need for consensus facilitated learning among delegates.[84] Members of the provisional constituency set it as their goal to "formalize the voice of the women's and gender civil society organizations present and regularly active in UNFCCC processes, and to debate, streamline and strengthen the positions which these organizations put forth." In the same document, Gender CC and GGCA members also agreed to a governance structure. These protocols created common ground to work together and in some ways helped the two groups "function almost as an alliance, in a cohesive way, leading to a huge change in terms of how we work together."[85]

Like labour, gender NGOs arrived at a broad frame that linked climate change to gender issues, postponing consensus on specific and perhaps contentious policy issues. This frame positioned women as both disproportionately impacted by climate change and as agents of change. The frame did not include any mention of reproductive rights, after the GGCA and Gender CC vetted the issue. There was considerable potential for gender NGOs to fracture into competing frames owing to their differing views, yet the groups collaborated to develop and use the gender frame in a consistent manner.

The first aspect of the frame was easier to arrive at, because Gender CC and the GGCA shared similar ideas about the relationship between gender inequality and women's vulnerability to the effects of climate change. Both networks linked gender inequalities to climate change outcomes. Gender CC members highlighted how gendered divisions of labour, income inequalities, and differences in power influence women's resilience to the impacts of climate change and their ability to influence climate policy. Similarly, the GGCA states in a training manual on gender and climate change that climate change impacts "affect men, women, boys and girls differently because of the inequalities between them caused by gender-based roles in society and the resulting levels of vulnerability" (UNDP, 2012, p. 5). While both groups agreed that women's roles in society ascribed by gendered norms can affect their vulnerability to climate change and that climate change policy should include women in decision-making, they differed on what those climate change policies should be.

Gender CC opposed market mechanisms, such as REDD+ and the Clean Development Mechanism. Among the problems Gender CC cited with market mechanisms was that they failed to tackle the causes of climate change, namely, excessive consumption in developed countries and ignorance of social issues disproportionately threatening marginalized people, particularly women (Gender CC 2009). By contrast, the GGCA took a more moderate approach, seeking to mainstream gender considerations and women themselves into the decision-making on market mechanisms. For instance, after a workshop in 2009 called "Engendering REDD+," the report highlighted that

> REDD+ clearly presents opportunities for positive outcomes for forest-dependent communities, but also risks serious negative outcomes, especially for women who rely on forest resources to sustain their families' livelihoods ... Since REDD+ is performance-based, it rewards programs that are more effective and more efficient. This provides a rationale for mainstreaming gender; it is important to demonstrate cases where women's involvement has [been] shown to make a difference in terms of effectiveness and efficiency. (GGCA, 2009)

Not until 2011 did the Women and Gender Constituency submit a shared view on REDD+. The statement outlined several concerns: REDD+ would contribute to land grabs, create perverse incentives and inequities, transfer mitigation responsibility away from developed countries, and ignore traditional and Indigenous cosmologies (Women and Gender Constituency, 2011). This was a mix of Gender CC and the GGCA's positions. While they worked in the constituency space to find agreement before 2011, the frame that solidified to highlight women's vulnerability *and* agency.

The frame, and the specific proposals it informs, did not include reproductive health issues as brought forward by the Population and Climate Change Alliance in 2009. This small group serves as a microcosm for viewing the consequences of a fragmented frame. Population Action International was the key organization linking reproductive health and population dynamics to climate change. Based on its experiences in other processes such as the Committee on the Status of Women and the Commission on Population Development, some Population Action International delegates expected that they could insert language on the need for family planning into the climate change agreement anticipated in Copenhagen.[86] In the run-up to the UNFCCC meeting held in June

2009, just six months before the Copenhagen conference, they realized
this goal was unrealistic. They instead started referring to the Copenhagen meeting as an opportunity to raise awareness on the links between
resilience, adaptation, and family planning.[87] Any potential inclusion in
the gender frame was unlikely, in part because Gender CC was against
its inclusion, and also because other organizations were advancing
more controversial ideas around population and climate change.

The frame advanced by Population Action International was based
on resilience and adaptive capacity to climate change. Perhaps this
could have found a place within the gender frame espoused by Gender CC and the GGCA. The Population and Climate Change Alliance
argued that providing universal access to family planning and the right
to reproductive health would reduce vulnerability at the household
and individual levels and moderate population dynamics in a way that
also increased resilience to the effects of climate change.[88] The focus
was on adaptation and reducing women's vulnerability.

But other organizations not aligned with the Population and Climate
Change Alliance linked population dynamics with mitigation, offering controversial solutions that muddied the political waters for any
group discussing reproductive rights. The Optimum Population Trust
advocated "PopOffsets" as a solution to climate change.[89] PopOffsets
were proposed as a mechanism for offsetting carbon emissions through
contributions to family planning projects in developed and developing
countries. Gender NGO representatives, most vocally those from Gender CC, were firmly against this idea, characterizing it as "tone deaf regarding the sensitivities between the global North and South, especially
regarding burden sharing."[90] Although not affiliated with the idea,
members of the Population and Climate Change Alliance found themselves confronted with questions about PopOffsets.[91] Their message
was diluted. Others could cherry-pick which frame to reject or accept.

The lack of coherence made it easier to vet the reproductive rights
frame. PopOffsets provided a reason for gender NGOs to dismiss the
claims of reproductive health organizations entirely. One delegate
working on reproductive health issues at the Copenhagen conference
recalls being surprised that Gender CC was so "vehemently opposed"
to the adaptation-based messaging.[92] Gender CC rejected population
growth as a key driver of climate change and any reframing of family
planning as a climate change solution (Gender CC, 2011 p. 1). Gender
CC was wary of a mitigation focus seeping in, as encapsulated in the
PopOffsets proposal.[93] For Gender CC, the real culprit was (and remains) overconsumption in developed countries: the network viewed
population dynamics discussions as shifting responsibility for reducing

emissions to developing countries (Gender CC, n.d.; 2011). PopOffsets distracted and detracted from any possible conversation, although one delegate believed that the opposition was in part principled and was always going to be difficult.[94]

Gender NGOs sidestepped the reproductive health NGOs, underscoring the ability of centrally positioned NGOs to set or vet the agenda. The organizations cooperated, striking an implicit bargain that the frame would centre on the issues on which they agreed, highlighting women's agency and vulnerability. Where there was disagreement – be it on market mechanisms, family planning, or population dynamics – the network sidelined the issues. Not all issues from the traditional regime make it in the target regime, and cooperation among lead NGOs may have required setting aside issues that one felt strongly must be vetted. The need for cohesion among GGCA and Gender CC members trumped any temptation to bring new organizations and ideas into the gender frame.

The experiences of gender NGOs and the labour movement varied, in part because of the different structures of their networks. The labour movement was centralized around the ITUC; gender NGOs were split into two coalitions with differing views and a third alliance with controversial views. Both networks confronted internal differences in views. How they dealt with them – through internal negotiations away from the UNFCCC, or through negotiations at the UNFCCC – was influenced by the degree of centralization in the networks. From these internal negotiations, both networks arrived at a broad frame that all could explicitly or tacitly support. These broad frames could then be applied to specific areas of negotiations in the UNFCCC, as labour and gender advocates sought to leverage the rules as entry points to the climate change regime.

Leveraging Rules

Both labour and gender advocates carved themselves an institutional place in the UNFCCC through constituency status, and both sought to link their issues to specific rules under development in the UNFCCC. Labour unions focused on setting targets and mitigation rules more generally, while gender NGOs started with adaptation rules before moving to finance and other areas of climate policy. These initial choices fit with their frames. The just transition frame focuses on how to protect workers and positions labour unions as leaders, as economies reduce their emissions and ultimately move to a low-carbon future. The gender frame highlights women's vulnerability and agency.

Discussions on how to build resilience to the effects of climate change was an appropriate place to underscore the need to consider gender.

These initial choices mattered. They kept the bargain made internally on the frame even while making it possible to find niches in the negotiations where climate delegates could recognize the validity of the new climate activists' claims. Neither group sought to undermine the rules. Instead, they sought recognition as actors very much like others already embedded in the UNFCCC process.

One way both labour and gender organizations sought recognition was through constituency status at a time when they were struggling to be accepted by climate actors. The view at the time was that social issues were, at best, a distraction from the core business at hand and, at worst, undermining the push for an ambitious climate agreement. One labour delegate cited the experience of being kicked out of a Climate Action Network meeting as a motivation for seeking constituency status specifically for labour.[95] Similarly, a reason for institutionalizing the GGCA with a Secretariat and formal structure was the pushback to securing constituency status; several felt that "if we couldn't have a formal space, we'd make the space." NGOs and states in the climate change regime were initially not open to the participation of labour unions or gender NGOs. But the first hurdle to constituency status – being recognized as a formal constituency within the UNFCCC – was the UNFCCC Secretariat.

Both groups used the constituency system from Agenda 21 to argue for a formal place in the UNFCCC system. As explained in chapter 3, the constituency system at the UNFCCC resembles, but does not follow, the Major Groups system established by Agenda 21, which gives special status to groups, including women and workers and trade unions. The UNFCCC does not have the same groupings and has admitted groups over time rather than automatically providing space. In 2007, labour delegates argued that as a Major Group under Agenda 21 they should have constituency status. After all, the other "Rio Conventions" and other UN environmental forums follow the Agenda 21 system.[96] They sought to import the norm into the UNFCCC. After labour unions were granted status, other groups with Major Group status, but missing from the UNFCCC constituency list, made similar claims and established constituency status.[97] The Women and Gender constituency was "provisionally" established in 2008 and granted permanent status in 2010.

The Secretariat established this stepwise system. First, parties were granted provisional (or as one delegate called it, "probationary") status. Two years later, if the group could demonstrate that it was organized and active and had a stable point person and organization to interact with the Secretariat, permanent status was conferred. For activists, this was labour-intensive. The ITUC put together four reports detailing how many delegates attended from the labour movement, side events they hosted, and other activities they undertook to demonstrate they were valuable stakeholders working for a positive outcome.[98] Gender NGOs set up a website to document their activities, and each coalition listed its side events and other activities to jointly submit to the Secretariat as a way to demonstrate its contributions to the process.[99]

Constituency status meant recognition by the UNFCCC, the official body convening the negotiations, and by the parties engaged in those negotiations. Tellingly, many union and gender activists specifically used the term "recognition" when discussing why constituency status mattered to them.[100] For unions, constituency status was a symbol that labour was a recognized actor in the UNFCCC. As internal meeting minutes show, those involved in securing constituency status framed it as an "acknowledgement [that] signals the importance given to our priorities and our involvement in the process" (ITUC 2008). It served as a symbol of recognition of unions' place in the negotiations.[101] For gender NGOs, constituency status represented recognition of their cause and helped garner attention in the cacophony of voices vying for attention in the UNFCCC: "Because we have this constituency, some people were willing to listen to us more than other issues than have not been as recognized."[102]

Constituency status also brings visibility within the negotiations. Both movements used this visibility to mobilize new supporters within the climate change regime that otherwise they would not have been able to attract. Having a seat at the table signalled to unions that they would be heard and that there was value in attending UNFCCC negotiations.[103] The office space, workshop invitations, and other material benefits of constituency space helped coordinate the growing labour contingent within the UNFCCC. As more unionists started to attend the annual climate meetings, the need to train newcomers on the challenges of engaging on climate change, and on how to deploy their just transition message, grew.[104] A simple thing – an office provided by the Secretariat – helped coordinate labour unions' delegates and their message.

Gender NGOs used their status to recruit from within the climate change regime. They took advantage of the public advertisements of all constituency meetings' times and locations and opened their meetings to anyone with an interest in gender–climate linkages. Women from international organizations, states, and other NGOs soon started to attend.[105] These meetings helped NGOs find new allies to raise their issues. For example, gender advocates raised the lack of attention to gender in the negotiations over the Paris Agreement "rulebook."[106] NGOs raised this issue among constituency members through internal communications.[107] The next day, Mexico, a regular participant in constituency meetings, publicly called for reflecting the preambular references to gender and other social issues throughout the negotiations (IISD, 2016). Constituency status provided visibility and recognition useful for mobilizing from within and outside of the movements. Labour and gender organizations used their status as dedicated spaces to recruit, teach, and deploy actors to advance their discursive frames.

While constituency space served as an official recognition of belonging and had other, more tangible benefits, on its own it did not guarantee that new climate activists would be accepted in the climate change regime. Labour and gender advocates needed to convince state delegates – those wielding decision-making power – that their issues were within the remit of climate policy. To do that, they had to link labour and gender issues to specific rules in climate policy. Both movements showcased their issues as potential solutions to problems faced by climate actors. Labour unions offered to help overcome opposition to mitigation policies, while gender advocates demonstrated how women could help advance adaptation solutions.

There were other substantive rules that the movements considered leveraging. Unions considered adaptation. Awareness was high among American unions after Hurricane Katrina and among unions from developing countries.[108] Unions in Kenya hosted round tables and discussed the climate impacts they were already experiencing in agriculture, forestry, and other sectors in 2006. These documented effects left an impression on those unionists who previously had thought of climate change in terms of mitigation.[109] Politically, one union member observed that speaking on adaptation would help achieve balance between northern and southern interests within the movement.[110] Before Copenhagen, labour delegates suggested text linking adaptation, technology transfer, and other non-mitigation rules in the draft agreement. But these suggestions were placeholders, meant to show the interest and commitment of the labour movement; there was little systemic evidence connecting labour to these institutions.[111]

Gender NGOs explored several rules as entry points, often realizing there was little traction among delegates for these ideas. Regarding mitigation, some argued that there was "little to be gained by looking at the responsibility for emissions on a gendered basis," in part because apportioning emissions by gender would be technically difficult and politically unpalatable (Wamukona & Skutsch, 2008). From there, gender NGOs tried to leverage the negotiations for a new "shared vision" in the agreement being developed before Copenhagen. The GGCA called for a vision that "effective and responsive implementation requires that gender considerations and gender balanced participation be incorporated at all levels in all areas of the Bali Action plan" (GGCA, 2009b). With Gender CC, the GGCA suggested a gender paragraph in the shared vision, which would state: "The full integration of gender perspectives is essential to effective action on all aspects of climate change, including adaptation, mitigation, technology sharing, financing, and capacity building. The advancement of women, their leadership and meaningful participation, and their engagement as equal stakeholders in all climate related processes and implementation must be guaranteed" (Women and Gender Constituency, n.d.).

These suggestions found little traction. Delegates viewed the shared vision in terms of emissions reductions and temperature goals. Most discussions and submissions included elaborate emissions pathway scenarios and mitigation targets commensurate with 1.5°C or 2°C average temperature increases. An environmental NGO delegate recalls that the shared vision discussions before Copenhagen "really required us to bring our technically minded delegates."[112] Laden with technical jargon and focused on environmental goals, these discussions did not provide an open space for social issues, and this left gender NGOs to focus on adaptation.[113]

Adaptation was the opening that gender NGOs found most useful, and it ultimately helped to explain their engagement in the UNFCCC. The negotiations for a new agreement included adaptation on the agenda, which "cracked open the sector-specific, isolated issues to new stakeholder groups."[114] Advocates could link gender inequalities to vulnerability to the effects of climate change, as many of the early reports produced by the GGCA and Gender CC documented women's vulnerabilities and their potential to build resilience in a world with a changing climate. As June Zeitlin, Executive Direction of WEDO in 2007, said in the press release launching the GGCA, "disasters, like poverty, have a woman's face," in this way closely tying development, gender, and climate-related disasters (GGCA, 2007).

The close identification of the adaptation issue with developing countries (see chapter 3) made adaptation a useful entry point. The four GGCA founding members, WEDO, IUCN, UNDP, and UNEP, worked extensively in developing countries. They could use that expertise to align their message with the emerging adaptation institutions. Such on-the-ground knowledge of development and gender issues was one reason why adaptation was a natural starting place for gender advocates, although later they branched into finance and mitigation (see UN Women, 2015; Williams, 2016).[115] While gender activists do not take credit for the emergence of adaptation on the climate agenda, several pointed out that adaptation became a useful entry point for gender.[116] Meanwhile, unions focused on mitigation in what proved to be internally divisive discussions.

Unions' focus on mitigation targets as an entry point was meant to signal to climate change actors that the labour movement was positively engaged.[117] Initial discussions considered advocating for temperature goals (e.g., 2°C), acceptable levels of carbon dioxide (350 or 450 ppm), or emissions targets against a baseline year (e.g., 40 per cent below 1990).[118] The ITUC's preferred position was to support the IPCC targets of 25 to 40 per cent reductions by 2020 below 1990 levels, and 85 per cent by 2050 (ITUC, 2007). The AFL-CIO could not accept those targets and timelines.[119] It had only recently accepted that "human use of fossil fuels is undisputedly contributing to global warming" (AFL-CIO, 2007). In a memo to the ITUC, the AFL-CIO acknowledged that the discussion of targets was causing disagreements between the organizations and expressed concern that the IPCC targets were unattainable, given the availability at the time of technologies such as carbon capture and storage (Sweeney, 2014). Still, the ITUC continued to support ambitious targets and worked within the response measures forum, another mitigation institution.

The response measures forum was designed to explore the implications of climate action. Its main supporters were, and remain, countries within the Arab Group, which pointed out that a move away from fossil fuels through mitigation policies would decimate their economies. The forum has often been seen as a "negative space," despite efforts by some countries to highlight positive consequences of climate action, such as green jobs.[120] Within the just transitions space created in the response measures forum, unions had the opportunity to present states with the findings of their research and to showcase how a just transition could help bring about political support for a low-carbon future.[121] Again, the goal was to use mitigation as an issue that positioned the movement as a political force that could support climate solutions.

There were two benefits for the labour and gender organizations in their respective mitigation and adaptation choices: they were able to position themselves as experts on an emerging niche area of climate policy, and to position themselves as part of a solution that aligned with the status quo of current climate policy. Both these strategic benefits were valuable to gain recognition and influence with climate governors.

Linking the frames to these institutions established unions and gender NGOs as expert authorities on the connections between their issues and mitigation or adaptation. They became the "go to" experts when policy-makers wanted to avoid pushback from workers, create green jobs, or include gender-sensitive language in the negotiations.

Both groups undertook significant research efforts to bolster their claims. Unions produced research focused on job creation and the effects of various climate policies on employment across and within economic sectors. A collaborative report produced by UNEP, the ILO, the International Organization of Employers, and the ITUC (UNEP, 2008) emphasized the need for systemic information on the links between climate change and jobs, despite the growing rhetoric of green jobs. That information gap was filled by others in the movement and later by the ITUC as well. The European Trade Union Confederation completed one of the most ambitious studies on the cross-sectional impacts on jobs, and opportunities for jobs. It estimated an expected 1.5 per cent net gain in employment by 2030 in the sectors considered, as a result of climate change policy (ETUC, 2007). It cautioned, however that both the quantity and quality of these new jobs should be considered, to guard against newer jobs being of a lower quality than jobs in established sectors (ETUC, 2007, p. 73). The labour movement produced the information needed to back up its claim that mitigation, employment rates, and workers' rights were all connected: "Unions are not experts about the science, so rather than argue that we should be inserting our views in areas that we do have expertise in – social policy, social justice, industry restructuring. Basically, saying to the climate negotiators 'if you want to achieve such and such reduction, you need to look at these issues if you are going to achieve them.'"[122] In response to the information and expertise presented, some state delegates began to see labour unions as unique contributors, the "only ones able to speak to the workforce in a low-carbon economy, while also supporting our calls for more ambitious mitigation."[123] It was also information produced by the movement's actors, making them the experts on the mitigation–labour link.

For gender NGOs, adaptation seemed like a natural starting point because they could use their expertise in development in the context of climate change. When adaptation was framed as a development issue (chapter 3), gender NGOs recognized themselves as implicated in climate change work. Gender NGOs recognized that climate change could impact the attainment of the Millennium Development Goals, including those related to gender equality.[124] Like labour, gender NGOs identified a systemic lack of evidence and sought to fill that gap. The IPCC was silent on gender issues because of the lack of peer-reviewed research on gender and climate change; this undermined the Panel's ability to consider gender issues because it reviewed only peer-reviewed publications (Hemmati, 2005). At the local level, women's roles in providing household energy, food, water, and care for children and the elderly increased their reliance on natural systems as well as their vulnerability to changes expected from climate change, as documented by Gender CC (Röhr, 2007). Other researchers amassed considerable evidence about how women's positions in the family, community, economy, and society were affecting their resilience to the effects of climate change (see Aguilar et al., 2009; Dankelman, 2010; GGCA, 2012).

This evidence base positioned gender NGOs as the experts on the links between gender and climate change. State delegates invited them to some of the informal negotiations, usually closed to observers, for the Lima Programme on Gender. One delegate underscored that gender NGOs "taught" delegates the differences between gender equality, gender sensitivity, and gender responsiveness.[125] Climate delegates were debating these terms yet had little experience with them. Gender activists were able to define and help shape the debate because others viewed them as experts in the field.

Second, and unlike the climate justice movement explored in the next chapter, unions and gender NGOs positioned themselves as part of the solution by forging links with these institutions. Both movements, as reformers, aligned themselves with current climate efforts and showcased how they could help bring about better climate outcomes. The just transition frame focuses on how workers can support mitigation solutions. Many of the core aspects of the just transition frame found ways to redeploy countries' labour forces in the service of a low-carbon economy. Workers can be retrained to work in renewable energy, public transportation, or other low-carbon intensive sectors. A strong social protection net can catch workers lost in the transition, helping provide for their families while workers find new roles in the new economy. Together, these elements demonstrate how including worker's rights can secure the political support necessary to take ambitious climate change action – that workers' support can help pass climate policies and reduce any potential risks to a politician who wishes to promote climate policies. As one of the term's originators argues:

> The sequence is important. A just transition is a prerequisite to all other progress on, for example, the climate issue. Just transition measures must be in place before workers will willingly accept stringent measures to protect the climate, and while it is easy to dismiss the power of unions in many contexts, workers allied with capitalists to oppose climate measures create an insurmountable barrier to change.[126]

Gender NGOs were equally focused on being part of the solution as a means to gain recognition. As Ulrike Röhr of LIFE e.V. and Gender CC stated in 2007: "The lack of gender perspectives in the current climate process not only violates women's human rights ... but it also leads to shortcomings in the efficiency and effectiveness of climate related measures and instruments" (Gender CC, 2007). Later, the GGCA (2013, p. 4) concurred that "women's greater participation is also likely to enhance the effectiveness and sustainability of climate change projects and policies." The consistent message of gender NGOs, like that of their labour counterparts, was "help us help you." By including gender issues in adaptation policy, and labour issues in mitigation policy, the climate institutions will be stronger and more effective. And these new climate activists will be useful, perhaps even political expedient, voices for climate action.

Aligning with the existing institutions of the climate change regime only seems straightforward in retrospect. As noted above, many labour and gender advocates encountered a steep curve while learning the informal and formal rules at the UNFCCC. Everything from how to get constituency status and engage with delegates to how to navigate the science and technicalities of mitigation and adaptation policy presented new challenges. Both these movements were aided by powerful allies that had standing and experience in the climate change regime and that were motivated to help labour and gender advocates gain a foothold in their new institutional context.

Finding Allies

International organizations were crucial brokers. UNEP was particularly key and in many ways was the model ally for both movements. Already embedded in the climate change regime, UNEP fulfilled all the main tasks to help labour unions and gender NGOs gain acceptance in their new social and institutional environment. The partnership between UNEP and the labour and gender movements dates to the mid-2000s when both movements started participating in the climate change regime. UNEP provided research documenting the links between climate change and labour and gender, respectively, in addition to training, resources, and, importantly, public support for labour–climate and gender–climate links and their associated movements. UNEP lent its support and climate credentials to the labour and gender movements at a time when many climate actors were, at best, sceptical of the value these social movements brought to climate governance.

Members of both movements cite UNEP as a key actor catalysing and supporting their entry into the climate change regime, although the partnership between UNEP and labour broke down over time.[127] Still, at the start of these movements' efforts to become recognized as climate activists, UNEP – and, for gender, UNDP as well – played crucial roles bringing together stakeholders, providing information linking climate change to labour and gender, and publicly supporting the new climate activists' efforts in the climate change regime.

The convening power of international organizations was useful in the early years to bring together various UN agencies and organizations within the movements. UNEP reached out to the ICFTU (ITUC's precursor) to organize the Trade Union Assembly on Labour and the Environment conference (referred to as the "WILL" conference), held early 2006. It was convened under the auspices of UNEP with several international labour organizations,[128] the ILO, and the World Health Organization, and brought together more than 150 representatives. Among the outcomes of the conference, the three UN bodies present committed to supporting trade union engagement on sustainable development.[129] This support included financial support to SustainLabour and funding for some unionists to travel to the Bali conference in 2007.[130] Later, an *ad hoc* working group with the ILO, UNEP, and the ITUC produced the first assessment of the implications for labour of climate change and transitioning to a low-carbon economy; it may have been here that the term "green jobs" was coined (see UNEP, 2007). For many, the conference and its subsequent workshops and projects constituted a turning point in the labour movement's thinking on climate change, as it engaged and trained dozens of new unions in climate change.[131]

The involvement of UNEP and the UNDP quickly became more institutionalized. UNEP and the UNDP are founding members of the GGCA. In forming the GGCA, both organizations were implementing agencies for "gender-responsive climate change initiatives and decision-making," which is the overarching project outlining the activities that UNEP, the UNDP, the IUCN, and WEDO will undertake through the GGCA. The UNDP served as the grant recipient and fund manager for the funds provided by the Government of Finland and, later, the Government of Denmark. The UNDP's Gender Team was a key part of the project's management, which had to manage and overcome difficulties around fairly distributing funds among the UNDP, the IUCN, and WEDO (Rao & Bazilli, 2013).

In its role in the project, UNEP supported research that was useful in the early days of the GGCA's advocacy efforts. UNEP was a key part of phases 1 and 2 (2007–9 and 2010–12), focused on knowledge generation, capacity building, and integrating gender into policy, but it stepped back from the project as it entered its third phase, to influence UN-FCCC negotiations (Rao & Bazilli, 2013). These early research-oriented activities were important convince climate actors of the links between gender and climate change. Many recognized the lack of data available on the gender–climate connections in 2007 and sought to fill these gaps (see Gender CC, 2005; Röhr, 2007). UNEP published research on the possible links between gender and various aspects of climate change policy, such as mitigation, adaptation, and capacity building (Wamu-kona & Skutsch, 2008). UNEP hosted reports provided by other gender advocates exploring the connections between gender, adaptation, and climate change, including a 2007 report by Ulrike Röhr, a driving force behind Gender CC.

The support of international organizations for the labour movement and gender NGOs extended into the UNFCCC, even if they did not directly aid efforts to influence negotiations. By providing public support and introductions to climate actors, UNEP – and, for gender, the UNDP – helped labour and gender organizations gain visibility and recognition. Essentially showing "they're with me," to their fellow climate actors, these international organizations provided a crucial introduction to climate actors. The international organizations opened their networks to the labour and gender movements to help persuade actors that labour and gender considerations should be part of climate policy. Key was UNEP's status and reach in the climate community, along with its capacity to frame and promote ideas such as green jobs and a just transition (Sweeney, 2014, p. 8). Similarly, in early discussions to form the GGCA, UNEP and the UNDP brought new audiences, member bases, and access to new circles that the gender NGOs would not easily have had access to otherwise.[132] The organizations co-authored reports, provided introductions to partner organizations, and participated in side events in the UNFCCC. UNEP participated in at least nineteen side events organized by the ITUC or by the GGCA (not Gender CC, notably) between 2007 and 2009. Then UNEP Executive Director Achim Steiner opened a side event titled "Green Jobs and Skills: Drivers for Climate Transitions" in 2007.[133] The involvement of international organizations at events held by labour and gender advocates was a very public act of support.

Why would UNEP and the UNDP engage social issues in the context of climate change when few others were drawing the links? UNEP hoped to increase its engagement with civil society groups outside of the usual environmental NGOs. It recognized labour as potentially a powerful voice for environmental action, in part because unions were, and still are, well organized and active on some environmental issues at the national and international levels.[134] Furthermore, by participating in the GGCA, UNEP and the UNDP gained access to the channels and advocacy tactics of the NGOs, allowing them to indirectly support types of activities that international organizations constrained by states are usually unable to undertake.[135]

The alliances could be uneasy at times. An ideological divide softened the relationship between UNEP and unions. Unions were focused on the role of government and the public sector in protecting workers' rights and on fostering social dialogue to facilitate a just transition. UNEP, to some in the labour movement, seemed more focused on engaging the private sector. Furthermore, UNEP viewed labour as another civil society actor, whereas unions sought a tripartite dialogue, with an place at the table equal to that of employers and governments, as at the ILO.[136] As outlined above, among gender NGOs, the inherent constraints (and to some, conservatism) of international organizations gave Gender CC members pause when they considered cooperation with the GGCA. Working with international organizations can open vital doors for non-state actors seeking entry and acceptance in a new regime, but these organizations have their own interests and mandates. Although not disinterested or entirely altruistic allies, international organizations can be helpful brokers in the process of forum multiplying.

Conclusion

The experiences of the labour movement's and gender NGOs' engagement with climate change demonstrates both the difficulties of moving to a new regime and how to overcome these challenges. Climate NGOs, state delegates, and the Secretariat, among others, ultimately accepted unions and gender NGOs as legitimate actors in the climate change arena. Such recognition was far from guaranteed, particularly given the chilly reception that labour and gender activists initially received.

With little initial enthusiasm for or uptake of their ideas, both labour and gender activists needed to engage in the long term and to remind themselves of their motivations to undertake climate work. Within both, there was a core of normatively committed individuals who capitalized on the openings provided when work in other areas of global governance dried up. Others in the movement were motivated by the need to remain relevant in global governance and to continue to advance their issues. This was particularly true when the issue of climate change confronted unions, as the prospect of mitigation policy seemed imminent. Similarly, gender NGOs' development work was increasingly threatened by climate change, pulling many toward the cause.

Once motivated, internal divisions threatened both groups. Yet the ITUC's ability to convene negotiations away from the climate space brought recalcitrant unions on board; meanwhile, the GGCA and Gender CC arrived at a common message through cooperation within their constituency space. Rules such as those relating to constituency status provide a measure of recognition. Leveraging those rules, and linking to substantive rules, further demonstrated that labour and gender issues were relevant to climate change discussions. Moreover, the movements used those institutions to position themselves on the right side of history, as actors that could help achieve a low-carbon, climate-resilient future. As reformers, aligned with international organizations and accepting most of the bases of current climate policy, labour unions and gender NGOs stood in stark contrast to the climate justice movement.

5 The Radical Challengers: Climate Justice Now!

The climate justice movement created a unique brand of climate activism and illustrated a different way to forum-multiply than the model illustrated by the labour and women's rights movements. Unabashedly antagonistic – that is, by the norms of traditional climate change activists – the climate justice movement set out to overturn the status quo of the capitalist system and the market-friendly approaches of the climate change regime. While traditional climate NGOs were quieter, lobbying from within the hallways of the UNFCCC for incremental change, the climate justice movement borrowed tactics from the global justice movement, including direct action. The complex critique of the climate justice movement, abridged under the banner "system change not climate change," loosely united a diverse group of organizations and individuals. The interactions among these disparate movements shaped their tactics and frames and, ultimately, their role in the climate process (Hadden, 2015).

Regarding the three aspects of forum multiplying, the climate justice movement meets the criteria, albeit in a different way than the labour or gender movements. First, the participation of the justice movement increased rapidly as it gathered itself around an evolving climate justice frame. The discursive frame highlighted the social justice issues associated with climate impacts as well as the capitalist roots of many of the climate institutions. Climate justice advocates declared many existing institutions to be "false solutions," including market mechanisms such as REDD+ that would pay others to plant forests and sequester carbon. Second, climate justice advocates expressed scepticism of many institutions even while showcasing their support for the regime's goals. They used the institutions they sought to overhaul or undermine as discursive hooks for their claims that they belonged in the regime.

Regarding the third aspect, recognition, several developing countries – including the Like-Minded Group of Developing Countries, a powerful coalition that includes China, India, Malaysia, and Saudi Arabia – publicly supported the frame. Yet other states did not. The opposition of developed countries in particular is why the Paris Agreement qualifies its reference to climate justice, in a strange turn of phrase for a treaty adopted by consensus: "The importance of ensuring the integrity of all ecosystems, including oceans, and the protection of biodiversity, recognized by some cultures as Mother Earth, and noting the importance for some of the concept of 'climate justice,' when taking action to address climate change" (UNFCCC, 2015, p. 21, quotes in original).

Others co-opted the frame. Several claimants unrelated to the movement have used the term climate justice (Bond & Dorsey, 2010). More moderate NGOs and others use the term to refer to the disproportionate effects that developing countries or peoples face despite contributing very little to the climate crisis. The climate justice frame is often used today in the context of loss and damage, even by environmental NGOs that were once critical of the movement (Allan & Hadden, 2017). Once meant as a critique of the neoliberal system – one that highlighted climate change as a dangerous consequence of that system – the term is now used by actors who are outside the movement, and in this way it deviates from the intended meaning, which is rooted in struggles for justice in international trade. As Hadden (2014) notes, the "inter-movement spillover" created as a result of the justice movement's participation in climate activism changed the future tactics, strategies, and discourses of climate activism.

The climate justice movement has drawn considerable scholarly and public attention. Many have commented on the mobilization of the climate justice movement at the 2009 Copenhagen conference (Chatterton et al., 2012; Fisher, 2010; Hadden, 2015). That movement's opposition to mainstream environmentalism has had wider implications; for example, it has challenged traditional climate activists' accountability politics (Newell, 2008) and their moderate, staid forms of activism (Hadden, 2015). Often overlooked are the years of mobilization effort preceding the movement's more visible emergence in 2009 (although see Hadden, 2015, ch. 5). This chapter augments these accounts by exploring the origins of the climate justice movement, particularly the motives of those actors from the trade regime that became key founding members. Internal divisions in the network, preferences for direct action, and tightened security influenced the movement's strategies, pushing the movement largely outside the halls of the UNFCCC. The movement's sheer diversity provided it with intellectual and strategic strength, but its decision to remain a loose network, unlike those of the more coordinated gender and labour movements, created coordination challenges.

The climate justice movement is diverse, with roots stretching back to several other movements and groups of NGOs. Bullard and Müller (n.d.) highlight the role of the justice movement, the environmental justice movement, and more radical environmental NGOs. Bond and Dorsey (2010) further cite the role of the late 1990s Jubilee movement and the 2000s justice movement in the climate justice movement's lineage. The justice movement includes organizations such as Focus on the Global South, ATTAC, Global Trade Watch, Jubilee South, and the Transnational Institute (della Porta & Tarrow, 2005), all of which engaged with the climate justice movement. Hadden (2015) traces the divisions among CJN! members and with more radical parts of the justice movement working in a coalition called Climate Justice Action to mobilize actions at the Copenhagen summit. Nicholson and Chong (2011) highlight the intersections of human rights and justice claims, although Bond and Dorsey (2012) and Chatterton et al. (2012) observe that human rights advocates and claims are not involved in the work of building the climate justice movement. While most concur that climate justice is a "movement of movements,"[1] and that it invokes the rhetoric of inclusion so commonly found within the justice movement,[2] another activist characterizes climate justice as a campaign.[3]

Here, I take the more widely held view: that the climate justice movement emerged from a diverse set of movements. I focus on the global justice movement, as the new climate activists working to bring to the climate change regime a new form of politics and contention focused on inequities and justice.

Moving to the Climate Change Regime

Unlike the labour and gender movements, the justice movement lacked even a minimal presence in the UNFCCC prior to its rapid start. As figure 5.1 shows, the only other appearance of justice-based organizations was in 2005 at the Montreal meeting, when three organizations attended, including San Francisco–based environmental justice and global justice organizations such as Redefining Progress. At the Bali climate conference in 2007, members of the justice movement met with like-minded environmental NGOs and Indigenous peoples' activists to launch the climate justice movement and bring a social justice critique to climate change.

From this initial meeting, there was a rapid increase in the participation of the climate justice movement. The data may underestimate the

Figure 5.1 Climate justice movement's participation in the UNFCCC

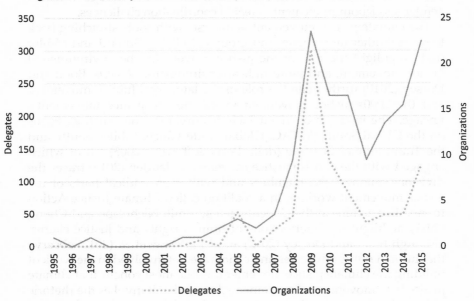

extent of the climate justice movement's engagement in the UNFCCC. That movement included several groups that, on their face, would be difficult to attribute to the climate justice movement. For example, the Indigenous Environmental Network served a key role in the formation of CJN! Based on the mission of the Indigenous Environmental Network,[4] it would be difficult to categorize that network as a justice movement member, although it is at times affiliated with the movement.

Furthermore, the participation data underestimate the size of the climate justice movement because of the outsider strategies the group employed and its mobilization at the national level. This underestimation is very likely to a greater extent and more systematic than with other cases explored here. Several larger CJN! members eschewed formal accreditation and participation within the UNFCCC. The global peasant movement La Via Campesina organized climate justice marches, caravans, and solidarity events around the UNFCCC conferences. Because they did not participate formally inside the venue, their role is missing from the data. Still, it is clear that 2007 was a pivotal year.

The origin of the climate justice movement is unique among new climate activists. In many ways, it was spontaneous, suggesting that forum multiplying could be an emergent property arising when international organizations serve as convening spaces for transnational actors. Several factors came together. First, the location of the 2007 meeting was decisive for the participation of many in the justice movement. A key mobilizing actor was the Indonesian People's Movement against Neocolonialism-Imperialism (Gerak Lewan).[5] Gerak Lewan reached out to its contacts within the justice movement to organize a mobilization at the UNFCCC COP.[6] Several key actors attended, including Focus on the Global South and the Jubilee movement located in Southeast Asia, for they viewed it as an opportunity to speak about the climate impacts and the importance of forests in the region.[7]

Second, a parallel space called the Solidarity Village for a Cool Planet served as an area for justice, Indigenous, and environmental activists to meet one another. In that physical space, NGOs and individual activists found common political space. Organizations with different concerns, including forests, Indigenous rights, trade, and the environment, connected and discovered they shared common views and challenges.[8] This was a synthetic process, one that forged links between environmental and social issues and viewed these issues as parts of larger processes at work – globalization, the ongoing marginalization of local communities, environmental destruction, and the impacts of climate change.[9]

Third, a key actor, Friends of the Earth International, joined the Solidarity Village. Multiple respondents retold the narrative of Friends of the Earth severing ties with the Climate Action Network and collaborating with the nascent CJN! group as a turning point in the group's formation.[10] Friends of the Earth had links to the justice movement fighting against Shell in Nigeria, coal in South Africa, and deforestation in Malaysia, and was collaborating with La Via Campesina in other forums. Some who worked with Friends of the Earth saw CJN! as a global expression of their national level campaigns, and the timing was viewed as right to link climate to these local justice movements.[11] Friends of the Earth's involvement signalled the importance of forming a new identity for the movement in the climate activism space and that a major NGO would support the effort. There was a sense of a common purpose and goals in the Solidarity Village, among organizations large and small, from a range of backgrounds.

CJN! brought a new form of contention to climate change activism. While labour and gender advocates worked to make inroads with state delegates, international organizations, and NGOs inside the UNFCCC meetings, CJN! used protest and direct action, which, as Hadden (2014; 2015) observes, was new to climate activism. These tactics quickly gained attention. Protesters disrupted a press conference held by Richard Branson in 2007.[12] On the last day of the negotiations in 2007,

130 protestors staged a "die in" to disrupt a World Bank press conference announcing the launch of the Forest Carbon Partnership.[13] These
tactics also helped CJN! get the attention of other environmental NGOs
that had been disenfranchised from the Climate Action Network and
that welcomed a new force in the environmental movement.

In the lead-up to the 2009 Copenhagen conference, there were two
major organizing groups at work, Climate Justice Action (CJA) and
CJN!. Their memberships somewhat overlapped, although CJA tended
to have more members from the justice movement, particularly the
more radical activists. The goal of many of these activists was to
"Seattle" Copenhagen: a direct reference to the Battle of Seattle protests at the WTO in 1999 (Bond, 2012). CJA organized the Reclaim
Power Peoples' Assembly, squatters' camps, and activist trauma centres in Copenhagen (for a complete look at the centres mobilized in
Copenhagen, see Chatterton et al., 2012). Disobedience occurred, but
not on the scale of the Seattle WTO protests, largely because of the
moderating influence of CJN! members, particularly more moderate
organizations like Friends of the Earth (Hadden, 2015). What emerged
was an inside–outside strategy: outside protesters would arrive at the
venue, and those working on the inside would go out to meet them.

Inside, many from the justice movement were exasperated by
the process. They found the UNFCCC a difficult space to navigate
in the early days, as had the labour movement and gender NGOs.
The jargon and complexity of the climate change negotiations created obstacles. In the beginning, some in the movement were frustrated by the lack of solidarity and support from many developing
countries. Members' prior experiences in the trade regime were not
helpful when it came to surmounting the initial challenges posed by
the UNFCCC:

> WTO is like checkers; UNFCCC is like chess. In the WTO [negotiating]
> positions are clear, the issues are clear, and the rules are known. The
> UNFCCC is always shifting, the ministers of agriculture, economy, and
> environment are all saying different things. It uses extremely technical
> language, which is deliberate to obfuscate and keep the public out of the
> negotiations.[14]

Despite the multilateral failure, CJN! members identified several successes for the movement from the Copenhagen mobilization. They
viewed their work as bringing an ethical perspective to the negotiations and highlighting how elites captured the UNFCCC (CJN!, 2009).
Some pointed to the successful recruitment of individuals from groups

that previously had not worked on climate change issues. One of the main successes identified was the securing of constituency space in the UNFCCC.[15] These successes signalled the dual nature of CJN! – it worked both *outside* the venue, through protests and by facilitating the participation of marginalized organizations, and *inside* the venue, to secure access to negotiations. However, working inside the venue would continue to prove difficult for many in the movement. Some self-described "policy wonks" would continue to engage in the details of negotiations; others would stick with the group's outsider tactics.[16] In part, the purpose of CJN! was to collaborate so as to provide space for both modes of contention. But over time, for reasons explored in the rest of this chapter, the outsider tactics would prove more fruitful to many looking to build the climate justice movement.

For a time, both the insiders and the outsiders maintained significant momentum. Inside the venue in 2010 and 2011, at least 125 and 75 activists (respectively) attended from the climate justice movement to try to influence the shape of the Cancun and Durban conferences. Outside, well-attended marches were held on the streets, particularly in Durban. La Via Campesina continued to engage, organizing caravans and other actions. In Cancun, activists formed a human chain in front of delegates to prevent anyone from leaving. After UNFCCC Executive Secretary Christiana Figueres came out to negotiate with the protesters, some lost their badges. A CJN! member who was at that action recalls: "They [the activists] got a lot more publicity from that. It was around that time that people really started talking about CJN!."[17]

While CJN! was garnering even more attention, internal debates and divisions continued. In the view of some, these fractured the movement. The Global Campaign to Demand Climate Justice (GCDCJ) emerged in 2011, formed by many CJN! members, including Friends of the Earth, Jubilee South, ATTAC France, and the World Development Movement (GCDCJ, n.d.). The GCDCJ ascribes climate change to profit-driven and growth-oriented extraction and consumption systems, unequal and exploitative economic and social structures, and policies and practices promoted by economic elites (GCDCJ, n.d.). According to some members of the Global Call to Demand Climate Justice, the new forum helped mobilize national groups and did not duplicate the work happening within or around the UNFCCC conferences.[18] Some founding members of CJN! Saw this as an "intentional undermining of prior commitments to CJN!" and worried that the movement might be losing steam.[19]

From 2012 through to the Paris Agreement, participation inside the venue waned somewhat; meanwhile, national mobilizations and outside actions continued. Justice delegates numbered 36 in 2012 and 49 in

2013 and 2014; then at the Paris Conference in 2015, 126 delegates were mobilized inside the venue. These numbers were in part a function of the location. CJN! members often struggle for funding for their participation, which makes their attendance more unpredictable, particularly at more difficult locations such as Qatar (the conference location in 2012).[20] At any given conference, different members will attend, and this can complicate efforts to plan strategies or actions.[21]

As the network's visibility inside the negotiations waned, the movement engaged in more outsider tactics, though it still attempted to keep the dual, insider/outsider strategy alive. Many movements at the local, national, and global scales followed the working principles of the climate justice movement.[22] The formal engagement that remained proved contentious – for example, there were concerns that northern voices were occupying the space that CJN! had carved out for marginalized groups.[23] Eschewing performances of insider politics, the movement pivoted more toward outsider strategies before the Paris conference.

In many ways, the mobilization planning for the Paris Conference mirrored what had been done to prepare for Copenhagen. A local organization and justice movement member, ATTAC France, convened many of the strategy meetings.[24] Other campaigns and actions were planned and discussed at the World Social Forum, such as the Reclaim Power campaign led by Friends of the Earth International, the Belgian Climate Express, and the Run for Life race from Norway to Paris. There was difficulty arriving at a shared message or a vision of what a 2015 agreement should look like; this was reflected in the diversity of messages on the CJN! listserv.[25] At a planning meeting held in Tunis in 2015, the Narrative Working Group reported that, based on the lessons learned from Copenhagen, the movement should not "tell a lie that Paris will fix the climate. People were arrested in Copenhagen for this lie. No unrealistic expectations – but we need to give people hope that there is a purpose to the mobilization" (Bond, 2015). This resonated with those who felt that "no agreement is better than a bad agreement."[26] At the meeting, Pat Mooney of the ETC Group[27] and others emphasized that "it [the march] should start like New York[28] and end like Seattle. Shut the thing down" (Bond, 2015).

The idea of a human chain or blockade around the venue's entrances gained traction. Then the terrorist attacks in Paris took place, in response to which the French government declared martial law. At least eight climate activists were put under house arrest, and others had restraining orders placed on them in advance of the conference, despite there being no connection between these activists and the terrorist attacks (*The Guardian*, 2015). On the last day of the conference, a human chain formed for two hours, causing minor inconveniences, and a large march was held through Paris in defiance of martial law.[29]

Having rapidly mobilized, the climate justice movement had made an abrupt appearance in the climate change regime. Despite having had no previous presence, climate justice activists found like-minded environmental and Indigenous rights groups with which to form a movement that would change the nature of climate change activism. Its efforts at forum multiplying reverberated: climate change is now a prominent topic of discussion at the World Social Forum, though in 2008 there had been no sessions devoted to the issue.[30] Institutional shifts toward market mechanisms brought the justice movement into the work of the climate change regime; they saw themselves as integral to this work – as a needed voice to save climate change governors from themselves.

Climate Justice Network

The climate justice network was founded through a merging of movements and grew rapidly from early beginnings at the UNFCCC in Bali. Figures 5.2 and 5.3 illustrate the extent of this growth. The movement expanded as more actors from the global justice movement joined and as new organizations devoted to climate justice were established. Various clusters grew or emerged, complicating organization within the movement. As had happened in the gender–climate network, the lead NGOs in the climate justice movement became more central over time. Jubilee South, an organization that was marginal in the early period (2005–8), became a key organization after 2009.

The original network, shown in figure 5.2, was relatively small, with three clusters. During this time, the most connected NGOs were the Transnational Institute, Friends of the Earth, the World Rainforest Movement, and Focus on the Global South.[31] Focus on the Global South was a key player in the early formation of CJN! and is shown in figure 5.2 as linking the nascent CJN! cluster to the justice movement; one staff member there, Nicola Bullard, was "the glue that held the whole thing together" in the early years.[32] Established in 1995, Focus on the Global South stands against neoliberalism, militarism, and globalization driven by corporations. Working at the global and local scales, Focus on the Global South sought to instil the approach it had used on trade and investment so as to serve as a platform for climate change regime participation and empowerment.[33]

The second cluster visible in figure 5.2, around the Corner House, is the Durban Group for Climate Justice, a group of environmental NGOs and individuals, some of them already in the UNFCCC, that rejected market mechanisms and the commodification of nature those mechanisms entail. The Transnational Institute was a member of the Durban Group and also became a key member of CJN!. Founded in 1974 as the

Figure 5.2 Climate Justice Network, 2005–2008

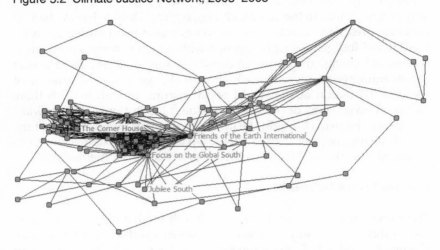

global program at the Institute for Policy Studies, which seeks to "speak truth to power," the Transnational Institute has engaged a network of activist scholars and grassroots movements on a wide range of issues, from African liberation movements to the global justice movement. It has a foot in both the climate change regime and the justice movement. Its ideas and approach were first articulated with others in the Durban Group for Climate Justice, and later CJN!.

In the early period represented in figure 5.2, Jubilee South stands outside the main action, but by the 2009–15, it has moved to the centre. Jubilee South was part of the Jubilee 2000 movement, which called for the cancellation of developing countries' debts. Through that work, Jubilee South was connected to many of the centrally located NGOs in CJN!. Jubilee South first participated in the UNFCCC in 2011. In the second time period studied, it would become the best-connected organization, followed by Focus on the Global South and Friends of the Earth.[34]

Figure 5.3 shows the near doubling of the movement. There were 482 organizations in the network in 2005–8, and 984 in 2009–15. The successful mobilization in Copenhagen played a significant role in this. The links between the Durban Group for Climate Justice and CJN! grew; in figure 5.3, CJN! appears to have absorbed the smaller group.

Growth was evident in the justice movement, leading to many influential actors. New organizations swelled the number of actors under

Figure 5.3 Climate Justice Network, 2009–2015

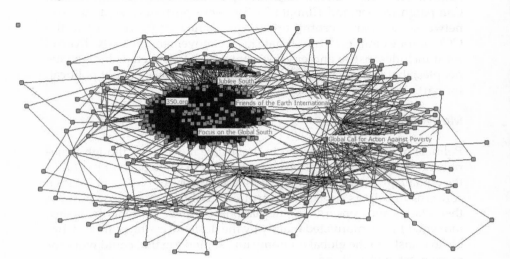

the climate justice umbrella. The Indigenous Environment Network had significant ties to the network (166 connections, 2009–15). La Via Campesina, the peasant movement, had not registered for the UNFCCC but had many (168) connections with key members of the climate justice movement. This conferred influence. For example, one internal planning meeting discussed the need to continue to ally with the peasant movement and support the actions of La Via Campesina in its climate caravan travelling toward the Cancun climate COP. La Via Campesina had not directly discussed these plans with those present at the meeting; instead, the participants said they had heard of the caravan and wished to support it.[35] In addition, Jubilee South became more important in the overall network, but also in the Global Campaign to Demand Climate Justice. The Global Campaign, which formed in 2011, shares many members and ideas with CJN!. As discussed below, this has created some tensions in the overall network.

The multiple key actors could all share information gathered from diverse sources. Successful mobilization and the emergence of multiple groups within the network increased its size, as well as the need for collaboration among these key actors and others in the network. Internal debates ensued on how to ensure that messages were coordinated and that the frame was coherent and that its strategies were united (see below). This was difficult to achieve, because CJN! and the Global Campaign to Demand Climate Justice were purposely kept as loose networks, without a central organizing secretariat (in contrast to the GGCA, for example).[36] The climate justice movement is clearly diverse, for it includes justice and environmental NGOs as well as Indigenous peoples; that said, its members did share motivations, mainly political, for participating in the climate change regime.

Motivation

Political motivations prevailed in the justice movement, though material and normative motivations were present in some parts of it. Within the climate justice movement, just as among gender NGOs, normative concerns to help its supporters nurtured a political impetus to buttress their claims and concerns in international forums. Those in the justice movement were motivated mainly by the desire to continue their struggle to transform the global economy into something that could work for those most marginalized.

The justice movement had several successes in the late 1990s. In Seattle, bringing together different movements created a "phantasmagorical mix of tens of thousands of demonstrators," from "teamsters to turtles," and this brought the issue of fair trade to the political agenda (Cooper, 1999). After raising the profile of fair trade, justice activists then "helped render the WTO a pointless talk shop" (Bullard & Müller, 2012). In the WTO, state delegates repeated the same discussions year after year. Stalemate in the WTO meant there was little left for the justice movement to speak out against, so they had few opportunities to advance their issues.

Around the same time, the term neoliberalism lost its resonance, frustrating many activists in the justice movement who had advanced the idea. At the G8 Summit in 2005, 300,000 people marched as part of the "Make Poverty History" campaign. Instead of protesting global capitalist powers conspiring together in a small, opaque process, people marched in support of the summit, apparently convinced that global elites could, and would, address global poverty. The logic seemed to be that neoliberalism could work for those who were poor – the opposite of ideas that justice advocates were trying to advance. This march signalled to many in the justice movement that the momentum they had sparked in Seattle had been captured and turned against them (Turbulence Collective, 2007).

When the G8 later started to discuss climate change, the justice movement lacked a response to this green capitalist agenda. As one justice campaigner explains, "movements need something to come up against, something for traction. After 9/11 and the collapse of the WTO, the wind was out of the sails of the anti-globalization movement."[37] Another climate justice activist stresses that "as much as we were a movement without a story at that point, there was also a story without a movement, climate change" (quoted in Hadden, 2015, p. 34). Politically, the trade regime offered little to the justice movement to keep its critique alive. Climate change offered a new cause.

Normatively, the effects of climate change in the Global South prompted action and provided a basis for the climate justice movement's claims. The problems related to climate change became more evident, having been underscored by the IPCC's 2007 Fourth Assessment Report. For some, the evidence amassed by the IPCC, particularly on the impacts of climate change, was a turning point.[38] As the IPCC's report outlined, developing countries were among the first and worst affected by climate change. With its roots in the Global South, the justice movement also came to see some climate solutions as problematic, particularly in countries that had already started REDD+ pilot projects that were negatively affecting local communities.[39]

There was a strong motivation to include perspectives from the developing world through an inclusive network. The disproportionate impact of climate change on developing countries was evident, and many climate justice advocates perceived those countries as having been excluded from the climate dialogue.[40] There was a strong motivation to create "another coalition of groups who were more representative of the CSOs [civil society organizations] and social movements from the South, and who rallied around climate justice."[41] Representatives of the Global South could not be brought to the global climate negotiations solely on the basis of normative or political desires. There was a normative motivation to address climate change in a way that recognized and empowered local communities.

Funding was a motivation for some organizations within the justice movement, although there was a strong sense that principled engagement needed to take precedence over the search for material support. The motivations in some ways came together: "If you've been in the NGO game for long enough you realize all these things are connected. It's no great hardship to digress from the core issue, and funding is part of it, but you certainly have to be genuine."[42] Similarly, while Focus on the Global South received funding to convene dialogues on climate change in Southeast Asia, those within the organization didn't view funding as a dominant reason to campaign on climate change issues. For them, climate change work had to match their goals and continue their critique of the system.[43] For many other organizations, the search for funding did not pay off. For example, organizations that actively took a stance against REDD+ *lost* funding: "We found out the hard way that NGOs are strongly funded by a quite conservative corporative elitist sector. There are no alternatives. Southern governments such as ALBA haven't been funding critical groups, and they have their own issues with funding NGOs. If people lack capacity, then simply don't have the money to work. It's a bitter reality."[44]

The struggle for funds would contribute to debates and divisions over strategy. Many of the tasks of organizing the network fell to activists volunteering their time, or to staff of organizations with other duties; a communications person, hired before 2009, was the only dedicated person for the network, in sharp contrast to the GGCA and the ITUC.[45] These debates perhaps hampered the network's ability to advance its frame within the UNFCCC (see below).

Means

The climate justice movement may have shared many motivations with other new climate activists, particularly the need to remain politically relevant. But the means used by the climate justice movement differed in several respects. Its central NGOs collaborated to construct the climate justice frame, but owing to divisions within the network and appropriation by some powerful actors outside the network, the frame lost its original meaning. To leverage rules, the climate justice movement argued for space within the environmental NGO constituency. Mitigation institutions, such as REDD+ and market mechanisms, were the central substantive rule that climate justice activists sought to undermine; in this, they took a different approach than labour unions, which sought to support countries' mitigation efforts. NGOs proved the key allies for the climate justice movement, helping provide orientations to the process.

Building Cohesion

By 2015, many were invoking the term climate justice, from French Prime Minister François Hollande in his opening address to the Paris conference to Pope Francis in his encyclical. The term's origins go back earlier than this, to 2001 at the UNFCCC conference in The Hague, where it was coined by environmental justice advocates at a time when the climate justice movement was emerging. The idea was used primarily at the domestic level by environmental justice groups working to reconcile the unique aspects of climate change with the environmental justice frame (Schlosberg & Collins, 2014). By the time of the Paris climate conference, the climate justice frame had been transformed and many NGOs inside and outside the climate justice movement were using it (Allan & Hadden, 2017). Ultimately, it meant many things to many people.[46] As a result of this widespread use of the concept of climate justice, CJN! and others who had redefined and popularized the term lost their central rallying point. The frame no longer meant a systemic critique. The movement's carefully crafted frame had slipped out of its control.

As articulated by CJN! in 2008, the climate justice frame emphasizes how injustices and inequities in the global system cause climate change. It prioritizes politics over science (Hadden, 2015). This reverses the logic of other new climate activists, who argue that climate change can exacerbate existing gender inequalities and who focus on the science in order to mobilize their movements. The justice frame is evident in CJN!'s founding press release, which listed many forms of inequities as central to the causes of and solutions to climate change. The press release outlined the group's founding principles:

- Leaving fossil fuels in the ground and investing instead in appropriate energy efficiency and safe, clean, and community-led renewable energy.
- Radically reducing wasteful consumption, first and foremost in the North, but also by elites in the South.
- Huge financial transfers from North to South, based on the repayment of climate debts and subject to democratic control. The costs of adaptation and mitigation should be paid for through redirected military budgets, innovative taxes, and debt cancellation.
- Rights-based resource conservation that enforces Indigenous land rights and promotes peoples' sovereignty over energy, forests, land, and water.
- Sustainable family farming and fishing, and peoples' food sovereignty. (CJN!, 2007; 2010)

The UNFCCC agenda did not include most of these issues. CJN! called for overturning the status quo, for moving from international policy to local control, and for the North to offer reparations for climatic effects in the Global South. The climate justice frame sought to overcome existing practices (Goodman, 2009), unlike the gender and labour frames, which sought to reaffirm or revise existing climate policies. It reframed the climate issue as a systemic critique of the neoliberal basis of the global economy; neoliberalism, that is, had *caused* climate change and served as a foundation for what was then the dominant approach to address-ing the climate crisis.

The frame emerged from the coming together of different groups and movements at the Bali climate conference. The Durban Group for Climate Justice provided the climate change expertise necessary to place the various ideas in context. As a loose network of think tanks, activists, and academics, the Durban Group shared its research on the perverse incentives and human rights abuses associated with carbon markets. This work provided a set of ideas and fact-based critiques that appealed to the other social movements under the banner of climate justice; espe-cially appealing to them was its critique of capitalist solutions. Perhaps more significantly, the Durban Group's small but growing member-ship showed there was a viable alternative to the dominant voice of the Climate Action Network and "its naive, weak, Northern middle-class-style sense of politics and movement building ... the Durban Group helped activists be more confident that a more effective alternative to CAN [Climate Action Network] was both necessary and possible."[47]

These critiques aligned with those of Focus on the Global South, and with other members of the justice movement that viewed market mech-anisms as an extension of their long-held critiques of neoliberalism. Concerns about the commodification of nature aligned with the cri-tique of neoliberalist globalization, premised on the idea "that we need to provide the services of nature; it's a new dimension of capitalism."[48] Climate change presented the opportunity to incorporate ecological issues into central concepts such as deglobalization,[49] a term coined by Walden Bello, a Philippine economist and founder of Focus on the Global South, as meaning "the transformation of a global economy from one integrated around the needs of transnational corporations to one integrated around the needs of peoples, nations, and communities" (Focus on the Global South, 2019). There was ample room for the var-ious movements present in Bali to construct a frame together, though their ideas and interests ranged across several distinct issues.

There was debate regarding which issues to highlight. REDD+ was a central issue for the climate justice network, bringing together In-digenous activists, environmental NGOs critical of land-based mitiga-tion, and justice movement members against the use of markets. Views differed regarding how much to focus on REDD+ and who could and should speak on the issue. Members found a compromise in the final formulation in the principle that CJN! "is against market-based mech-anisms, such as REDD+." This compromise satisfied both those who wanted to focus solely on REDD+ and those who wanted to advocate against *all* market mechanisms. The wording also recognized that

Indigenous groups were the ones with legitimacy to speak on the issue. CJN! members wanted to open space for Indigenous voices critical of REDD+, particularly since Indigenous peoples' organizations were split on the issue.[50]

Working through all these issues, from markets to land tenure, and from military occupation to consumption, CJN! members created a frame that could serve as common ground so that those with more radical politics could bring their claims to the UNFCCC. The frame created space for "lefty politics" and for the voices of those who had long been marginalized in global governance.[51] Goodman (2009, p. 499) notes that with its inclusive formulation that challenged the status quo, the climate justice frame could serve the needs of many groups, including the global justice movement, environmentalists, environmental justice activists, and Indigenous rights activists. Southern-based NGOs could focus on development and inequalities, and northern-based NGOs targeting large corporations[52] could equally claim space under the climate justice banner. As an early CJN! member characterized the days developing the climate justice frame:

> When we were looking for linkages, there was a beautiful spider's web that emerges. Beautiful in the sense that it was so cohesive. It all makes sense when you join all those issues and create a jigsaw puzzle of a picture of the problem of which climate change has become the iconic feature because it has linkages to all of these issues.[53]

But the potential for inclusivity inherent in the climate justice frame left it vulnerable to co-optation by others. Several groups unrelated to the movement sought to claim the term climate justice. Bond and Dorsey (2010) highlight five such claimants, including those focusing on per capita emissions, who attempted to insert the principal of climate justice into carbon markets and pivot toward rights to development and rights to pollute. The proliferation of the term weakened its power, rendering it meaningless for many in the movement.[54]

Among those organizations that took up the frame, the Mary Robinson Foundation drew the ire of many climate justice activists. Robinson's foundation uses the term climate justice even while – according to several in the climate justice movement – remaining firmly entrenched in the political and economic elite (Bond & Dorsey, 2010). The Foundation uses climate justice to tie together human rights and development[55] in a way that is anathema to the systemic critique inherent to the original version of the climate justice frame.[56] In the hands of the Mary Robinson Foundation and other articulators among the elite such as then French President Hollande,

Pope Francis, the WWF, and even Shell,[57] the climate justice frame was transformed to highlight only the disproportionate impacts of climate change. Stripped of its systemic critique of the capitalist system, climate justice now stands as a meme of its formulation by CJN! members.

This co-optation of the climate justice frame raised difficulties for the movement; some even viewed it as a failure. For all they had done to mobilize so many under the climate justice frame, there was no longer an anti-capitalist discourse that could be widely understood, beyond climate experts (Bullard & Müller, n.d.). The status quo had won out. Climate justice no longer promised to "substantially reconfigure the political field around climate change."[58] Some thought that the frame's success had been the very reason for its co-optation, but even so, it presented a challenge for the movement: How was it to move forward with a term that had been appropriated by others for different ends?[59]

Internal disputes about how best to disseminate and defend that frame grew more pronounced. There were internal debates about how to organize. Some preferred a loose network of many movements that would converge on some common activities or campaigns without the requirement for consensus among members on all aspects. Others wanted to tighten the movement, perhaps with a Secretariat to coordinate activities and claim a representation role for the group.[60] There were tensions about tactics, when to use direct action and when to work within the UNFCCC to influence the negotiations in more discreet ways. There was a temptation to work in the "grey areas" rather than hold the hard line maintained by many climate justice activists.[61] Concerns over accountability within the network were evident. Some members did not complete tasks or did not disclose that they had funding to carry out some types of work.[62] Some did not volunteer funding; others avoided doing "the dirty work." Lack of accountability and disagreements between those interested in a radical agenda and those interested in more moderate claims led some groups to leave CJN!.

The emergence of the Global Campaign to Demand Climate Justice sparked further debate. Some original CJN! members viewed the Global Campaign as a deliberate attempt to undermine CJN!, including by organizing parallel meetings while not organizing CJN! meetings and by not sharing information between the groups. There was overlap between the two groups; several members were on the international facilitation team for CJN!, including Friends of the Earth and Jubilee South.

Whether the Global Campaign to Demand Climate Justice actually split CJN! is debatable. The Global Campaign stresses the need for mobilization and collective action at local, national, and regional levels. For some, the differences were crucial: while CJN! focused on global negotiations and mobilizing, the Global Campaign would mobilize at other scales.[63] For those involved in both networks, CJN! was a space to share information, not to develop strategies; the new campaign was a platform for groups to work in a more coordinated manner to build the movement.[64] Yet the new group adopted a tone and demands that several CJN! members found unacceptable because they seemed too moderate.[65]

Leveraging Rules

The justice movement carved space for its claims in the climate change regime, using market mechanisms as discursive hooks. The movement members were innovative in securing procedural recognition for themselves, but the preference among some for direct action created challenges for its activities in the UNFCCC. Ultimately, the same norms that had facilitated labour and gender advocates' recognition and acceptance, and that rewarded their ability to behave as climate insiders, proved to be constraints for the climate justice movement.

CJN! applied the climate justice frame to critique what it saw as the neoliberal foundations of the climate change regime, particularly its use of market mechanisms and land-based mitigation. These "false solutions" were the first institutions CJN! sought to end. Those institutions had powerful backers, most notably developed states that used markets heavily and that sought to expand their use. The climate justice movement maintained that markets commodify nature, fail to reduce emissions, and reinforce the power of multinational corporations. It followed that markets allow rich countries to pay for projects in developing countries and then claim for themselves the emission reductions thereby achieved. Markets provide emissions reductions on paper while allowing business as usual to flourish. The Transnational Institute and Carbon Trade Watch, a member of the Durban Group for Climate Justice! and CJN!, exemplified this view:

> Industrialized societies can continue to use up fossil fuels until there are none left worth recovering. At the same time, they can create new markets that make it possible to claim that others can clean up the mess, and that it will be economically efficient for them to do so ... Carbon trading is aimed at the wrong target. It is not directed at reorganizing industrial societies' energy, transport and housing systems – starting today – so that they don't need coal, oil and gas. It is not contributing to the de-industrialization of agriculture or the protection of forests through the recognition of local and Indigenous Peoples' tenure rights or food sovereignty. Instead, it is

organized around keeping the wheels on the fossil fuel industry for as long as possible. (2009, 14–15; see also Durban Group for Climate Justice, 2004)

Such a view did not gain much traction among developed countries. They use markets and argue that such mechanisms spur innovation and create incentives necessary to transition to a low-carbon economy. Climate justice activists characterize markets as representing a "reconfiguration of capitalism,"[66] which developed countries would view positively, as using the market to the benefit of climate action. These ideological differences would limit developed countries' support of the climate justice movement. Gaining the support of developed countries was never the goal of the climate justice movement; instead, it sought to work with and empower developing countries.

The climate justice movement sought to delegitimize institutions related to reducing or sequestering emissions from forests or agriculture. This left some developed and developing countries out of the potential group of allies. CJN! members were the strongest opponents of the use of forests, agricultural soils, and other lands as sinks to sequester carbon dioxide. They argued that markets and land-based mitigation would lead to land grabs and the forced relocation of Indigenous peoples for the sake of afforestation or reforestation projects or biofuel agriculture, in the name of what activists saw as a dubious way of saving the climate.[67] The inclusion of afforestation and reforestation in the Clean Development Mechanism, and rumours that agriculture would be included in market solutions, further fuelled CJN!'s critique of land-based sinks.[68]

Among these land-based mitigation institutions, CJN! singled out REDD+. First proposed by a group of developing countries called the Coalition for Rainforest Nations as a market mechanism for reducing emissions from deforestation in developing countries, REDD+ encapsulated CJN!'s opposition to land-based mitigation and market mechanisms in one emerging institution. According to CJN!, this had created the conditions for abuses they viewed as common in other markets, so that unscrupulous carbon traders would be able to exploit local communities to maximize their profits in a market.[69]

CJN! members focused their critiques largely on mitigation and the use of market mechanisms. Some that were emerging as negotiators – including REDD+ – debated whether to further open the forest sector in developing countries to market approaches. Others, such as the Clean Development Mechanism, were increasingly being used in the mid-2000s (see chapter 3). These institutions proved to be useful discursive hooks in that they allowed members of the justice movement to link their critiques of neoliberalism to climate change and provided specific areas of negotiations for members to target. Being heard in the UNFCCC is a difficult task, especially given the growing number of civil society actors vying for attention and recognition. To distinguish themselves, CJN! members found a way to be recognized as part of a constituency.

Some environmental NGOs already in the climate change regime were helpful when it came to navigating the UNFCCC system to secure part of the environmental NGO constituency.[70] In 2008 around a dozen CJN! members petitioned the UNFCCC Secretariat, stating that CJN!'s hundred-plus organizations held views irreconcilable with those of the Climate Action Network.[71] The Climate Action Network was an umbrella for hundreds of environmental NGOs, but it did not represent *all* environmental NGOs in the constituency. Yet it had absorbed all the available benefits of constituency status and had excluded non-members from planning meetings.[72] This practice angered several environmental NGOs that held divergent views. As Michael Dorsey explains:

> [Those who] were advocating against the use of market mechanisms, and there has been a sizeable coalition since 1992, were being purposely, physically blocked from CAN [Climate Action Network] meetings. It was a quasi-apartheid system – CAN had a badge system, selectively targeting people to not get access to rooms. CJN! isn't a coincidence, there was a critical mass of people tired of the level of assholery from CAN management that actively blocked the participation of some individuals.[73]

Finding space as half of the environmental NGO constituency was secured through negotiations. CJN!, representing roughly 4 per cent of environmental NGOs, reached a provisional compromise with the Climate Action Network, which represented around 14 per cent of environmental NGOs.[74] Under the arrangement, the two groups would split the benefits of constituency status. For example, each group would speak for one of the two minutes allotted to each constituency during plenary, and invitations to technical briefings would be decided based on the proportional representativeness of each network. The arrangement was intended to be provisional but remains unchanged.[75]

There was important value in the negotiated constituency space for CJN! activists. The space clearly and publicly distinguished CJN! from the Climate Action Network, which was an important goal in itself for many in the movement.[76] Presented one immediately after the other, the CJN! and Climate Action Network statements would starkly highlight the differences, both in substantive content and in the tone each group assumed (although some observers wondered whether state delegates really noticed the difference).[77] Where CJN! sought a voice for the Global South and critiqued market mechanisms and the corporate takeover of the UNFCCC, the Climate Action Network was predominantly Northern-based and helped advise on markets.[78] Using the constituency space, CJN! could present itself as an alternative to the Climate Action Network.

This procedural recognition helped the burgeoning movement recruit new members. Many environmental NGOs wanted to attend the environmental constituency coordination meetings but had been excluded because they were not Climate Action Network members. These NGOs found a new home within CJN!.[79] The scale and speed of CJN!'s mobilization surprised members of Climate Action Network.[80] The visibility and recognition facilitated by constituency status helped these environmental NGOs find CJN! and helped build cohesion in the movement: "It [constituency status] is pretty token, but it did have an impact. It gave a sense of cohesion and recognition. Everyone that considered themselves part of CJN! would align themselves with a statement. It gave some authority to our words."[81]

For those in CJN! more interested in and adept at outsider tactics, the norms and rules about how observers to the UNFCCC "ought" to behave could be constraining. Rules instituted after Copenhagen tightened access for observers, and security restricted some types of demonstrations. Both these developments uniquely hampered the climate justice movement in ways that did not affect many other new climate activists. CJN! members reported that under the post-Copenhagen rules, accreditation became more difficult to secure, badges were more closely controlled, demonstrations more strictly monitored, and fewer observers granted access to the plenary, where decisions were being made.[82] Some members feared they would lose their access and badges if they participated in unpermitted actions. Furthermore, UNFCCC security had started cracking down on unregistered protests, which further dampened members' enthusiasm.[83] The arrest of climate justice activists and the imposition of martial law before the Paris conference in 2015 resulted in a last-minute scramble to reorganize and re-envision the planned disruptions to the conference. The rules favoured those who were willing to lobby and demonstrate quietly. This approach was not in CJN!'s repertoire. The movement chose to protest en masse outside the walls of the UNFCCC in part because the forum's rules proved too cumbersome. Over time, the outsider tactics of the climate justice movement became more prominent, particularly among members of the justice movement that found participation within the UNFCCC too restrictive.

Finding Allies

The justice movement and others in the climate justice movement were often critical of international organizations and could not turn to UNEP, UNDP, or other international organizations to facilitate their entry into the climate change regime. These organizations did not offer help. Instead, it was the environmental NGOs that had joined the justice movement that fulfilled many of the functions of a broker. These NGOs were already inside the climate change regime, connected to the justice movement through the climate justice movement, and they worked to help the new climate activists navigate the UNFCCC.

Friends of the Earth was a well-placed and highly visible organization, but it ultimately proved too moderate for some of the climate justice movement's tactics. Friends of the Earth International was already positioned within several networks, including the justice movement and the climate change regime. It could broker between these two worlds. Some national chapters of Friends of the Earth and Friends of the Earth International had been a member of the Durban Group for Climate Justice since the mid-2000s and had forged a "strategic alliance" with the justice movement and La Via Campesina focused on trade issues.[84] On climate change, Friends of the Earth International decided to shift its strategy toward a more social movement–oriented approach that would link with its lobbying efforts within the UNFCCC.[85] This internal decision coincided with the justice movement's mobilization at the Bali conference and helped motivate the organization's involvement in the nascent climate justice movement.

Yet it was a difficult relationship at times. Friends of the Earth is a large, well-resourced organization with a global brand. But to avoid any appearance that it was dominating the agenda, it did not provide resources to the climate justice movement.[86] In the lead-up to the Copenhagen conference, CJA and CJN! members debated tactics, and the more radical members of CJA from the justice movement would not commit to non-violence or to avoiding the destruction of property. This led Friends of the Earth to leave the group (Hadden, 2015). Despite the rift, others in the movement note that the media paid more attention to the Friends of the Earth delegates who were barred from the conference venue than to the arrest of 230 activists.[87] Friends of the Earth was a recognizable brand, so it was mentioned specifically while arrested activists and their concerns were lumped together in the media.

Still, Friends of the Earth and other environmental NGOs used their connections and experience in the UNFCCC to make political space for the movement. Friends of the Earth publicly broke away from the Climate Action Network after growing disagreements with the network, particularly on REDD+ and issues around the representation of southern views and voices more generally.[88] CJN! defined itself in many ways in opposition to the Climate Action Network, and the environmental NGOs in the climate justice movement helped foster the separation of the environmental NGO constituency. CJN! claimed its own political space and gained recognition as a major grouping in the environmental NGO constituency as a result of the brokerage efforts of the environmental NGOs in the movement.

Like the brokers for labour and gender networks, Friends of the Earth reaped benefits from associating itself with the climate justice movement. Friends of the Earth International struck new alliances on key issues such as carbon trading; it also strengthened existing collaboration with Via Campesina and Jubilee South.[89] The movement also shifted the organization's climate and energy program somewhat, hiring coordinators experienced in organizing social movements to address internal concerns about the narrow focus on the UNFCCC.[90] This was a mutual exchange: Friends of the Earth International (and some of its chapters) possessed characteristics that were able to garner attention for the movement; and the movement, in turn, helped Friends of the Earth move out from the shadow of the Climate Action Network and pursue its own strategy.

Recruiting other allies proved difficult. The effort to overturn the status quo meant that states and NGOs invested in the UNFCCC were reticent about accepting CJN!'s messages. Some countries, such as China, India, and the more socialist Latin American countries, were receptive to the climate justice movement's message. For the justice movement, the unique political dynamics of the UNFCCC negotiations proved surprising and challenged its efforts to recruit more allies. Members of the justice movement had expected to be able to bring developing countries onside as allies, as they had done at the WTO, where developing countries were more united, but this strategy proved less effective in the climate change regime because of shifting coalitions and interests.[91] The problem in the WTO was that developing countries had little voice or influence;[92] the obstacle in the climate change regime was that these countries were less united, and sometimes invested in or in favour of either REDD+ or markets that CJN! opposed. REDD+ was a reality in Southeast Asia, where several climate justice organizations were based. They were already hearing about problems associated with REDD+ pilot projects in Indonesia, Malaysia, and the Philippines.[93] In the negotiations, however, these three countries were strong supporters of REDD+ (Allan & Dauvergne, 2013). Through the Coalition of Rainforest Nations, these Southeast Asian countries were refusing to ally themselves with CJN! and against REDD+.

Similarly, some activist groups refused to support disrupting the status quo. The Climate Action Network eventually adopted the language of climate justice, but not its deeper critique of the capitalist system (Allan & Hadden, 2017). The two major groups in the environmental NGO constituency never reconciled their differences in their provisional arrangement. Other NGO groups were also split. Among Indigenous peoples' activists, some sought to stop REDD+ and joined CJN! while others viewed REDD+ as inevitable and sought seats at the table for Indigenous peoples to push for social safeguards.[94] Mobilizing a movement to disrupt the UNFCCC proved difficult, as so many allies that had existed in the WTO or elsewhere had been social justice advocates and were heavily invested in the path then being taken in the climate change regime.

Conclusion

The climate justice movement represents a different type of new climate activism. The reformers, the labour unions, and gender NGOs that claimed space in the UNFCCC thought they would be able to help realize and implement UNFCCC institutions, whereas the climate justice movement saw UNFCCC institutions as a reification of many of the problems in the current global system, particularly the capitalist system and the inequalities it fostered. The justice movement demonstrated that even challengers can successfully forum-multiply and influence the politics of the regime into which they move.

The justice movement's experience has all the markers of successful forum multiplying. It constructed the climate justice frame, a public discursive act. It espoused the goals of the UNFCCC, arguing that the best way to avoid dangerous climate change would be to keep the oil in the ground and stand up to multinational corporations, rather than trade carbon credits in markets. It used these "false solutions" as discursive hooks to show it had a contribution to make to the climate change regime. The climate justice movement and its frame came to be recognized by others in the climate change regime, either as a new ally to fight for greater equality and participation for the Global South, or as a group and an idea to avoid. The Climate Action Network, some other NGOs, and several developed states avoided the movement: they recognized its involvement in the UNFCCC as something new and as representing views that diverged wildly from their own. The climate justice frame spread in directions the members of the justice movement never intended, morphing into a shorthand for the disproportionate impacts of climate change on vulnerable peoples. The many meanings of the term, and disagreements among states regarding its use, muted its recognition in the Paris Agreement. Still, the term climate justice will remain in the UNFCCC in the Paris Agreement preamble alongside references to various social issues espoused by other new climate activists.

Despite all the differences between the two, the climate justice movement multiplied into the climate change regime as a result of the same mechanisms as the labour and gender movements had used. The justice movement had significant – largely political – motivations for finding a new issue and regime. With those motivations, it found allies to help navigate its new forum and leveraged rules to demonstrate why it belonged. The gender NGOs had had to collaborate to bring together the network; the climate justice movement succeeded in doing the same, albeit in a more informal manner. Preferring a loose network to a formalized constituency with agreed rules or a Secretariat, major NGOs in the climate justice movement collaborated to disseminate their frame. Over time, that informal collaboration proved more difficult to maintain, and this left the frame vulnerable to appropriation. The climate justice movement remains entrenched in the climate change regime and continues to urge climate justice and to bring leftist politics to the UNFCCC.

6 The Uninterested and Impeded: Health and Human Rights

The cases of health and human rights reveal how promising discursive links can fail to mobilize NGOs or gain them recognition in another regime. These cases also underscore the importance of motivated NGOs at the centre of the network; of allies to serve as brokers; and of finding entry points within the regime's institutions. Some environmental health advocates engaged in the UNFCCC, but they struggled to convince public health NGOs to participate. Human rights NGOs were left at the first stage of the forum multiplying framework, for the key NGOs lacked motivation to multiply their presence entering the climate change regime.

Both networks amount to null cases: forum multiplying did not occur. Key human rights NGOs had little motivation to engage on climate change. On their part, there was little participation or other forms of public engagement. In terms of a commitment to the institutions and shared goal of the climate change regime, the human rights network remained virtually silent. Instead, environmental NGOs and environmental lawyers linked human rights issues and climate change and advocated successfully for the inclusion of human rights in the Paris Agreement's preamble. It was actors within the climate change regime that brought about recognition of human rights issues. Human rights NGOs from outside the regime were not involved. Amnesty International and Human Rights Watch remained unmotivated to participate.

Similarly, in the health network, public health NGOs were largely uninterested. In terms of public acts of participation or other sustained engagements, a small group of environmental health NGOs from outside the climate change regime participated, trying to advocate for the links between climate change and health. Some NGOs in the network had been created solely to address climate change and health. However, this informal alliance was largely unable to convince key public health NGOs such as the World Medical Association (WMA) to join.

While few public health NGOs participated vocally in the climate change regime, a handful of NGOs working on environmental (specifically, climate) and health issues did develop a frame linking health issues to climate change. This frame was unfocused, split as it was between mitigation and adaptation institutions as advocates tested different possible entry points. This broad frame proposes that climate change is a health issue – which could motivate actors – but it struggles to show commitment or to offer novel approaches that could help the climate change regime achieve its goals.

There is broad acceptance that climate change is bad for health, but, as this chapter shows, there is little understanding or recognition that health NGOs offer anything to further the climate cause. For a time, early drafts of the Paris Agreement referred to public health. In the end, however, the only reference to health was in the preamble, and the issue was clustered with other human rights (i.e., the "right to health") (UNFCCC, 2015). Climate–health advocates often encounter delegates who question or even dismiss their presence even while showing awareness that science has linked climate change to health.[1] It seems that the link between health and climate change has been recognized, albeit minimally, but it is not yet recognized that health NGOs should be part of the climate change regime.

The human rights and health frames both have the potential to link to climate change negotiations. A health frame for climate change can elicit support and even inspire hope for climate change action in individuals (Meyer et al., 2012). In its Second Assessment Report, the IPCC devoted a chapter to the risks posed to population health, and the Third Assessment Report, released in 2007, documented the emergence of health impacts arising from climate change (IPCC, 1995; 2007a; 2007b).

Those linking human rights to climate change often take a legal rather than a scientific tack. An example here is a 2009 resolution on human rights and climate change by the UN High Commissioner for Human Rights. Beyond the legal foundation, a human rights frame is politically attractive. Nicholson and Chong (2011) reviewed the legal and institutional foundations supporting the links between human rights and climate change, and explained:

> The human rights regime ... does not just provide a legal and institutional architecture of use to those seeking action on climate change. It also provides language, tropes, and framing devices that can be used to mobilize support for a new type of climate politics – a politics that properly recognizes, and that seeks to fully accommodate, the fact that traditionally marginalized nations and communities are suffering and will continue

to suffer from the worst impacts of climate change (Nicholson & Chong, 2011, p. 123).

The health and human rights frames do not lack scientific or legal support. The case could be made for the viability of claims that climate change exacerbates health and human rights concerns. As these cases underscore, forum multiplying is a political process, not a function of our understanding of how issues are connected. Efforts to forum-multiply are often undermined when there is little motivation among key network actors, or, if motivation *is* present, when network members are unable to carry authority or find institutional hooks for their claims. For the key actors in the human rights and health networks, their absence and lack of motivation was especially detrimental to the network's prospects of forum multiplying.

Moving to the Climate Change Regime

Figures 6.1 and 6.2 below show how few human rights and health NGOs participated in the UNFCCC, respectively. It also shows how these groups attempted to join the climate change regime later than the other new climate activists. Their limited engagement largely began in 2009 at the Copenhagen conference, two or three years after labour, gender, and justice organizations brought their issues to the climate change regime.

The human rights chart (figure 6.1) reveals limited and sporadic engagement. Participation is limited mostly to the historic conferences in Copenhagen and Paris, when many expected treaties to result from the negotiations. The highest level of engagement was eleven delegates from four organizations in 2015 in Paris, a conference that had the highest attendance in the history of the climate change regime. In addition to these landmark meetings, one NGO, the International Council on Human Rights Policy, attended in 2007 in Bali with the delegation for the Centre for Sustainable Development Law.[2] In 2009, Amnesty International participated as a partner in the Global Call to Climate Action's *tcktcktck* campaign, signing its Call to Action.[3] Amnesty International's involvement was at the request of the Global Call to Climate Action, not of its own initiative. The organization signed reluctantly and issued an internal memo that outlined and limited the extent to which it would engage.[4] When the three delegates arrived in Copenhagen, they were greeted warmly by other organizations; the common sentiment was "finally, you're here."[5] But the organization wouldn't stay. By 2010, Amnesty International had decided to end its engagement with

Figure 6.1 Human rights NGOs' participation in the UNFCCC

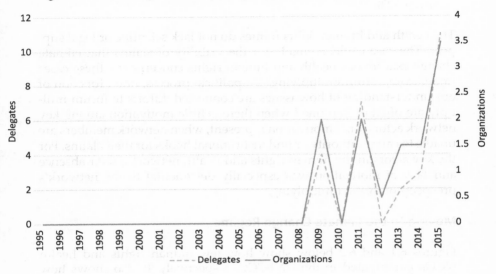

Figure 6.2 Health NGOs' participation in the UNFCCC

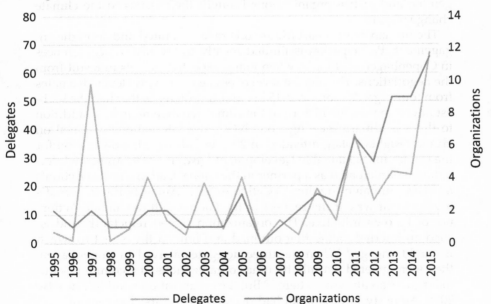

the UNFCCC and the Global Call for Climate Action to focus on its core areas of work.[6]

The heavyweights in the human rights NGO network, Amnesty International and Human Rights Watch, would occasionally participate, usually at historic gatherings in anticipation of a major international event. Otherwise, the human rights NGOs were uninterested and disengaged. Their story ends at the first stage of the framework, largely as a result of their lack of motivation (see below).

A small contingent of health NGOs continued, but struggled to mobilize, as figure 6.2 shows. That their engagement was limited qualifies the health network as a null case. Their maximum presence in 2015 was sixty-six delegates from twelve organizations, twice their previous high mark in 2011. By comparison, gender NGOs mobilized sixty-three delegates at Warsaw in 2013, one of their smallest delegations since they began forum multiplying. Even at a historic conference with more than 35,000 in attendance, the health network mobilized few people, many of whom were from environmental health organizations, not public health NGOs.

The few health organizations that participated in 2009 started informally collaborating among themselves. As with the climate justice movement, many of these actors met once they arrived at the UNFCCC rather than coordinating beforehand. The group was comprised of delegates interested in health, including representatives from WHO, health advocacy organizations, and one environmental research institute. As that member recalls, the discussion centred on how health could motivate policy action and how to leverage a reference to health in a footnote on one page of the draft negotiation text.[7] Through indirect personal relationships, ten like-minded people among the thousands participating at the conference connected.[8]

By 2011, momentum seemed possible for health advocates. The Global Climate and Health Alliance (GCHA) formed with the goal of minimizing the health effects of climate change and maximizing the health co-benefits of climate change action.[9] Founded by Health Care Without Harm and the Climate and Health Council, the Alliance had grown to sixteen members by 2015; three of these were public health NGOs that did not make explicit reference to environmental or climate issues in their mandates.[10] Other health NGOs such as Nurses Across the Borders that had participated in the UNFCCC did not join the Alliance. The Alliance held the first Global Climate and Health Summit at the 2011 Durban conference. These Summits became regular events held on the margins of UNFCCC meetings, with other meetings held in 2013 and 2015.

Still, the health network lacked critical mass. Speaking in 2014 after the 2013 Conference in Warsaw, Nick Watts, founder of the Climate and Health Council and coordinator for the GCHA, lamented that "five years ago there were two of us. We get excited, but it's a bit depressing, that there are twenty of us."[11] The few health NGO delegates participating in 2014 and 2015 – twenty-five and sixty-six respectively – continued to seek inroads into the negotiations.

Human Rights and Health–Climate Networks

The limited participation of human rights NGOs renders a social network analysis of the human rights–climate network essentially meaningless. The highest level of attendance was four organizations in a single year. There are no networks dedicated to the link between human rights and climate change, as there are for gender, climate justice, and even health. Murdie and Davis (2012) mapped the overall transnational advocacy network for human rights, identifying Amnesty International and Human Rights Watch as the network's central NGOs. Below, using these findings, I focus on the motivations of Amnesty International and Human Rights Watch as well as the two other human rights organizations that participated in climate change between 1995 and 2015.

The health–climate network shows none of the traditionally influential or well-connected actors associated with global health advocacy. Murdie and Davis (2012) also investigate the health network, arguing that it is a small network composed mainly of service providers, such as NGOs that undertake water sanitation or vaccination programs. None of these organizations are to be found in the health–climate network. The network seems to be similar in size (603 organizations) to the other networks of new climate activists. Unlike what is found in those other networks, however, many of its member organizations (135) have only one connection. There are many organizations that could hear information about climate change, or could be mobilized to participate in the UNFCCC, but have chosen not to. Instead, the network is populated by environmental health NGOs and NGOs created solely for climate–health linkages. Very few public health NGOs appear, most notably the WMA, which has little incentive to participate in the climate change regime (see below).

The WMA is one of only two central actors in the health–climate network, and even it participates only sporadically.[12] The WMA is a global organization that represents physicians and serves as a platform for discussing and developing standards of medical ethics and competence. It works on human rights issues related to health but has no programs for environmental health. The connections it has in the health–climate network arise from work on other, non-climate issues. The climate change regime falls outside the WMA's remit, and its engagement with that regime is limited – it has attended only twice. In 2015, only nine delegates from the WMA attended.

Besides the WMA, the International Federation of Medical Students (IFMSA) is the only other actor with significant connections within the network. IFMSA is a global alliance of medical student associations from 127 countries. It works to provide leadership opportunities for medical students early in their careers on a variety of issues. However, its connections to others in the network are not built upon strategizing and sharing information; they usually involve internships and some research and advocacy.[13] The IMFSA has some history with some actors, such as WHO staff working on climate change.[14] The existing ties have been built on professional opportunities, not campaigning. While the IFMSA works with the Youth constituency,[15] and its collaboration with others in the health network is strained by differing ideas of how to progress work on climate change in the UNFCCC.

Figure 6.3 shows three main clusters of organizations. First, the core of much of the advocacy work on climate change and health is undertaken by a cluster of organizations connected to Health Care Without Harm, IFMSA, and the GCHA. This cluster represents the Global Climate and Health Alliance (GCHA), which was founded in 2011 and by 2015 had sixteen members. This group includes many of the principal advocates from environmental health NGOs and climate–health NGOs. Many of these organizations, like the Alliance itself, were founded as hybrid organizations working at the intersection of health and environment (particularly climate) issues.

The second cluster is connected to the WMA and is comprised mainly of public health NGOs. This group includes the World Health Professionals Alliance, the International Hospital Federation, and the International Council of Nurses. None of these organizations have attended a UNFCCC meeting, save the WMA, which has participated only a few times. Public health organizations are reticent to engage in climate change work (see below). It is these organizations, in this cluster, that the climate–health NGOs seek to convince.

Third, there is a small cluster of environmental NGOs in this network. Greenpeace, Friends of the Earth International, and the Climate Action Network appear largely due to connections that some of the environmental health NGOs forged through other campaigns. Friends of the Earth International, however, has not engaged with the health network often on climate issues and has not acted as a broker for the

Figure 6.3 Health–climate network, 2009–2015

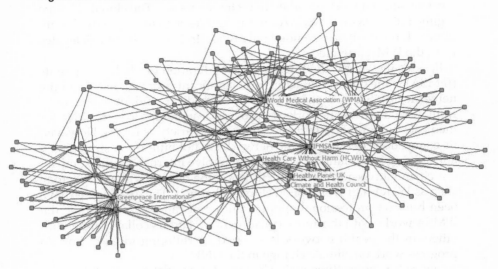

network. As a key climate and health person explains, "no environmental NGOs want to take on health and almost no health NGOs do climate advocacy. This leaves very few of us working on both."[16]

Motivation

Stage One of the forum multiplying framework is about motivation. Central NGOs must have a political, material, normative reason to engage in a new arena in global governance and to bring others along with them. As the other cases of the new climate activism show, political motivations tend to be most relevant. The lack of political motivations on the part of human rights and public health lead NGOs to engage in climate change work on a sustained basis tells much of these networks' story. Political, material, and – to a lesser extent – normative motivations were largely absent for the key NGOs: the WMA, IFMSA, Amnesty International, and Human Rights Watch. Without these motivations, there is no presence of human rights NGOs in the climate change regime and only limited participation by health NGOs, mostly environmental health NGOs.

There is little political motivation to find a new regime because the health and human rights regimes both remain viable options for public health and human rights organizations respectively. Within the health regime, there is little political motivation to engage in climate change among public health NGOs. It is not that the health NGO network refuses to travel to other regimes: it *has* engaged in forum multiplying. The WMA has participated in discussions on leaded petrol, road safety, tobacco, nuclear weapons, and human rights.[17] The International Society of Doctors for the Environment has worked on nuclear weapons and small arms and light weapons, inviting other health organizations to speak.[18]

The WMA issued the Delhi Declaration on Climate Change and Health in 2008 after some members sought to engage on the issue in much the same way as had been done on human rights.[19] The five areas of the Declaration are all inward-looking: they consider how to advocate, show leadership, undertake education and capacity building, undertake surveillance and research, and collaborate with others in the health sector (World Medical Association, 2008). But there are no references to actors outside the health sector. At a 2013 conference, Climate Change and Health, the GCHA asked the association to sign its statement, which included calls to keep fossil fuels in the ground and references to the UNFCCC negotiations.[20] The WMA viewed the GCHA's declaration as too focused on climate change; the Delhi Declaration was as far as it was prepared to go.[21] Any discussion of climate change and health would have to keep the WMA firmly planted in the health regime and not venture into messages that were strictly related to climate change.[22]

For human rights NGOs, there is considerable work remaining on human rights issues and they still have considerable authority in this regime. Amnesty International often receives requests to undertake new campaigns on human rights and other issues and faces internal tensions between those seeking to uphold its moral authority as a witness and those seeking to build political authority, taking a stance as an advocate (Hopgood, 2006). Climate change presents challenges to human rights NGOs that wield their moral authority. They built their authority by documenting abuses as defined by the specific legal framework defining state responsibilities enshrined in human rights treaties. Human rights NGOs operate according to a specific methodology for documenting and proving human rights abuses, according to human rights law. This methodology does not lend itself to climate change:

> There are some challenges to addressing climate change from [the] perspective and methodology we use. We document abuses that have occurred using testimony etc. Speaking about potential abuses in the future involves different methodology, such as modelling or predictions, which we are not accustomed to using. There is a recognition that we need to

be smarter and engaged [on climate change], but there are resource constraints and we have human rights violations to prioritize.[23]

Climate change could threaten the enjoyment of some human rights,
but it a probability rather than a provable fact based on demonstrable
actions by the state. When it comes to climate change, moral authority
built on documentation is not possible. Such an exercise would involve
apportioning blame for an event, for example a super-typhoon, to a
country or countries that emitted the greenhouse gases causing that
natural disaster. That is an exercise for modellers in a scientific lab, not
for those who gather testimonies in the field. Human Rights Watch and
Amnesty International have built their reputations and authority on
demonstrating that human rights violations occurred. Climate change
would extend the limits and plausibility of human rights NGOs' methods beyond what may be credible and doable based on their expertise,
potentially undermining their authority.

It is unclear how climate change could fit into the legal framework of
the human rights regime. At one time, the Maldives pushed the issue,
hoping to add moral weight to its case for climate action heading into
the Copenhagen climate conference later that year (Knox, 2009). In 2009
the Office of the UN High Commissioner for Human Rights undertook
research, ultimately adopting a decision on the link between human
rights and climate change. The decision states that climate change
threatens the enjoyment of several human rights, but that climate
change does not necessarily violate human rights. It further states that
human rights law places duties on states concerning climate change,
including an obligation of international cooperation (OHCHR, 2009).
As Knox (2009, p. 478), a UN Special Rapporteur on Human Rights and
the Environment, explains, the main obstacle is the difference between
magnifying or multiplying human rights problems and violating those
rights:

> While the distinction between an adverse effect on the enjoyment of hu-
> man rights and a violation of human rights may seem arcane, it is well
> grounded in human rights law. A violation of human rights is commonly
> understood to imply a breach of a legal duty under human rights law.
> Not all adverse effects on human rights necessarily imply such a breach.
> A mudslide that results from heavy rains, for example, may well interfere
> with, or even destroy, the right to life of those harmed by it, but it is not
> caused by a state acting in violation of its legal obligations and, in that
> sense, is not a violation of human rights.

So it is unclear how human rights NGOs can engage in climate change work using the legal framework on which their authority rests, and this has added to their reticence. For a time, the International Council on Human Rights Policy sought to fill this gap in understanding through a climate change project undertaken in 2008 (ICHRP, 2008). The author of the report, Stephen Humphreys, explains that the intent was to inform human rights organizations that were not participating in the UNFCCC, because so few were engaging.[24]

Given the mismatch between the legal framework of the human rights regime, and the methodologies underpinning human rights NGOs' authority, human rights NGOs had little political motivation to participate in the climate change regime. Human rights issues remain the priority. Climate change was not seen as a human rights issue; it was viewed as too different in nature from human rights and human rights governance, in which NGOs still had considerable authority and influence.

Also, there were no material motivations for these networks to participate in the climate change regime. The health NGOs had few resources to undertake climate change–related work and little funding forthcoming to support their work. Nearly all of the climate–health and environmental health NGOs reported they had little funding for their work and that they relied on volunteers, all of which ultimately impacted their ability to realize their strategies and undertake campaigns.[25] Some, such as the International Society of Doctors for the Environment, rely on retired doctors with time to pursue advocacy.[26] Even the WMA has limited capacity to undertake new and complex issues, particularly to learn about issues and the UNFCCC so as to strategize and implement an advocacy strategy.[27] After years of trying to secure funding for their work, the GCHA received some funding from the Global Call for Climate Action to produce a website on the health-related aspects outlined in the IPCC's Fifth Assessment Report.[28] The lack of internal capacity to expand into new issue areas, and the lack of funding, dampened any incentive for other health NGOs to participate.

For human rights NGOs, it was unclear whether multiplying within the climate change regime would help secure donor funds; indeed, doing so might even detract from their pool of resources. Human Rights Watch has a strong foundation of donor support; however, while some of these donors suggested they could support work on climate change, others intimated that they would not.[29] There are concerns about overextending staff and being able to find a niche where human rights

NGOs can show they are "in it for the long haul" by claiming expertise and establishing long-term relationships and engagement.[30] Without a clear signal of support from donors for work on the links between climate change and human rights, there is little incentive to take on new issues and the associated costs. Building long-term engagement would require normative motivations as actors internalize the view that climate change is a health or human rights issue. Here, both networks struggled to motivate a wider movement.

Unlike in the labour movement, and to an extent the climate justice movement, where a few normatively committed individuals were able to convince a wider group to engage in climate change, the lead NGOs in the human rights and health networks remained unpersuaded. A few human rights NGOs working on climate change tried to entice Amnesty International and Human Rights Watch. Some invoked climate justice to refer to human rights (for an example, see Nicholson & Chong, 2011), in part because

> it is difficult to make a good case using human rights law alone, so anyone interested in the human rights implications of climate change tends to widen the lens to "justice," whatever that is. Anyone I have worked with has tended to use both terms, not quite interchangeably. I am aware that there are some using the term "climate justice" who have a more radical agenda in mind than usually found among human rights people. I have always hoped the climate change issue might radicalize human rights activists a bit. Unsurprisingly, though, this doesn't seem to have happened.[31]

The climate justice frame offered a way around the human rights regime's strict adherence to the legal framework and methodologies. Yet while human rights discourse is invoked by environmental lawyers – and sometimes by others under the rhetoric of climate justice – the principal human rights actors remain outside of the climate change regime.

Among health NGOs, there was (and remains) a cadre of environmental health NGOs and other groups devoted solely to the links between climate change and health. The IFMSA is the only public health NGO in the network normatively motivated to undertake climate change work, which it does in conjunction with the Youth Constituency in the UNFCCC. It invokes this role as an organization of future leaders in the medical profession in its advocacy work on climate change, to prepare future health professionals to take on climate change as a public health issue.[32] Despite the normative motivations of some and support from academic work such as *The Lancet*, these groups struggle to convince doctors and other public health NGOs of the need to take on climate change campaigns.

The normatively committed environmental health and climate–
health NGOs faced pushback from doctors and some public health
NGOs. Variations of the mindset that "I already save lives, why are
you asking me to save the planet as well," were recalled by several respondents and, as well, were stated by a few participants at the WHO
Conference on Climate and Health held in 2014.[33] Those words sum
up doctors' responses to calls to campaign, advocate, or educate others on climate change and its implications for public health. Doctors
are patient-oriented – their goal is to take care of one person, it is not
to address the effects of other people or environmental trends on the
patient.[34] Those few health organizations – already devoted to environmental issues – involved in the climate change regime struggle to
motivate the wider health network.

Beyond their reluctance to get involved in an issue they view as unrelated to their work, some doctors and public health NGOs questioned
what the science linking health and climate change means in real-world
terms. At the 2014 WHO Conference, some delegates discussed what
the IPCC's confidence intervals meant, including whether a "moderate" increase in some health outcomes, such as vector-borne disease,
would mean a large number of affected people.[35] One public health
NGO, Safe Observer International, stressed the need to focus attention
and resources on water quality and sanitation, underscoring that the
health sector has expertise in handling these issues, which have a direct
impact on improving health; that sector hasn't the ability to address
climate change as effectively (IISD, 2014b). Climate science itself is not
being questioned here – rather, there are questions about whether there
is a strong enough link between climate change and health to warrant
action by the health sector, particularly given that the sector cannot on
its own mitigate emissions or build resilience to climate impacts on a
scale large enough to see an impact on health outcomes.[36]

The WMA's Delhi Declaration on Climate Change and Health reflects
the reticence of some in the health sector to take up climate change issues. In 2008, some members wanted the organization to treat climate
change in much the same way as it had addressed links between human rights and health. The WMA has made statements linking human
rights to health and outlining how doctors are affected by and can affect
human rights such as the right to health, rights for LGBT people, and
prevention of torture.[37] Other members, however, did not want to address the issue. Ultimately, its WMA settled on a broad statement that
lacked the specificity of the human rights declaration.[38] Few elected
members of the WMA have shown interest in attending UNFCCC
meetings since the Delhi Declaration in 2008.[39]

Unlike the labour, gender, and justice networks, the lead NGOs for human rights were unmotivated to campaign on climate change. Only the IFMSA, one of the two health NGOs in a leadership position, showed normative motivations. Without well-connected actors motivated to use their ties throughout the network, there is little that actors with fewer connections can do. The doctors, public health NGOs, and human rights NGOs remain unconvinced, perhaps even unaware of the connections between health or human rights and climate change. As a result, the mobilization of these networks in the UNFCCC requires only a brief account. For the human rights network, the story ends at the motivations stage. For the health network, a handful of delegates participated from environmental health NGOs or climate–health NGOs, trying to mobilize their network and gain recognition in the UNFCCC.

Means

Health advocates struggled to find their way in the UNFCCC. Numerically, there were few of them, and they lacked larger organizations such as the WMA, though WHO had started engaging on climate change in 2009. On each front – building cohesion, leveraging rules, and finding allies – the health network fell short when trying to navigate the social and institutional landscape of the UNFCCC. Few state or non-state actors engaged with health arguments or with the NGOs trying to advance them.

Building Cohesion

The health NGO network that was attending the UNFCCC meetings has put forward several ways to link climate change and health. Three frames have emerged: that the health sector can act to reduce its emissions; that climate change will exacerbate health outcomes; and that mitigation policies can bring about better health outcomes as a "co-benefit." Interestingly, many of the same actors espouse these frames concurrently. Rather than a clash between ideologies, as seen with the gender network and the labour movement, or a merging of complementary ideas, as with CJN!, the health NGOs working on climate change put forward several frames at once. The co-benefits frame seems to be gaining some traction among the three frames, as a possible way to bring together the network and settle on one message.

Regarding the first frame – that the health sector can itself undertake mitigation – health advocates argue that it is about leadership, though few in the sector are willing to make the investments or take up the idea. As WHO outlines in a discussion draft, hospitals account for 10.6 per cent of the United States' commercial energy consumption and health care buildings are the second most energy intensive commercial sector buildings. Some estimates show that in the United States and Britain, the health sector may account for 3 to 8 per cent of national emissions (WHO and Healthcare Without Harm, 2013). Health Care Without Harm has established the Global Green and Healthy Hospitals network to shrink the footprint of hospitals, including their greenhouse gas emissions. The Durban Declaration of the GCHA commits signatories to, among other actions, "lead by example and reduce the carbon footprint of our own institutions, practice and activities" (GCHA, 2011). Few actors have seemed willing to make these changes to their operations. In breakout sessions devoted to reducing emissions from the health sector at the 2014 WHO Conference on Climate Change and Health, few participants called for drastic action to reduce emissions; instead, participants noted the need for greater information about and understanding of the problem, and for funding to "green" their systems (IISD, 2014b; see also WHO and Healthcare Without Harm, 2013).[40]

The GCHA has drawn attention to the IPCC's findings on the health impacts of climate change, iimpacts that include heat-related and extreme weather-related illnesses and injuries; aggravated chronic illnesses; vector-, water-, and food-borne infectious diseases; asthma and respiratory disorders; malnutrition; and stress-related and mental health disorders (GCHA, 2011). Similarly, WHO has focused most of its work on how health and adaptation are related.

The adaptation link was often too hypothetical, outlining the potential health effects, at a future date, caused in part by climate change. This weakness in the frame led some NGOs that had previously used it to back away from it. The frame didn't show that health effects are already occurring from climate change, although the methodologies for attributing health outcomes to climate change impacts is still under development. The message that health effects from climate change are already happening wasn't resonating with other delegates, or with fellow physicians, and this prompted advocates to move toward the co-benefits argument.[41]

The co-benefits argument highlights that acting on climate change can improve public health. Examples offered by the movement include closing coal-fired plants can reduce air pollutants that contribute to asthma and mortality for those with cardiovascular problems; and investing in active transport can reduce obesity and thereby reduce rates of non-communicable diseases such as diabetes.[42] As more fully explained by WHO:

> There is a particular opportunity to reduce the roughly seven million deaths a year associated with air pollution, while also reducing climate warming. Approximately one in every eight deaths globally is now attributable to ambient and household air pollution. Inefficient combustion of fossil fuels and biomass creates releases particles including black carbon, which is both a major contributor to air pollution mortality, and a short-lived climate pollutant. (WHO, 2014, p. 7)

Much of the work of Health Care without Harm and others in the GCHA is focusing increasingly on the links between climate change, coal, and health. Put briefly, the frame states that "doing well for the climate will also help improve health outcomes." It offers no new solutions to climate change, nor does it propose new causes of the problem; instead, it tries to offer another reason to act on climate change, using air pollution as an intermediary step.

This broad frame, with its rather indirect logic, accrued favour among the health NGOs working in the UNFCCC. For some, the co-benefits frame was useful because it sent a general message to communicate health as a new link to climate change and could accommodate several specific health issues.[43] Others pointed to the frame's potential to motivate climate action, particularly by highlighting the potential savings to public health systems that could be achieved through mitigation.[44] Also, using the co-benefits frame as a discursive infrastructure to discuss health spending, WHO estimates that climate change could result in between US$2 and US$4 billion per year by 2030 in health-related public spending (WHO, 2016).

By 2015, there was still little uptake of this frame by others in the network. Unlike the broad frames such as climate justice or a just transition, the co-benefits frame did not mobilize a larger movement. Physicians still did not attend, and many public health officials still did not accept or use the co-benefits frame.[45] Environmental NGOs likewise were reluctant to include health messaging. When the Climate Action Network discusses health, it focuses on the health effects occurring after climate change, rather than on the co-benefits frame: "A lot of health people believe health is a fundamental message to send and reasons that a health perspective could be game changing. The message doesn't get picked up anywhere near as one might expect from environment groups or physicians."[46]

Divisions among those working on the links between climate and health further weaken the cohesiveness of the network and its ability to speak loudly to convey the co-benefits frame. The GCHA is a significant alliance bringing together some but not all of the NGOs engaged in the UNFCCC. Not involved is Nurses Across the Borders, a small NGO based in Nigeria that has sent one delegate to the UNFCCC since 2007, before many other health or environmental health organizations were involved. Nurses Across the Borders has engaged in projects on the ground to train nurses and in some advocacy work, using research and partnerships with the Seatrust Institute.[47] The Alliance also has to navigate several internal tensions with its membership, and as with the ITUC, this restricts the types of statements and tactics it can use. With national constituencies and international NGOs, the GCHA needs to maintain a more conservative line to ensure it does not alienate any members.[48]

This can create difficulties with the IFMSA, which coordinates with the Youth constituency in the UNFCCC and sometimes adopts messaging that the GCHA cannot sign on to. For some health advocates involved in the UNFCCC, the IFMSA's demonstrations, such as wearing their white coats or scrubs, chanting, and carrying large signs, are useful to visually draw attention to health issues, but these are not actions they would consider joining. One advocate referred to such demonstrations as "too shouty" for senior physicians to engage with, particularly as they are already new to and leery of engaging on climate change.

The small number of organizations working within the UNFCCC are divided. Some work on research and training. Others engage with and through the GCHA, focusing more narrowly on health issues as they relate to climate change. IFMSA has its own tactics and is more willing to promote climate action, whether it is linked to health or not. These divisions, and the multiple frames espoused by these groups, complicate the health messaging related to UNFCCC delegates. Because there is no unified voice putting forward a single idea, the message is diluted. Climate actors are left wondering whether to address climate change as mitigation or adaptation issue or to focus on health first, or on climate. Similarly, the health network has struggled to focus on one discursive hook and lacks the ability to use procedural rules to gain recognition.

Leveraging Rules

The health advocates struggle to find a firm connection to climate change institutions. The health frames highlight worsened health outcomes as a consequence of climate change and improving health as a co-benefit of climate action. The frame related to health outcomes caused by climate change could link to adaptation in a similar way that the gender frame linked to adaptation – by highlighting that efforts to adapt to climate change must include health considerations to avoid climate impacts falling disproportionately on some segments of society.

The co-benefit aspect of the frame did not have a direct tie into the negotiations. There is no institution devoted to the co-benefits of mitigation or adaptation policy.[49] There is the response measures forum, which convenes to discuss the consequences of mitigation. Originally, this forum was requested by oil-producing states, which remain the strongest proponents for the forum's continuation and consideration of ways to avoid or minimize the negative impacts that some countries may experience when climate policy is implemented. Some have characterized this space in quite negative terms.[50] WHO was invited to present the co-benefits of climate action at one session of this forum in 2014 and met with a somewhat terse response from some delegates, who asked what role health had in the forum and asked the Secretariat to choose the topics presented with more care to the forum's mandate.[51]

The small network struggled to locate an institutional foothold for its claims. Health–climate NGO delegates tend to be split among those frustrated with the UNFCCC process and those that are interested in the "nitty gritty of the text and the streams."[52] Those who are interested in closely following the negotiations divide their time between adaptation, focusing on the Nairobi Work Programme on impacts, vulnerability, and adaptation (commonly called the Nairobi Work Programme) and on the Clean Development Mechanism, particularly the modalities that award emissions reductions credits to coal-fired plants.[53] The work related to the Clean Development Mechanism is technical and low-profile; it entails reviewing the rules for crediting coal-fired plants if they can demonstrate the use of technologies to reduce emissions. It is "technical and far removed from what else is happening in the process ... a tough sell to the health community."[54]

Almost by default, the primary link for the health network is adaptation. Unlike the gender NGOs that linked to adaptation in the early days of the institution's formation, health advocates started linking health and adaptation issues after the Copenhagen conference in 2009. By that time, several of the institutions had been set, primarily the Nairobi Work Programme. Gender advocates could help shape the understanding of climate adaptation to include the disproportionate effects experienced in developing countries, namely among genders, in the institution's formative years. Health had to find space within an already formed set of norms, rules, and negotiation bodies devoted to adaptation.

Within adaptation, there are routine meetings and continued discussions on the implementation of national adaptation plans, national adaptation plans of action, the Nairobi Work Programme, and the Adaptation Fund, among others.[55] Health advocates largely ignored the funding aspect of adaptation until 2015. Initially, their focus was on national adaptation plans and primarily the Nairobi Work Programme. Some health advocates attempted to get experts on the review of the Work Programme, which was expected to lead to recommendations for new focal areas for future work.[56] Still others prefer to take a broader approach to the issue, focusing less on technical aspects than on trying to get across the message that climate change and health are connected.[57]

Some of the directions taken focused on the Clean Development Mechanism, others on adaptation issues; still others eschewed a narrow focus on technical negotiations altogether, and spread the resources and attention of the network. Further complicating matters was the network's late emergence in the UNFCCC. Its claim to belonging was premised on adaptation, an institution that by 2010 was firmly established in various work programs. The health network had to take the institutions as they were rather than try to shape them by teaching new ideas and norms, as the gender advocates had when bringing gender into the adaptation and, later, into other areas of the UNFCCC. This left technical solutions in corners of the UNFCCC negotiations that were difficult to describe to the wider health community, never mind mobilize that community. As the other cases show, broader frames can unite a network. Here, technical issues hampered mobilization efforts.

The health network found itself at a disadvantage procedurally as well. Unlike the successful new NGO networks, health could not leverage the rules about observer participation to increase their resources for mobilization. Health was not a Major Group in Agenda 21 as established in 1992. As chapter 3 outlined, the UNFCCC mirrors the UN Major Group system but does not follow it precisely because environmental and business and industry constituencies had organized themselves organically during negotiations for the Convention before 1992. Still, labour and gender groups argued that they, as Major Groups, also should act as constituencies in the UNFCCC (see chapters 4 and 5). Health had no such leverage vis-à-vis the institutions. Accepting this norm, members of the network did not seek constituency arrangements.[58]

In terms of aligning with expected norms of observer behaviour, the network seems divided on what its repertoire of contention should be. Some of these organizations had not worked together before entering the UNFCCC, or they are new, such as the organizations created solely to address climate change and health. There is no shared identity and repertoire of contention to draw upon. Some, like the IFMSA, prefer more contentious forms of politics, such as actions within the negotiations. Others have sought a strictly insider approach and without constituency status have faced difficulty pursuing this tactic.

Members of the health network met informally in Copenhagen. Yet as one health researcher explains, "it was odd, there were no developing countries represented, there was no one from the people we were talking about."[59] The health network tried to align itself with the adaptation institutions but lacked any route to communicate with developing countries.

Frustration at the difficulties of gaining recognition and developing connections within the UNFCCC led to this group continuing to organize and calling itself the "Friends of Public Health Contact Group."[60] The purpose of the Friends of Public Health Contact Group was to reach out to health organizations and "non-health people." These people were identified through a rather laborious process of selecting a few health-specific people from the list of participants sending out invitations.[61] Without the benefit of constituency status, the health network had to try to organize itself. Even finding one another proved difficult in the large climate conferences.

However, the group's name proved somewhat problematic and perhaps revealed a lack of understanding of the UNFCCC process. In the UNFCCC and other multilateral environmental negotiations, a contact group is a negotiation forum where states discuss and negotiate text on discrete issues for later decision by a higher body. By calling themselves a contact group, Friends of Public Health created confusion. The UNFCCC Secretariat contacted some of the organizers to clarify, as one recalls:

> They saw us organizing something non-traditional. We explained that it was not anything weird, just trying to build consensus around a non-controversial topic. After some consultations with the Secretariat, they were more relaxed, but there were difficulties. There is a bureaucracy to it, we've found a lot of constraints within the UNFCCC system.[62]

The Friends' efforts to organize initially confused climate governors but provided a way for the members to interact.

These informal meetings did garner some resources useful for further mobilization. Several of the NGOs in the network and WHO met through the "contact group," and some initial connections were made with a few interested countries, although often there were very few people in the room due to meetings held in parallel that had priority.[63] These initial activities helped form the network, ultimately contributing to formation of the GCHA and its collaboration with WHO.[64] It was still a small group, trying to work around the institutions of the UNFCCC.

One could argue that it is only a matter of time before this small network manages to convince public health NGOs to participate in the UNFCCC. This seems unlikely. Other networks managed to mobilize quickly, rapidly increasing their numbers after key actors began participating. The first step would be to secure sustained engagement of the WMA, including its commitment to articulate a health frame to its network and to climate change governors. Even then, there will be barriers. Some of the organizations connected to the WMA are issue-specific, such as the International Hospital Federation, the International Pharmaceutical Federation, and the midwife, psychiatric, and veterinary organizations. These organizations may be hard pressed to find a role for themselves under a health frame that is currently focused on the intensified health impacts wrought by climate change.

This in turn may add to the sense that there is little the health community can offer to the global effort to mitigate emissions and build resilience to climate impacts beyond (yet) another reason why these actions should be undertaken. The unique skill set and knowledge of health NGOs does not increase understanding of how to mitigate emissions or, as in the case of the labour network, reduce political barriers to doing so. Regarding adaptation, health becomes another issue to consider in planning. Health NGOs know how to vaccinate and even eradicate disease; they have less input into how to undertake climate change planning. If anything, health NGOs have made the reverse case: that health policy-makers need to consider environmental factors, most notably climate change.

Unlike the gender NGOs, the health community cannot argue that its inclusion creates a new group of agents already on the front lines of climate change impacts and able to contribute new solutions to the problems. While women foresters and farmers can participate directly in improving flood resistance, altering irrigation systems, and sharing knowledge about changing crop yields, doctors can only report changing disease patterns and pursue traditional ways to cope, such as sanitation practices, water quality improvements, and vaccination campaigns. None of these are in the remit of climate change governors or directly affected by climate change policy. The health frame's prognostic and diagnostic elements will need to change or expand if it is to find a niche that only the health network can occupy to transform the network's members from cheerleaders into integral actors that must be part of future climate action and policy discussions.

Furthermore, the health community continues to lack a broker. WHO has yet to gain acceptance as a key climate change actor. Most climate and environmental NGOs have not engaged with health NGOs. The Union for Concerned Scientists has produced a series of reports and hosted workshops on the health-related impacts of climate change in the United States in 2011 and 2012, but this work seems to have ended.[65] Without an organization that is a recognized climate governor to provide introductions and lend its authority to the health network, these actors may remain on the outside.

Finding Allies

Unlike the new climate activists previously explored, the health advocates did not have an international organization or NGO ally that was already embedded in the climate change regime. Many pointed to WHO as a potential broker with a trusted reputation and resources, but it cannot fulfil this role for the network. WHO was an outsider to the climate process and was unable to bring health concerns into the UNFCCC – it started its own climate change work only in 2008 and attended its first UNFCCC conference only in 2009.[66] Unlike UNEP, which was an effective broker for labour and gender networks, WHO was not engaged in many environmental issues or climate change work before 2009, when the NGOs also started attending. WHO was not well placed to be a broker. It was on the outside, striving for recognition.

The social network analysis showed connections between WHO and climate change actors such as UNEP; however, these connections are not evident when it comes to health–climate linkages. Internal coordination mechanisms in the UN system established informal working groups on climate change, including a task group on the social dimensions of climate change. This informal group included twenty UN agencies and organizations, including WHO. UNEP is absent.[67] WHO and UNEP may be linked through other programs, such as water sanitation, but those programs do not seem related to climate change.

Many actors in the health network looked to WHO to take a leadership role on climate change issues. The group working on climate change in WHO is quite small, ranging between two and four staff. NGOs question whether climate change has the support of the organization and observe that WHO struggles to get much recognition or respect in the UNFCCC.[68] Internally, WHO has few levers for addressing climate change. Unlike with health issues, such as vaccinations, WHO cannot directly intervene or achieve results on the drivers of climate change, such as emissions from the energy sector. The inability to directly influence results makes it difficult to find interventions for WHO to view as worth investing resources toward.[69] So WHO has sought and secured funding to support the inclusion of health in the national adaptation plans of developing countries and is supporting students from the IFMSA in internships.[70]

Some of these resources are of value to the NGO network. All the submissions on health made before 2013 were from WHO. Furthermore, WHO has developed guidelines for least developed countries (LDCs) and other developing countries aimed at helping health ministries assess the impacts of climate change and find suitable adaptation strategies. As underscored by a 2012 submission by WHO to the UNFCCC's work on adaptation, WHO's technical work comes after the "strong political mandate" from the World Health Assembly's 2008 resolution on climate change:

> WHO supports countries in planning and implementing health adaptation to climate change, contributing to the implementation of the decisions of the UNFCCC COP [Conference of the Parties], and its support mechanisms, such as the Nairobi Work Programme. WHO is currently executing major projects to pilot adaptation to climate change in 14 countries in all six WHO regions, and has provided support for assessments of health vulnerability and adaptation to climate change in over 30 countries. (UNFCCC, 2012)

These tools were useful for some within the network. The GCHA does not include WHO as a member but closely collaborates with it. As the Alliance's coordinator explains, WHO's resources and its collaboration with the GCHA have meant that the Alliance is "the first point of call for civil society who want to engage around the WHO, and work on NAPs [national adaptation plans] as a result."[71]

WHO did not bring the IFMSA into the UNFCCC, which is what one would expect of a broker. A health advocate who has been involved in the UNFCCC explains that the IFMSA and WHO met "by chance" in 2009, and since then, WHO has hosted IFMSA students as interns to complete climate change–related work. The IFMSA plays a liaison role, linking WHO to public health NGOs working on climate change:

> We've been lucky that we met the IFMSA in Bangkok [in 2009]. They are very good, students that got involved as medical students with their own

internal program on climate change. We met them by chance and started offering them internships. Now [we] have a regular program with interns from IFMSA coming regularly. For us they are a liaison with public health NGOs working on climate change.[72]

Rather than serving as a broker, WHO used its connections with other health organizations to help increase its capacity to work on climate change. WHO was limited in its capacity to address climate change and participate in the UNFCCC; it also lacked connections to climate actors. In many ways, it was finding its way just as the small health community of advocates were struggling to find a foothold in the UNFCCC.

Conclusion

The human rights and health frames both hold considerable promise on scientific or legal grounds. They could help motivate people who otherwise would not care about climate change to act to protect their own rights and health, or those of others. New claims can be made that, if one is a parent of an asthmatic child or cares about the right to shelter, then one should also support climate change policy. These claims could motivate others to engage in the issue, although so far only a small number of activists have made these connections. Primarily it is environmental lawyers rather than NGOs that make human rights claims. A few environmental health NGOs, and activists that have started their own organizations devoted to the links between climate and health, are carrying the torch in the absence of public health NGOs. As these cases show, *who* participates in global governance is political. There may be a scientific or legal basis for connecting issues. Yet some networks are not interested in participating in other areas of global governance, while others find themselves unable to mobilize a presence.

The first lesson these null cases show is that, at least in the context of the climate change regime, one will not be recognized as a member of the governing club simply by offering further motivation for climate action. Unless they offer new solutions or causes, health and human rights join the long list of reasons why climate change action makes sense. They are speaking to the proverbial choir whose members already know they need to act but face geopolitical and economic barriers. Offering additional reasons to act does not help climate actors.

Second, many in these networks do not see themselves as implicated in the climate change regime. Labour activists saw themselves threatened, or possibly empowered, by mitigation institutions; gender activists viewed adaptation discussions as extensions of their development work; the global justice movement saw market mechanisms as another instance of capitalism run amok. Few health or human rights advocates see how to extend their current work into climate change. The institutional changes creating overlap and the implications for networks from other regimes did not similarly trigger health or human rights actors to forum multiply.

These unique lessons aside, these cases confirm many of the central dynamics of the forum multiplying framework. First, motivations, particularly failure in other regimes, must be present before a network undertakes forum multiplying. The health and human rights regimes are still fruitful areas for these networks. Expanding outward is a risky, unnecessary endeavour. At this stage, the human rights NGO network filtered out.

Second, cohesion matters. The health network was unable to find a single frame or to collaborate to forward just one frame. Spreading multiple frames in different ways diluted the potential that one frame would have offered.

Third, frames must link to substantive institutions. Climate delegates are working on discrete areas of negotiations, each devoted to a given issue. They need to know where a new issue would fit. An indirect frame, such as the health co-benefits frame, doesn't provide an actionable call to delegates. They may understand why health and climate change are connected but not know what to do with that information in the context of the institutions and negotiations of the UNFCCC.

Finally, procedural institutions matter, in that they separate NGOs that are recognized by the Secretariat from others that are not. By leveraging these procedural institutions, networks can borrow the legitimacy of the regime's institutions. Backing that up with behaviour conforming to norms can solidify a new network's place in the regime. Procedural institutions alone cannot guarantee successful forum multiplying, but the recognition these institutions provide can be a useful sign that the regime accepts the actor and can provide resources to help the network amplify the frame and build alliances.

7 The New Climate Activists' Future

NGOs are mobile actors in global governance, which is particularly surprising because their authority does not easily travel, and because political opportunity structures can impose constraints. NGOs are not free to move at will, yet they still manage to traverse the boundaries of regimes. Through routine interactions with states and others within their target regime, NGO networks can navigate relationships and institutions and find recognition, even influence. This uncovers a new way to look at regime complexes, one that shifts emphasis away from the overlapping rules and mandates of organizations and instead focuses on networked actors building connections and creating links among issues. This chapter provides an overview of the research contributions and the generalizability of the framework and findings. I then turn to the theoretical and substantive implications of this book, outlining areas for future research and drawing on the arguments to posit what lies ahead for the new climate activists in the climate change regime governed by the Paris Agreement.

This book has sought to explain both NGOs' mobility and the limits of that mobility by exploring why NGO networks participate in a forum in which they have no expertise or experience and why some networks successfully forum-multiply into that regime while others do not. I began by exploring the observed but untheorized phenomenon of NGO forum multiplying, which happens to summarize many of the findings of this book. The framework I provide, which helps advance our understanding of the complexities around forum multiplying, has two stages. First, political motivations often outweigh material or moral ones. Stagnation in the home regime can be a powerful motivation to undertake forum multiplying. When political opportunity structures become more constrained, one would expect to see non-state actors seeking new regimes to advance their causes.

This book uncovers some of the dynamics that enable some NGO networks to find acceptance in the target regime. Centralized networks or networks with cooperative central NGOs are better able to rally around a single coherent frame. Finding actors within the climate change regime has been of vital importance for introducing the new climate activists to the social and institutional environment of the regime, which NGOs would otherwise struggle to navigate. There have been strong institutional effects. NGOs had to find a way to link their frame to substantive rules in order to demonstrate that their issue belonged in the climate change regime, that they had a valid claim. Other institutions – these related to how observers are categorized and supported, or allowed to participate – influence the strategies and recognition of NGO networks. Constituency status, which may seem a token institution, is important to the new climate activists symbolically and materially, because it helps them mobilize new supporters in the climate change regime.

Second, I join a growing literature that views NGO networks as heterogeneous groups. I contribute to our understanding of how and why NGOs can influence the network's actions and global governance outcomes. This book builds on work on intra-network dynamics and expands on it to nuance our understanding of the power allowed to and limitations placed on lead NGOs. Central NGOs are important actors in forum multiplying. They can introduce an issue generally perceived to be unrelated to the core work of the network; essentially, they vet the network's agenda (Carpenter, 2014). This is a significant ask of others in the network, for it promotes expensive work to link disparate issues and engage in a new regime whose institutions network members do not yet understand.

Yet there are checks on this power. While the literature tends to characterize the process as unilateral, I have shown that considerable internal negotiations are often required. Even the most centralized network, labour, still had to moderate its claims and convene negotiations among members. The presence of multiple central NGOs in the network was not necessarily detrimental but did require close coordination and internal negotiation. Less centralized networks can draw upon the strengths of each actor. The climate justice movement brought together the climate-specific knowledge of the Durban Group with the systemic critique of the global justice movement to devise the climate justice frame. But organizing loosely can undermine the network's overall goal, which is to develop and defend its frame in the target regime.

This book makes an original contribution by underscoring the role of brokers, particularly international organizations. Brokers act as conduits through which some new frames and understandings enter regimes and thereafter influence how governors understand and govern. Among the cases studied here, only those with brokers to the climate change regime succeeded in forum multiplying into the UNFCCC. Often, the brokers were international organizations. These actors have a legitimacy that spans regimes and have staff able to conduct research. Legitimacy and expertise seem to be valuable resources for NGO networks seeking acceptance in a new regime.

Third, I have introduced NGOs to the literature on regime complexes. This book takes a different view of regime complexes, focusing on actors and agency rather than on overlapping formal rules and structures. There are examples of traditional, state-centric forum shopping; for example, the Marshall Islands put climate change on the human rights agenda, which led to resolutions at the UN High Commission for Human Rights. There is also a case of Secretariat influence on international organizations managing regime complexes (see Jinnah, 2014; Hall, 2015). In 2008 the World Health Assembly adopted a resolution on climate change and devoted some resources to it (not many, mind)[1] before even the early few health NGOs had started working on climate change. Beyond these few examples, this book uncovers the role of NGOs.

This book suggests how NGOs matter in regime complexes. It seems that their influence on regime complexes is double-edged – they both contribute to the expansion of regime complexes and, perhaps, help manage the growing fragmentation of global governance. Zelli and van Asselt (2013) posit that bandwagoning behaviours, such as an NGO network joining the climate change regime in order to advance its own issues, are a way of managing the fragmentation inherent in regime complexes. This book shows that such strategies can do the opposite: rather than manage overlapping mandates, NGOs can expand the number of institutions engaged and further fragment their authority on a given issue. Forum multiplying strategies can increase the number of rules governing the issues that NGOs seek to advance into multiple regimes. Here, NGOs stretched the mandate of the climate change regime, creating new overlapping sets of rules and norms with other, social regimes. The politics of NGO agenda-setting and influence can extend beyond a single regime, thus contributing to the fragmentation of global governance as more organizations' rules overlap on a similar issue.

NGOs can serve as conduits between regimes. This can help manage fragmentation by creating consistent or compatible understandings of the issues and the corresponding rules. New climate activists forged new connections among social regimes and the climate change regime. The ILO adopted guidelines on climate change and a just transition, using its tripartite decision-making structure (i.e., governments, labour organizations, and employers participating in decisions), supported by key individuals such as Guy Ryder, Director General of the ILO and a former union representative active on environmental and climate issues.[2] The Committee on the Elimination of all Forms of Discrimination against Women adopted a decision and established a working group on climate change that included individuals who worked to bring gender issues into the UNFCCC. The World Social Forum increasingly discusses climate change, in a new Climate Space in part organized by those in the global justice movement and their climate allies, such as 350.org. NGOs' forum multiplying strategies can link regimes because, unlike with forum shopping or forum shifting, the NGOs do not leave their home regime. They straddle multiple regimes, and this enables them to feed information to and from those regimes, building support and allies on all sides. In addition, they can propagate shared understandings of how the issues should be governed, which can lead to more compatibility and less conflict in the regime complex. How these mechanisms work more precisely is a promising area for future research (see below).

Moving to Regimes beyond Climate Change

Climate change is a "tough test" for NGO mobility because of the many barriers to NGO entry that would lead one to expect little engagement by those outside of groups that are directly affected (e.g., environmental NGOs or business groups). But climate change governance shares some features with regimes that experience influxes of new NGOs. These features, which may be key background mechanisms, are shared by many regimes, showing the potential generalizability of the arguments of this book.

Scholars have noted that many of the regimes in which NGOs from other regimes participated were high on the international agenda. Regimes such as trade and human rights drew considerable attention from the media, states, UN leadership, and even celebrities. This privileged place has implications for forum multiplying, for NGOs know more about these regimes. Information is more readily available, so NGOs are more likely to hear of developments that may implicate their work. Regimes that are not in the policy-making spotlight, may be more insulated from outsiders, because those outside the process are less likely to know whether the rules or norms of that regime have implications for other regimes.

Of course, greater public and state attention is also an incentive for NGOs to participate in these regimes and for international organizations to seek out NGO participation. By linking their issue to a high-profile issue, NGOs can garner greater media attention for their causes, perhaps finding new supporters. International organizations that are in the spotlight may feel pressure to adhere to a wider range of social norms. For example, in 2018 the UN Organization for the Prohibition of Chemical Weapons, a treaty-based organization with a small Secretariat, aligned some of its work with the Sustainable Development Goals (which were adopted in 2015),[3] and member-states called for greater consideration of gender.[4] Both of these developments occurred after the organization was called upon to enforce the elimination of chemical weapons in Syria. This broadening of the agenda could be a way for an organization to signal that it is legitimate and inclusive and ascribes to global norms. Or it could be a way for states and international organizations to show some progress while avoiding the central issues at hand – for example, by taking leadership on gender issues while continuing to emit greenhouse gases at rising annual rates. The gender–chemical weapons link was made in 2018 at the same meeting that states failed to agree on the outcome document owing to disagreement over Syria's use of chemical weapons. There are many reasons why international organizations may welcome the participation of new NGOs in its work as it becomes more high-profile. NGOs are often happy to participate in work that attracts more attention to their causes. There is, perhaps, an implicit bargain in play here.

Not all NGOs try to move to all regimes, which suggests that some regimes are more opportune targets than others. It also seems, based on the anecdotes in the literature and on the logic of this book, that wider, more diverse groups of NGOs tend to participate in regimes governing more complex and encompassing issue areas. There may be "latent regime complexity" – that is, a propensity for a regime to attract a diverse group of NGO claimants, with some regimes' remits becoming more malleable, and open to expansion, over time simply because there are many facets to the issue being governed. Some issues are more malleable than others. Or, they may be complex and thus offer several discursive hooks for incoming NGOs. Or, they may be more contested, accommodating more than one take on what is "really" going on. This malleability can provide openings for NGOs to link their issues to regimes such as trade, human security, human rights, development, and others that are broader and more "holistic."

Issues are also malleable because that is how they have been reframed over time. Political processes are inherently tied to the governance of issues, from problem identification to rule formulation. There are few "natural" ways to understand an issue detached from political dynamics (Carpenter, 2014). Here, the climate case is instructive: in the mid- and late 2000s, when many of the new climate activists started participating in the climate change regime, the issue was thought of as a distant environmental problem with economic implications. Our understanding of climate change today, as an issue deeply intertwined with our present-day economic, social, and political structures, has been shaped in part by the new climate activists. Even seemingly smaller, more discrete issues can be politically reshaped and expanded to take on new connotations. An example of this is the persistent organic pollutants regime. The Stockholm Convention governs the production, use, and disposal of this discrete class of (currently) twenty-five chemicals.[5] It was expected that the regime that oversees this small group of chemicals would be limited to environmental issues, yet environmental and health activists have succeeded in reframing the issue to highlight gender, Indigenous rights, health, and children's and other human rights–related aspects of those issues. Many issues may be malleable, or open to new interpretations, but institutions don't necessarily change as easily. NGO forum multiplying strategies seem to be triggered at least in part by institutional change.

Latent regime complexity is a political process involving, and perhaps triggered by, expansion of the zone of issues a regime considers. The WTO, the UNFCCC, and development organizations, among others, all engage in ongoing negotiations, in renewed rounds of commitments, in stalemates and breakthroughs. Similarly, the human rights regime launched and navigated multiple waves of new human rights that expanded their governance remit. These ongoing processes of renewal can be strategically useful for NGO forum multiplying. NGOs can enter the regime when state and public attention is high and when new rules are in development and more open for influence. This in part explains the rise and fall of environmental NGOs' participation in the WTO (Casula Vifell, 2010). That is, when there are political openings conductive to NGO participation and influence, NGOs may participate, then leave when such openings close.

Ongoing rounds of negotiations can be a key factor on the "demand side" for NGOs' participation. New negotiations allow opportunities for agenda setting and for issue linkage, which can introduce new issues to the regime. States may have incentives to link new issues to the regime in order to widen the zone of agreement (Haas, 1980). International organizations may welcome NGOs' expertise on new issues or look to them for help bringing clarity to the uncertainties involved in negotiations (Jönsson & Tallberg, 2010). New issues, introduced for any number of reasons, including NGO lobbying efforts, expand the remit of the regime and implicate the work of others in its mandate. NGOs from further afield, even another regime, may see their work as necessarily now linked, thus triggering forum multiplying.

There is a need for comparative work on the supply side of NGOs' participation to complement the demand side. We have some understanding of why international organizations or even states may want to entice NGOs to participate in their regimes (Jönsson & Tallberg, 2010). Expanding from the logic of this book to a comparative exploration of why NGOs choose some regimes over others would broaden our understanding of NGOs in global governance, including how they can expand the regime complexes governing issues.

Theoretical Implications and Future Research

This book set out to explore a phenomenon previously not systematically researched: NGO forum multiplying. As with any fresh concept, several potential directions emerge from it. This book raises new questions about NGOs' influence and authority, their mechanisms and variations across regimes, and regime complexes' expansion over time.

It is striking that the NGO networks studied here vary greatly in their ability to influence the politics of the climate change regime. This marks the most obvious area for future research. Gender NGOs proved remarkably influential, despite considerable opposition from some countries. Labour was less successful, carving a smaller niche into the institutions. Climate justice received a small mention in the Paris Agreement, which many were reluctant to approve, thus the hedging words "of importance to some." Much of the literature on NGO influence focuses on the organizations most closely associated with the regime; the influence of newcomers is a new question to explore.

From roughly the same starting line – as climate politics rookies – some newcomers were able to exert influence, while others were less successful, which suggests that NGOs' strategies matter when it comes to the likelihood of gaining influence. The networks studied here had different levels of success despite similar structural conditions. My research suggests, echoing Betsill and Corell (2008), that building alliances with states is a vital strategy. Yet in contrast to their finding that "key" states matter, it seems that a critical mass of state allies or states with moral authority or issue-specific power may be the most potent allies, as posited by Price (1998) and Finnemore and Sikkink (1998). Gender and climate justice advocates forged alliances mainly with developing countries, which are objectively less powerful but enjoy many cohesive negotiation coalitions as well as moral authority. These findings are suggestive, and the research design used here – varying the NGO network while keeping the regime constant – could be useful in studying NGO influence.

Looking across issues and regimes, however, several questions emerge regarding how NGOs choose their strategies. One such research question emerges from a surprising finding. A reference to human rights was included in the preamble of the Paris Agreement despite the near total absence of human rights NGOs. Environmental lawyers, often working with environmental NGOs, succeeded in convincing states to accept the human rights frame and admit a few carefully chosen human rights into the Paris Agreement. This was not a given, or a case of states accepting "easy" issues; indeed, there was considerable debate, and some developing states worried that such a principle could be used to tie the provision of climate funding to the upholding of human rights (IISD, 2015). Still, climate governors accepted a frame not articulated by the NGOs most closely associated with it. There seem to be instances where frames can be separated from their traditional articulators and still prove influential.

Indeed, there may be something unique about the human rights NGO network. Carpenter (2007) notes the prevalence of buck-passing strategies by the network. Forum multiplying is the opposite – a refusal to pass on an issue and leave the work to another network. Here, only human rights NGOs engaged in buck passing, while labour, gender, global justice, and even some health activists refused to do so. These latter networks took up climate change despite the many environmental and climate change organizations already involved. Many environmental health NGOs also tried to take up climate change, believing they had a valuable contribution to what the environmentalists were already offering. The comparative nature of this project suggests that buck passing may not be a trend, or even common, but perhaps is rather unique to one network. Further comparative research could focus on this trend, to determine the extent of buck passing and why NGO networks choose to remain isolationist, devoted to one cause.

A second area relates to how NGOs choose among the potential sources of their authority. Many NGOs are in a position to draw on their expertise, their moral claim to represent a marginalized issue or people, or their capacity to realize change on the ground. Authority, it seems, is carefully constructed and strategically deployed. It is a resource, or set of resources, that NGOs protect (Stroup & Wong 2017) and, as seen here, selectively use. Most of the networks sought to extend *expert* authority into the new regime, rather than moral or capacity-based authority.

It is not that these groups could not have made a moral claim; there is certainly a principled claim to be made on behalf of disadvantaged workers and vulnerable populations. It may be that expert authority travels well among regimes or helps demonstrate relevance and connections to the issues in the target regime. Perhaps expert authority helps new NGOs gain allies, particularly among epistemic communities in the target regime, or that it fulfils some states' need for information to facilitate their participation. Expert authority can be a strategically advantageous way to establish a political niche that only the network members can fill, besides increasing their access to delegates. Some NGOs are traditionally associated with the use of some types of authority over others, yet even this appears mutable. For example, Climate Action Network has recently shifted away from a technical, expert-based set of claims toward more justice-oriented frames (Allan & Hadden, 2017). Such questions could help expand our understanding of authority and its construction and use by NGOs in global governance.

A third strategy that varies among the networks studied here involves their relations with international organizations. Labour used UNEP's resources and connections to facilitate its entry, then later the two collaborated less after ideological differences arose. Climate justice activists rarely engaged with international organizations. By contrast, some gender NGOs embraced relationships with international organizations at the outset, while others were wary of the limitations that can arise when collaborating with international organizations. International organizations can provide strategically useful resources that network members can tap in order to increase their political heft. However, international organizations can also impose constraints. Both international organizations and NGOs are traditionally considered weaker actors in interstate negotiations. The relationships among these actors as they form coalitions could provide an interesting avenue for approaching questions of power at the margins, with implications for how these actors influence global governance.

The Future of the New Climate Activists after Paris

In their efforts to claim space in climate governance, these incoming NGO networks have changed climate activism. The civil society voice in the climate change sphere is today more fragmented than ever before. Writing on the mobilization of NGOs in the early 1990s, Clark, Friedman, and Hochstetler (1998, p. 5) expressed hope that the "cross fertilization" of NGOs across conferences on the environment, women, and human rights would contribute to the growth of a global civil society able to increase political representation and safeguard public freedoms at the international level; but they ultimately conceded that "the construction of a global civil society is under way but is far from complete." While such cross-issue fertilization has occurred, the process has not been easy or entirely harmonious. As this book shows, relations among NGOs can be as fraught as those among states.

This diverse group of NGOs now must engage with the rules as outlined in the Paris Agreement. As chapter 3 noted, the Paris Agreement has rearranged the rules into a five-year cyclical system of pledge and review. Countries submit, or update, their nationally determined contributions (NDCs) every five years. Three years after submission, countries engage in a Global Stocktake, which involves expert and political views on how countries are faring, in aggregate, in their efforts to reduce emissions, adapt to climate impacts, and provide support to developing countries. The Paris Agreement has reorganized existing climate institutions, including by codifying the "bottom-up" approach that permits countries to design their own targets and policies as they see fit (Allan, 2019; Falkner, 2016). There are now to be regular and predictable political moments when states announce their intentions and when the world reviews progress with the explicit aim of inspiring more ambitious climate action in the future. Such predetermined events could help new climate activists plan, organize, and influence the post-2020 process.

It seems that if they couple up with a host of institutions created to facilitate the engagement of non-state actors in the UNFCCC process, new climate activists could have considerable influence in the post-2020 system. A unique feature of the negotiations before 2015 was the considerable mobilization of non-state actors, which included creating new institutions to facilitate their long-term engagement. The Global Climate Action Agenda has grown from a one-off meeting featuring high-level speakers, to year-round events and initiatives bringing together actors publicly that announce commitments and reflect upon progress and challenges. The aggregation of non-state actors' announcements and pledges resides in an online platform, the Non-State Actor Zone for Climate Action (NAZCA) portal, launched in 2014 and "revamped" in 2018. The portal logs the actions pledged by cities, regions, corporations, investors, and civil society organizations.

How will the rules of the post-2020 regime shape the new, diverse civil society campaigning on climate change? Global climate activism – those attending the UNFCCC – may contract; national-level and transnational activism may thrive. The future of NGO participation in the UNFCCC may look more like the past, largely dominated by environmental NGOs and businesses, with only a few new climate activists remaining. Just as shifts in the rules and norms created opportunities for some NGO networks and not others, the post-2020 climate change regime will potentially reward some efforts over others.

Even those institutions devoted to engaging non-state actors privilege those with certain forms of authority. Cities, regions, and corporations – all primarily located in the Global North – constitute the majority of actors involved in the Global Climate Action Agenda and those pledging commitments on the NAZCA portal. The portal is designed to catalogue promises related to reducing emissions. Even recent efforts to include adaptation-related actions still involved efforts to link these entries to mitigation, such as actions taken related to water, which, as the website states, "is also critical to successful climate change mitigation, as many efforts to reduce greenhouse gas emissions depend on reliable access to water resources."[6] The focus is on mitigation probably because emission reductions are quantifiable and can more easily be aggregated to show what non-state actors are achieving. The UNFCCC can show that it is catalysing climate action, and businesses and cities can publicize their association with the UN. These institutions do not exist in the Paris Agreement, but only in the decision that adopted that agreement, which placed them on weaker footing. The platforms need to be shown to work effectively – a need that marginalizes those that are unable to contribute directly to the quantitative mitigation effort. NGOs working to include the voices of women, people from the Global South, and others are excluded. Groups involved in the labour movement and that are trying to support climate action by mobilizing worker's support (or at least removing their opposition) also don't fit into the schema of the new UNFCCC institutions.

The Paris Agreement itself will shape the prospects for new climate activists in different ways, primarily by privileging those with strong national bases and expert-based authority, as well as networks that have tied themselves to institutions that remain salient post-2020 (Allan, 2018). The NDCs are entirely the product of national processes. Countries, notably the United States, China, and India closely guarded their capacity to develop their contributions free of the influence of other states. Opportunities to influence climate change policy now rest largely at the national level – which could undermine global activism – but also allow national and transnational activism to grow.

Those groups with institutions closely associated with their cause likely have bright prospects in the global climate regime. While the Paris Agreement reaffirms most institutions, there have been subtle shifts in the relative importance of some institutions, which holds implications for the new climate activists. There are legacies to the framing strategies used to gain recognition in the climate change regime. NGO networks linked themselves to specific rules and in so doing became closely associated with *only* those rules. Some of those institutions are now less important in the post-2020 regime, and this has likely diminished NGO networks' prospects for influencing the regime.

Several of the institutions that the new climate activists have associated themselves with are outside the Paris Agreement. The Local Communities and Indigenous Peoples' Platform, meant to be a forum for knowledge exchange, and the Gender Action Plan, an ongoing negotiation to mainstream gender into the UNFCCC's activities, were both celebrated by activists. But how any outputs of these initiatives will be integrated into NDCs, the Global Stocktake, or other aspects of the Paris Agreement is unclear. The response measures forum, a key foothold for the labour movement, remains contentious. The work area for a just transition remains, yet the forum is as politicized as ever, with the Arab Group continuing to use the forum to highlight the negative effects of climate action and with developed countries trying to reduce the forum's scope and profile. The labour movement is caught in between, associated with a forum with a difficult and contested future. In 2019 only climate justice activists have the same battle on their hands, as market mechanisms remain one of the only unfinished areas of work related to the Paris Agreement. The REDD+ mechanism they fought to stop appears to be languishing in the implementation phase, despite the recognition of forests in the Agreement. The institutional niches that many new climate activists have found are largely outside the core of the post-2020 regime, leaving these NGO networks on the margins unless they find new areas to advance their issues and their vision of climate action.

A new round of issue linkage may be extremely difficult because there are no new negotiations in the foreseeable future. The Paris Agreement is designed to endure. Some technical guidances will be reviewed in the future, as agreed at COP 24 in 2018, but the basic cyclical structure of the Agreement will not be reopened. If new climate activists do not have their issues written into the Agreement or its supporting rulebook, there will be few opportunities to reset the agenda.

Ultimately, the core institutions of the post-2020 regime will favour those NGOs that use their expert-based authority over those making moral claims. As noted earlier, the capacity to implement climate policy will favour the participation of some NGOs. Similarly, the Global Stocktake, NDCs, and the transparency framework will require expert interpreters who are able to make sense of the technical information and scientific inputs for the world. The Global Stocktake aggregates all parties' efforts, at the insistence of countries such as China that do not want to be singled out, particularly if they fail to reach their goals because of a lack of support from developed countries. By design, it will be difficult to know which countries are lagging behind their potential. By contrast, the NDCs come in a variety of forms, mixing types of targets and policies, thus complicating efforts to assess their aggregate impact. The transparency framework for national reporting may help fill this gap between individual action and aggregate assessments, but there too countries may submit differing amounts and types of data based on their capacity.

NGOs with the expertise to interpret and analyse technical climate information on mitigation, adaptation, or finance could have a significant role in the future climate change regime. They can estimate the global temperature rise associated with NDCs, as some think tanks did for the intended NDCs submitted in 2015. They can also assess the ambition of successive NDCs. While each NDC is to be more ambitious than the last, this term is not operationalized or otherwise defined. NGOs can help shape a common understanding of the important, but vague, "no backsliding" principle. Also, experts can interpret and shape states' understandings of the outcomes of the expert phase of the Global Stocktake, before the political phase occurs. There are significant opportunities for those able to engage in the weeds of climate data and make sense of this information for a broader audience.

Yet those making moral claims highlighting the climate-related vulnerabilities of marginalized peoples or of the environment itself will have few such opportunities for influence. The idea of equity was never operationalized in the Global Stocktake, and the preambular paragraphs related to gender, human rights, and other social issues remain solely in the preamble, not reflected elsewhere in the Agreement or its rulebook. This again hinders the likelihood of continued influence of Indigenous peoples, climate justice activists, and others. It is harder to see how their expertise, tied to social issues, can influence the core institutions of the Paris Agreement. It seems that the post-2020 climate change regime may favour established, traditional climate actors, with technical expertise, over the new climate activists.

Lastly, the post-2020 regime favours those with strong national bases. NGOs and movements with strong national roots in key countries will be best positioned to continue to advance their goals linked to climate change. The post-2020 regime has relocated decision-making to the national level; there will be little for the UNFCCC to do most years. NGOs with an existing national presence will be able to contribute to

NDC development, whereas foreign NGOs will face challenges establishing themselves in new countries. Transnational ties will be more important after 2020.

Only some networks have a national presence in key states and transnational coordination mechanisms. The Climate Action Network is an umbrella of 1,100 organizations in more than 120 countries, with then regional nodes. The international Secretariat tries to bring together the hubs to serve as the face of the global movement. Similarly, the global labour movement has national affiliates and five regional organizations, with the ITUC fulfilling a transnational coordination role. Working at the national level became a growing focus for the labour movement after Copenhagen. It proved a difficult line to walk – bringing all national unions on board, and lobbying for national climate action, without overstepping the national unions' efforts to represent their workers. The climate justice movement is more informally organized but still has considerable grassroots support at local and national levels. The climate justice movement is strong in the Global South and could influence local or regional climate politics among those countries. These three movements – the Climate Action Network, labour, and climate justice – will be best placed to influence the post-2020 regime.

Recently, other transnational movements have emerged without using the UNFCCC as a hub. Extinction Rebellion and the Strike for the Climate movement, led by Greta Thunberg, started locally and rapidly expanded to other countries. Extinction Rebellion uses disruptive tactics, from disrupting traffic with boats to blocking bank entrances by gluing people to them. Perhaps Extinction Rebellion has employed these tactics more effectively at the local, national, and transnational levels than CJN! and others in the climate justice movement did at the UNFCCC. The Youth Climate Strikes had small beginnings – one girl going on strike for the climate – and has since become a monthly event in cities and towns around the world.

These types of transnational activism may be the future for climate activism. The pressure must be at the national level, to make leaders do more. The Paris Agreement binds the hands of global negotiations and interventions. But organizing, mobilizing, and disrupting across borders may still hold promise.

Several of these transnational activist networks perhaps owe a debt of gratitude to the new climate activists. Many frame climate change in terms of justice, such as intergenerational justice. They draw on the effects of climate change on society at large and call for urgent transformation of economic systems, led by political leaders. The tactics, particularly of Extinction Rebellion, align with those brought into the climate change regime by the global justice movement. The broader claims related to disproportionate effects, equity, and rights – in other words, why climate is a social issue, too – are now commonplace calls to action.

Perhaps the greatest victory of the new climate activists, and now the transnational movements, is that they have mobilized a cross-section of society to engage in the climate cause. Organizations and individuals that had never seen themselves as part of the climate movement now see their struggles intertwined with the fate of the earth. Supporters for climate action come from all sectors of society and reside around the globe. Pipeline protests have invoked climate concerns. Indigenous farmers are suing multinational energy companies, inspired by strategies first used by tobacco activists. The LGBT community has linked the violence and denial directed toward LGBT people to the existential threat climate change poses for humanity. Children are striking for climate change, drawing directly from the strategic playbook and discourse of climate justice activists. The climate movement is more than environmental activists. The new climate activism has generated a wave of supporters and helped trigger even wider social engagement.

The climate crisis requires a systemic transformation in our technological landscape and economic system. It is now understood to require a societal transformation as well, one that will change how people travel, consume, and work. Widespread support has brought new segments of society into the discussion and drawn them toward local and global solutions. These newcomers to climate politics have brought new ways to challenge the power of states and multinational corporations that so far have failed to address climate change. Once an abstract, narrowly defined, environmental issue, climate change finally has a human face.

Appendix: Multimethod Approach to Studying NGO Forum Multiplying

The politics of non-state actors can sometimes be notoriously difficult to study from a methodological standpoint. Those studying the influence of NGOs, for example, have to contend with issues of multiple causation, selection bias, and direction of bias (Allan & Hadden, 2017; Betsill & Corell, 2008; Arts, 1998). Transnational advocacy networks, of which NGO networks are a part, are geographically dispersed, hold varying assumptions and priorities, and use different terms and language to describe similar phenomena. As Carpenter (2014, 155) observes, "transnational ideas are both everywhere (that someone subscribes to or invokes them) and nowhere in particular. For that reason, such communities are challenging to identify in a way that allows for comparison, and an accurate picture of their discourse and impact is difficult to capture."

Here, I specify the multi-method approach I used to study forum multiplying among NGO networks. Each method served a unique purpose in the research. Social network analysis was useful for uncovering social structures and relationships among the organizations. It highlighted broad trends in their coalition-building and mobilization over time. Process tracing allowed a fine-grained description and analysis of underlying mechanisms, and this complemented the social network analysis. Interviews and participant observation tested the network analysis by uncovering the quality and the nature of the ties. For example, the IFMSA in the health network was not as central is it initially seemed because the connections were largely for internships and other reasons unrelated to activism. Extensive participant observation was valuable as a means to understand the social environment of negotiations and which organizations and issues were included/excluded from social relationships and institutions.

Capturing the NGO Networks

There are two quantitative parts of this project: an original database of NGOs' participation in UNFCCC negotiations, and the social network analysis. The database served as the foundation for establishing the overall trend of the fragmentation of NGOs in the UNFCCC, the increase in social NGOs' participation, and variation among social NGOs. It was integral to specifying the puzzle driving the central questions of this book.

To create the dataset of NGO participation, I logged the name of every NGO reported on the official participation lists of the UNFCCC at the annual COP meetings and the size of the delegation. I used the organizations' mission statements to identify categories. Much like Muñoz Cabre (2011), I did not impose categories, instead allowing the categories to be determined by the organizations. The majority of NGOs fit into discrete categories, such as labour or gender. The "other" category was something of a catch-all and remained relatively small. The database also provided the "starting points" for the social network analysis, the second quantitative part of the methodology.

The purpose of the social network analysis was to find out which organizations were most important within these new networks and to locate these NGOs within their larger network centred on their traditional issue in their home regime. Here I grappled with the "boundary specification problem," that is, how to determine the extent of the network, as well as which actors count as within the network and which do not (Laumann, Marsden, & Prensky, 1989; Marin & Wellman, 2010; Scott 2000). Too narrow a specification risks missing key actors, too wide risks diluting the information and the density of the network. To address this issue, I adopted a realist approach:[1] the researcher adopts the vantage point of the actors, which "by definition assumes the proposition that a social entity exists as a collectively shared subjective awareness of all, or at least most, of the actors who are members" (Laumann, Marsden, & Prensky, 1989, p. 21).

I started with the social NGOs that participated in the UNFCCC. Specifically, I used the list of NGOs participating in the UNFCCC that work on labour, gender, climate justice, health, and human rights. These starting points are summarized in Table A.1 below. I expanded from that initial list to identify connections among NGOs, following the relational approach[2] to addressing network boundaries (Marin & Wellman, 2010). I used Ucinet to analyse the data (Borgatti, Everett, & Freeman, 2002).

From this list, I used two types of relationships to connect actors. The approach was to start from those social NGOs working on climate

Table A.1

Organization	Year(s) participated
Labour	
2005–2009	
Confederación Sindical de Comisiones Obreras	2006
Construction, Forestry, Mining, and Energy Union	2008
International Confederation of Free Trade Unions	2005, 2006
International Trade Union Confederation	2007, 2008
International Union of Architects	2006
Japanese Trade Union Confederation	2006
Norwegian Confederation of Trade Unions	2006
Union for Jobs and the Environment	2005, 2006
United Mine Workers of America	2007, 2008
2009–2015	
American Federation of Labor and Congress of Industrial Organizations	2013–15
BlueGreen Alliance	2011–15
Construction, Forestry, Mining, and Energy Union	2009–15
IndustriALL Global Union	2015
International Trade Union Confederation	2009–15
International Union of Architects	2011, 2015
Norwegian Confederation of Trade Unions	2010–15
Southern African Confederation of Agricultural Unions	2015
Union for Jobs and the Environment	2009–15
United Mine Workers of America	2009–15
Work and Environment Association	2015
Gender	
2005–2009	
Asia Pacific Forum on Women, Law, and Development	2006
Club UNESCO de Centre d'Action Femme et Enfant	2006
Gender CC[3]	2007–8
International Council of Women	2007
LIFE – Women Develop Eco-Techniques	2005–9
Women in Europe for a Common Future	2005–8
Women's Environment and Development Organization	2008
Women's International League for Peace and Freedom	2008
2010–2015	
Abibimman Foundation	2010–15
All India Women's Caucus	2013–15
Asia Pacific Forum on Women, Law, and Development	2013–15
Gender CC	2010–15
Global Peace Initiative of Women	2009, 2015
Grassroots Organizations Operating Together in Sisterhood	2009, 2011
Huairou Commission	2009–12
International Planned Parenthood Federation	2009, 2015
League of Women Voters in the US	2009
LIFE – Women Develop Eco-Techniques	2010–15
National Federation of Women's Institutes	2009

(Continued)

Table A.1 (*Continued*)

Organization	Year(s) participated
Population Action International	2009, 2011, 2014, 2015
Réseau international d'information de communication et d'action pour le developpement des femmes et des enfants défavorisés	2009, 2013
Sustainable Population Australia	2009, 2012, 2013, 2015
UNANIMA International	2009–11, 2015
Women Environmental Programme	2012–15
Women in Europe for a Common Future	2010–15
Women Organizing for Change in Agriculture & Natural Resource Management	2012–15
Women's Earth Climate Caucus	2015
Women's Environment and Development Organization	2010–25

Justice

2006–2008

Action pour la taxation des transactions pour l'aide aux citoyens (ATTAC)	2007–8
Citizens' Movement for Environmental Justice	2005–8
Focus on the Global South Ltd.	2007–8
Gesellschaft für Bedrochte Völker	2008
Global Humanitarian Forum	2008
Global Justice Ecology Project Inc.	2006–8
International Forum on Globalization Inc.	2008
Redefining Progress	2007–8
The Corner House	2005–2006, 2008
World Development Movement	2008
The Transnational Institute	2005–8

2009–2015

Action pour la taxation des transactions pour l'aide aux citoyens (ATTAC)	2009–21, 2014–15
Corporate Europe Observatory Foundation	2009, 2013–14
Environmental Justice Foundation	2009
Focus on the Global South Ltd.	2009–11, 2014–15
Gesellschaft für Bedrochte Völker	2009–11
Global Exchange	2009–10
Global Humanitarian Forum	2009
Global Justice Ecology Project Inc.	2009–11, 2015
International Forum on Globalization Inc.	2009–15
National Association for the Advancement of Colored People	2013–15
Redefining Progress	2009–10
Society for Threatened Peoples International	2015
The Corner House	2009–15
The Transnational Institute	2012, 2014, 2015
World Development Movement / Global Justice Now	2009, 2011, 2015

Health

2009–2015

Association congolaise d'éducation et la prevention contre les maladies et drogues	2011–12

Table A.1 (*Continued*)

Organization	Year(s) participated
Climate and Health Ltd.	2011–15
Global Health Ltd.	2014–15
Hacey's Health Initiative	2014–15
Health and Environment Alliance	2009–15
Health Care without Harm	2011–15
International Federation of Medical Students' Associations	2010–25
International Society of Doctors for the Environment	2013–15
Nurses Across the Borders	2009–15
World Information Transfer, Inc	2010–11
World Medical Association	2011, 2013, 2015

change, then to expand from that initial list to identify the wider net-work in which their advocacy took place. The first connection was relationships among organizations that were in the same coalition or partnership. For example, all of those in CJN! were connected to one an-other. Given the coordination and communication systems established in such advocacy partnerships, it is a reasonable assumption that actors sharing membership would exchange information and be aware of one another's work on related issues. These partnerships exist to encourage coordination, making it a useful and accurate signal of relationships among organizations. Table A.2 below lists the coalitions included.

Second, I used self-reported relationships captured in the *Yearbook of International Organizations* published in 2007 and in 2013 for the 2005–8 and the 2009–15 time periods, respectively. The *Yearbooks* allowed organizations to specify which other organizations they routinely worked with. This was a highly accurate measure because it involved self-reporting (i.e., we can trust that the organizations were accurately reporting the organizations they partnered or interacted with). This was useful for identifying connections outside of climate change advocacy work. For example, ITUC reports relationships with several labour organizations that have not participated in climate change work. Similarly, the relationships of several organizations in the climate justice movement to the debt forgiveness movement were visible through these self-reported connections. This approach situated the network's climate change connections within the wider advocacy network. It also helped identify NGOs that were central, but not working on climate change, particularly for the health and human rights cases (the null cases).

Others have used different indicators of links among NGOs, notably hyperlinks (Carpenter, 2011, 2014; Lake & Wong, 2009), or event participation (Orsini, 2013). For practical or methodological reasons, neither of these approaches proved fruitful for this research. One of Carpenter's key data sources for identifying network ties and actor centrality is a

Table A.2 Data sources for coalitions for each network

Network	2005–2008	2009–2015
Labour	N/A	N/A
Gender CC	Membership list from 2008	Membership list from 2014
Global Gender and Climate Alliance	Membership list from 2008	Membership list from 2014
Climate Justice Now!	Signatories to the founding statement of the network (CJN! 2007)	Membership list from 2014, excluding national and local level organizations. I included only international, regional, and transnational organizations due to the size of the coalition
Durban Group for Climate Justice	Membership list from website in 2007	Unchanged
Global Campaign to Demand Climate Justice	N/A	Membership list from 2014
Global Climate and Health Alliance	N/A	Membership list from 2014

hyperlink analysis, which appropriately assumes that "linking practices between organizational websites function as academic citations, providing indicators of who is considered a member or a player within a specific community of shared knowledge and practice" (Carpenter, 2014, 160). When I attempted to replicate Carpenter's methods using my starting points, I found that very few of the organizations had pages listing links to other organizations, even in 2006 or 2007 (I used versions of webpages from the internet archive, the Wayback Machine). This is perhaps not surprising, given that the rise of Google in the mid-2000s signalled the end of "surfing" the Web and that Web designers stopped including pages for links to other organizations to direct interested information consumers.

The use of common event attendance required me to make assumptions that I was less confident asserting. UNFCCC meetings can be very large; during the period focused on in this book, 2007 to 2015, COP attendance often exceeded 10,000. I was reluctant to assume that mutual attendance at the same conference meant that two organizations interacted. It is more likely that two organizations attending a COP will not interact, and many people report interacting only with their pre-existing contacts.

With the network data, each empirical chapter reports the centrality of key NGOs and the size of the network for the two time periods. The centrality measure for the NGOs indicates how many organizations are connected to a given NGO, or, in network analysis terms, the degree to which they are. The size of the overall network is the total number of organizations appearing in the network. This does not double-count organizations that participate in multiple years. It only counts those organizations that participated at least once (the starting points) or that are connected to one of those organizations. The substantial mobilizations in 2009 and 2015 drew on several of the same organizations. Because organizations are only counted once, these two large mobilizations did not independently increase the numbers. Several of the organizations attending in 2015 had already participated, so they did not increase the size of the network.

Brokers cannot be measured quantitatively because of data limitations. Without mapping the climate change network and connecting that information to the social NGO network, it would be impossible to calculate a "betweenness" centrality score to identify a broker. To identify brokers, I cross-referenced the nodes in a social NGO network with the database of NGO participation to identify actors that attended UNFCCC meetings and were not social NGOs. I then cross-referenced this short list with actors mentioned in the interviews as important to facilitating the entry of the social NGOs into the UNFCCC.

The social network analysis identified key actors in the network and helped reveal the overall structure of the hybrid social climate network, including how that structure influences the capabilities of those key actors. Taking two snapshots illustrated changes over time, as the network grew through acquiring allies and mobilizing traditional network members. It further revealed that many of the central actors in the initial years of forum multiplying became further entrenched in the network during the second period. How these trends developed was beyond the remit of social network analysis and required in depth case studies.

Exploring Forum Multiplying Processes: Process Tracing

The interviews, document analysis, and participant observation seek to explore the interactions between incoming NGOs and existing climate governors, the perceptions of social NGOs regarding entry points in the climate change regime, and those of others within their network. Key terms, such as *recognition* and *motivations*, are intersubjective, requiring qualitative methods. Beyond the motivations of NGOs, these three methods sought to uncover causal mechanisms that could explain why a given network structure or type of frame mattered.

The semi-structured interviews followed a similar pattern. First, I asked for a brief account of the individual's involvement (or lack thereof) in the UNFCCC. From there, I asked questions within four clusters, selecting questions that were the most appropriate given the individual's experience. The first cluster asked questions about the NGOs' work before starting climate change. Questions such as "What was your organization's focus before climate change came onto your radar" or "What work occupied your time from 2•••–2••• [years before the NGO participated in the UNFCCC]" were asked to people who were present in the initial years of their organization's involvement. The second cluster asked about motivations and included broad questions such as "Tell me about the decision to undertake climate work, what was that conversation like?" or "What were the arguments of those for and against?" as well as narrow questions like "Was there funding available at the start?"

The third and fourth clusters related specifically to their experiences in the climate change regime. The third cluster asked about their experiences in the UNFCCC, including key issues ("What negotiations were you keen to follow and why?") and experiences with the institutions, such as "What was your relationship with the Secretariat?" and "What stands out for you in those early years?" The final group of questions related to interactions with others in their own network – "Which other [social issue] NGOs did you work with most closely?" – and with climate change governors – "Who did you speak with and how were you received?" or "Did anyone particularly 'get' what you were trying to say and back you up? Did anyone refuse?"

Interviews were conducted in a wide range of locations, mostly at UNFCCC meetings, and varied in length from fifteen minutes to two hours. After each interview, I followed up with the respondents to thank them for their time, and to ask if anything else occurred to them after our interview and if there were any key documents I should read. Several people provided draft or internal memos that were otherwise unpublished. These documents and interviews were invaluable for providing specific information for my cases, informing general conclusions, and rebutting alternative explanations.

When seeking interview respondents, I sought a representative reflection of the network's membership, both those in the central organizations and those on the periphery. I initially approached the focal points for those networks with UNFCCC constituencies, and for health and human rights I approached those few individuals who had attended a recent meeting. In total, I requested interviews from 107 people, of which 31 people did not respond and 3 refused. The representativeness of this sample is outlined in Table A.3 below. More than half the organizations in the networks were interviewed.

Table A.3 Representativeness of the interview sample

Organizations from the networks interviewed	44
Organizations from networks in UNFCCC 2005–15	77
Percentage of organizations from attending networks in the interview sample	57.1

The 57.1 per cent representation of the sample glosses over two important trends. First, I interviewed some actors who had not participated in the UNFCCC but were included in the network because of their ties to another actor who *had* participated. Second, I interviewed multiple people from the same organization in the case of some key organizations, as explained below. These interviews captured views from people with different roles in the organization – for example, a board member and a policy officer. I also interviewed members of the UNFCCC Secretariat, past and present, as well as state delegates, to triangulate the claims made by NGO representatives.

The final component of the case study research was participant observation in most UNFCCC meetings leading to the Paris Agreement, from June 2012 to December 2015. My role as a writer for the *Earth Negotiations Bulletin* does provide privileged access to climate negotiations and a fair degree of visibility among civil society and delegates who use the *Bulletin* as a transparency tool in the negotiations. This visibility provided me with interviews that otherwise would very likely not been possible because I had strong rapport with several NGO and state delegates.

This unique access provided several opportunities. First, I could observe which actors were interacting. I could identify NGO representatives trying to collaborate or lobby other NGO or state representatives. My access to negotiations meant that I could identify which NGOs were in a given negotiation room (or were absent) and which issues NGOs mentioned in their formal statements. It helped identify the key institutions that NGOs were trying to influence.

Several years of experience embedded in the negotiations also socialized me into the norms and other social practices of the UNFCCC. These could include anything from norms about how observers approach delegates, how they demonstrate, and when and how they make statements. Some demonstrations and claims were simply "tone deaf," given the social and institutional context of the climate change negotiations; for example, anyone embedded in the UNFCCC would view the suggestion of population offsets as a non-starter (or, worse, dangerous). More recently, many NGOs have tried to mainstream gender or other human rights into the Paris Agreement rule book, mostly completed in 2018. But these efforts fell on deaf ears, as delegates viewed the negotiations as being in a "technical phase."

Care was also taken to ensure that my role as an expert with the *Earth Negotiations Bulletin* would not influence the results of the interviews. It was clear at the beginning of each interview that I was acting in a personal academic capacity, as per the consent form, and not as an *Earth Negotiations Bulletin* writer. Information provided in interviews would not appear in a *Bulletin*, and information exchanged in a closed negotiation session would not appear in any publications related to this research.

Interview Respondents

The following individuals were interviewed for this research.

Gotelind Alber, co-founder and board member of Gender CC. Former focal point for Women and Gender Constituency.

Joe Amon, Director of the Health and Human Rights Division, Human Rights Watch.

Teresa Anderson, Policy Officer, Climate & Resilience International, ActionAid. Formerly with Gaia Foundation, a CJN member.

Anonymous Climate Justice Now! organizer. The respondent was involved in organizing several of the demonstrations and actions of the Climate Justice Now! network that occur during climate meetings.

Anonymous delegate from Environmental NGO. This delegate represents an environmental NGO that is a member of the Climate Action Network.

Anonymous developed country delegate.

Anonymous developing country delegate.

Anonymous developing country delegate.

Anonymous environmental NGO delegate.

Anonymous former UNFCCC Secretariat member.

Anonymous (Health network).

Anonymous (Justice network).

Anonymous (Justice network). This delegate worked with several members of Climate Justice Now! and was present at the Bali conference in 2007 when CJN! was formed.

Anonymous (Labour network).

Anonymous (Labour network). This delegate attended several UNFCCC meetings with a labour union from 2005–2010 as well as multiple ITUC Congresses.

Anonymous UN staff member.

Anonymous UN staff member.

Anonymous UN staff member.

Anonymous UN staff member.

Lois Barber, co-creator and Executive Director, EarthAction.

Cara Beasley, Coordinator, Global Gender and Climate Alliance.

Sabine Bock, Energy and Climate Change Coordinator, Women
in Europe for a Common Future.

Isobel Braithwaite, Healthy Planet UK.

Nicola Bullard, Focus on the Global South.

Bridget Burns, Director, Advocacy and Communications at Women's
Environment & Development Organization. Focal point for the
Women and Gender Constituency.

Peter Colley, labour advocate. Requested that his name not be affiliated with an organization.

Irene Dankelman, board member, Women's Environment and Development Organization and Lecturer, Radboud University Nijmegen
(the Netherlands).

Clarisse Delorme, Advocacy Adviser, World Medical Association.

Benjamin Denis, adviser, European Trade Union Confederation.

Kelly Dent, Economic Justice Coordinator, Head of Climate Change
Delegation, Oxfam International.

Roger-Mark DeSouza, Director of Population, Environmental Se-
curity, and Resilience, Wilson Center. Former Vice-President for
Research and Director of the Climate Program, Population Action
International.

Michael Dorsey, Interim Director, Program on Energy & Environment,
Joint Center for Political and Economic Studies.

Fergal Duff, International Society of Doctors for the Environment.

Cathey Falvo, President at International Society of Doctors for the
Environment.

Tamra Gilbertson, co-founder, Carbon Trade Watch. Former Coordinator of the Environmental Justice Project of the Transnational
Institute.

Patricia Glazebrook, Board of Directors, Gender CC and Professor of
Philosophy, Washington State University.

Dorothy Guerrero, Research Associate, Focus on the Global South.

Ashley Haugo. She asked that her name not be affiliated with an
organization.

Wael Hmaidan, Director, Climate Action Network.

Charlotte Holm-Hansen, International Federation of Medical Students.

Stephen Humphreys, Associate Professor of International Law,
London School of Economics. Former Research Director at the
International Council on Human Rights Policy.

Saleemul Huq, International Institute for Environment and
Development.
Sebastien Jodoin. He requested that his name not be affiliated with an
organization.
Muhammad Zakir Hossain Khan, Research Coordinator, Transparency
International, Bangladesh.
Brian Kohler, Director for Health, Safety and Sustainability at Industri-
ALL Global Union.
Chris Lang, REDD Monitor.
Larry Lohmann, The Corner House.
Simone Lovera, Executive Director, Global Forest Coalition.
Sam Lund-Harket, Global Justice Now (formerly the World Develop-
ment Movement).
Marianne Marstrand, Executive Director, Global Peace Initiative of
Women.
Claire Martin, Research and Capacity Building Coordinator, Transpar-
ency International.
Imogen Martineau, independent consultant.
Wally Menne, Project Coordinator, TimberWatch.
Kathleen Mogelgaard. Requested that her name not be affiliated with
an organization.
Laura Martin Murillo, Executive Director, SustainLabour.
Peggy Nash, MP. Formerly with Canadian Auto Workers Union.
Cate Owren. Requested that her name not be affiliated with an
organization.
Claudel P-Desrosiers, Think Global Coordinator, International Federa-
tion of Medical Students.
Philip Pearson, Senior Policy Officer within the Economic and Social
Affairs Department of the Trades Union Congress. Former Chair of
the ITUC working group on climate change.
Anne Petermann, Executive Director, Global Justice Ecology Project.
Aida Ponce, Head of the Health & Safety, Working Conditions Unit,
European Trade Union Institute.
Eva Quistorp, former member of the European Parliament. One of the
first gender advocates in the UNFCCC.
Camille Risler, Program Associate, Asia Pacific Forum for Women,
Law, and Environment
Ulrike Röhr, Director General, LIFE e.v., Gender CC member.
Anabella Rosemberg, Policy Officer Environment & OHS at Interna-
tional Trade Union Confederation. Focal point for the Trade Union
NGOs Constituency within the UNFCCC.
Lucien Royer, National Director, Canadian Labour Congress.

Pascoe Sabido, researcher and campaigner, Corporate Europe Observatory.

Tara Shine, Head of Research and Development at the Mary Robinson Foundation – Climate Justice.

Christian Teriete, Communications Director, Global Call for Climate Action.

Nick Watts, Executive Director, Lancet Countdown to 2030: Public Health and Climate Change, and Coordinator, Global Climate and Health Alliance.

Lynn Wilson, Executive Director, SeaTrust Institute.

Notes

1. Introduction

1 The original database catalogues every NGO that participated in every Conference of the Parties (COP) of the UNFCCC between COP 1 in 1995 and COP 21 in 2015. To determine the type of NGO, I reviewed the vision and mission statements for the organization. Environmental NGOs here are those devoted to environmental, sustainable development, and forest/agriculture issues. Social NGOs are those working on Indigenous rights, youth, justice, human rights, development, gender, labour, health, and religion. Few organizations cross the broad categories of environment, economic, social, climate, or other. Think tanks and universities are included in the database and excluded from figure 1.1.

2 Based on the database developed for this research of all NGOs participating in every COP of the UNFCCC, Médecins Sans Frontières did not participate between 1995 and 2015.

3 This follows George and Bennet's (2005) definition of a case as "an instance of a class of events." An "event" refers to an instance or phenomenon of scientific interest (George and Bennet, 2005, 17–18). Or, as Gerring (2014) notes, case studies are intensive studies of a unit with the aim of understanding similar units. A case is a unit broadly understood. In other words, a case need not be a country or a regime; it can be an NGO network engaging in forum multiplying.

4 The opposite strategy would be to examine the same network across different regimes. This implicitly is the strategy adopted by Betsill and Corell (2008) in their study of NGO influence. They study environmental NGOs in the climate change, desertification, forest, whaling, and biosafety regimes. Their work is strong regarding the conditions under which NGOs can achieve influence and when regimes are amenable, but has less certain claims regarding the nature of the network that is able to influence a regime.

5 As one indication, Google Trends reports that there were far more news headlines about climate change during 2007–9 than ever before. The relative interest in "climate change" at the time of the various conferences (generally late November or early December) was as follows: 2004, 26; 2005, 28; 2006, 32; 2007, 52; 2008, 40; 2009, 86; 2010, 35; 2012, 27; 2013, 21; 2014, 26; and 2015, 32. The numbers represent the level of search interest relative to the highest point on the chart (labelled as 100) for a given time. A value of 100 is the peak popularity, and 50 means that the term is half as popular. For this search, the peak popularity of the term was in September 2014, when media coverage spiked around the UN Climate Summit and People's Climate March, the largest climate march in history, with more than 2,646 solidarity events in 162 countries (see http://2014.peoplesclimate.org).

6 The Earth Negotiations Bulletin team members have Secretariat badges and an understanding with the Secretariat that we may attend and report from plenary sessions, contact groups, and informal consultations. With the permission of parties, we may attend and often can report without attribution from closed-door negotiations, which are otherwise closed to NGOs and other observers.

2. Forum Multiplying to New Regimes

1 A quantitative measure of forum multiplying would miss the qualitative aspects of the concept, particularly recognition, and might risk overreductionism. Furthermore, a quantitative measure is not possible due to data limitations. An absolute measure of how many NGOs or delegates participate in a given forum would ignore that some networks are larger or more geographically dispersed, which would boost the numbers regarding participation at various conferences around the world. A relative measure, such as the proportion of organizations in the original network that participate in the forum in the target regime, would be more appropriate. There is no reliable and comparable way to measure the size of a network. Different social network analysts may set different boundaries of the network and use different indicators of ties among actors, with the result that some actors would be included by one analyst but not by others (see the Appendix for a discussion of how those issues are addressed here). When looking for evidence of ties, some networks are more easily delimited. For example, labour unions, women's rights, health, and human rights are recognized categories of organizations in the Yearbook of International Organizations. The global justice, or alterglobalization, movement is not. Without a reliable measure of the size of the original network, a proportion is

impossible to ascertain, particularly one that is comparable and meaningful across cases.

2 In social network terms, brokers have a high "betweenness centrality," a measure used to indicate the number of connections an actor has in otherwise discrete areas of the network, or between different networks. For reasons explained in the Appendix, this is not a useful indication of a broker in my network. Rather, qualitative information can be used for NGOs to identify which climate actors also worked in their regime, and provided resources, if any.

3. Understanding and Governing Climate Change

1 This is derived from the NGO participation database.

2 This information is derived from the NGO participation database developed for this research. I calculated the number of environmental and climate NGOs as "environmental NGOs" and traditional and renewable business NGOs as "business NGOs" for this measure.

3 "Entering into force" relates to the moment when the provisions of the legal instrument become legally binding for those countries that have ratified the treaty. Signing the Convention is a largely symbolic act that indicates that a country intends to ratify. Ratification means that a country uses domestic processes or measures to indicate that it intends to be bound by the provisions of the international treaty. For the Convention to enter into force, fifty countries had to ratify the Convention. The 21st of March 1994 was the ninetieth day after the fiftieth country notified the UN that it had ratified the Convention.

4 To enter into force, the Protocol had a double threshold mechanism. It requires at least fifty countries, representing at least 55 per cent of global emissions, to ratify. At the time, the United States represented nearly 36 per cent of global emissions.

5 Russia at the time represented approximately 18 per cent of global emissions. Its ratification was vital for the Protocol to enter into force.

6 For one example of environmental NGOs using this frame to explain the otherwise technical issues, see New Scientist, 8 November 2003: https://www.newscientist.com/article/mg18024200-300-kyoto-lite-fails.

7 The Toronto Declaration cited several problems associated with climate change, including that it threatened human health, global food security, freshwater resources, political stability, sustainable development, and ecosystem diversity and productivity.

8 Developing country delegate, interview with author, 2013.

9 Rule 7 of the UNFCCC draft rules of procedure specifies that "observers may, upon invitation of the President, participate without the right to

vote in the proceedings of any session, unless at least one third of the Parties present at the session object." COP decision 18/CP.4 clarifies that this rule also applies to open-ended contact groups.

10 The Major Groups established by Agenda 21 are: business and industry, children and youth, farmers, indigenous peoples and their communities, local authorities, non-governmental organizations, the scientific and technological community, women, and workers and trade unions.

11 This information is derived from the NGO participation database constructed for this research. As above, environmental NGOs are environmental and climate NGOs. Business and industry NGOs encompass both traditional and renewable businesses. The remaining NGOs reported include social NGOs as well as other NGOs but not universities and think tanks.

12 Derived from data publicly available at http://cdm.unfccc.int/Statistics /Public/CDMinsights/index.html.

13 The full name of REDD+ is Reducing Emissions from Deforestation and Forest Degradation in Developing Countries; its activities encompass conservation, sustainable forest management, and enhancement of carbon stocks. In 2005, it was introduced as Reducing Emissions from Deforestation (RED). The other elements were included in 2007 as a compromise among the Coalition for Rainforest Nations, Brazil, India, and Congo Basin countries.

14 Anonymous, interview, 20 May 2014.

15 The last two pages of the Accord contain blank tables, one for developed countries to register their quantified economy-wide emissions targets for 2020, and the other for developing countries to register their nationally appropriate mitigation actions.

16 Developing country delegate, interview, 19 March 2014.

17 Anonymous former Secretariat member, interview, 11 June 2015.

18 Saleemul Huq, IIED, interview with author, 2015.

19 Saleemul Huq, IIED, interview with author, 2015.

20 Many respondents – two from the labour unions, one from youth, and two from women and gender – expressed dissatisfaction with the reporting requirement under the provisional system.

21 Anonymous UN employee, interview with author, 2014.

22 Anonymous UN employee, interview with author, 2014.

23 This information is derived from the NGO participation database constructed for this research. As above, environmental NGOs are environmental and climate NGOs, and business and industry NGOs are both traditional and renewable businesses. This measure includes only social NGOs, excluding those categorized as other, universities, or think tanks.

24 Countries, such as China, that have decided to have ten-year contribution periods will be invited to update their contributions every five years.

25 The Paris Agreement addresses mitigation, adaptation, and loss and damage in separate articles, creating conceptual separation between these issues. This separation was achieved through compromise: developing countries agreed to remove any reference to liability or compensation from the Agreement and to state in the decision that adopted the Agreement (1/CP.25) that liability and compensation would not be considered.

26 Examples of loss and damage in developed countries could include the pine beetle epidemic in British Columbia and Hurricane Katrina or Superstorm Sandy in the United States.

27 Discussion with Anabella Rosemberg, ITUC.

28 Some activists have been debadged temporarily. Others, such as the 3rd Viscount Monckton, who is a long-attending, infamous climate change denier, lost his badge permanently for impersonating a state and making an intervention during plenary.

29 In 2011, Kumi Naidoo, Executive Director of Greenpeace, lost his badge for participating in a sit-in (there were questions as to whether he actually organized it or was a late participant). It was announced that he would be barred from the UNFCCC permanently, but this was later reversed. In 2012, Viscount Monckton impersonated a party and permanently lost his right to attend UNFCCC meetings.

30 Anabella Rosemberg, ITUC, interview, 3 March 2014; Ulrike Röhr, LiFE e.V., interview with author, 2014.

4. The Reformers: Labour Unions and Gender NGOs

1 Wael Hmadian, Executive Director, Climate Action Network, interview with author, March 2015.

2 Lucien Royer, interview with author, 2015. Mr Royer led the ICFTU's work on health and safety and was a key actor advocating for the inclusion of climate change in its work.

3 COP1 is shorthand for the first meeting of the Conference of the Parties to the UNFCCC. Such COPs are the annual conferences of the highest decision-making body of the UNFCCC.

4 A labour union delegate present at the Bali Conference, who asked that these comments be anonymous, interview with the author, 2014.

5 Lucien Royer, Canadian Labour Congress, interview with the author, 2015. Mr Royer was with the ICFTU at the time. The ICFTU later merged with another international federation to become the ITUC.

6 Lucien Royer, Canadian Labour Congress, interview with the author, 2015; Anabella Rosemberg, ITUC, interview with the author, 2014.

7 Interview with the author, 2014.

8 Anonymous labour advocate, interview with author, 2014; Cate Owren, interview with the author, 2014.

9 Ashley Haugo, interview with author, 2014.

10 Cate Owren, interview with author, 2014.

11 Gender NGO representative who asked that these comments be anonymous, interview with the author, 2014.

12 This labour advocate asked that these comments be anonymous; interview with author, 2014.

13 Anabella Rosemberg, ITUC, interview with author, 2014. Ms Rosemberg was at the time a key member of the ITUC and SustainLabour working on the inclusion of climate change in the agenda of the international labour movement. She is currently the Policy Officer Occupational Health & Environment at ITUC and the UNFCCC focal point for the Trade Union NGO constituency.

14 According to the UNFCCC SEORS database of side events: https://seors .unfccc.int/seors/reports/archive.html.

15 "TODs" are training-of-delegate sessions – the informal, internal name for these events among gender advocates. They are formally known as "delegate orientation sessions."

16 See draft text FCCC/AWGLCA/2009/INF.1 (22 June 2009).

17 Unpublished memo cited in Sweeney (2014).

18 PCCA became the Population and Sustainable Development Alliance in 2012. For information on the alliance's background, see http://psda.org .uk/background.

19 Roger-Mark DeSouza, interview with author, 2014.

20 Kathleen Mogelgaard, interview with author, 2014.

21 Participation database developed for this book; Ulrike Röhr, LiFE e.V, interview with author, 2014.

22 Wael Hmadian, Executive Director CAN International, interview with author, 2014.

23 Anabella Rosemberg, ITUC, interview with author, 2014; anonymous delegate from an environmental NGO, interview with author, 2015.

24 Anabella Rosemberg, interview with author, 2014; Ulrike Röhr, LIFE e.V., interview with author, 2014; Bridget Burns, interview with author, 2014.

25 Ulrike Röhr, LIFE e.V., interview with author, 2014.

26 The response measures forum was created as a compromise to appease some countries in the Arab Group, which pushed for a discussion of the negative impacts of climate change policies on oil-producing countries. The forum remains controversial even after the Paris Agreement.

27 Anabella Rosemberg, ITUC, interview with author, 2014.

28 Oral statement delivered to the SBSTA opening plenary, 1 December 2015.

29 This respondent asked that this comment be anonymous. Interview with author, 2014.

30 Ulrike Röhr, interview with author, 2014.

31 Ulrike Röhr, Interview with author, 2014.
32 The Lima Work Programme aims to promote gender balance and achieve "gender-responsive climate policy, developed for the purpose of guiding the effective participation of women in the bodies established under the Convention" (UNFCCC 2014, decision 18/CP.20). It largely focuses on increasing the amount and quality of women's participation in the Convention, and thus does not fundamentally diverge from the Doha decision on the involvement of women. The same decision calls for a series of workshops on gender and mitigation and technology development and transfer, and on adaptation and capacity building. It was reviewed and renewed in 2016.
33 As explained by Bridget Burns of WEDO in a meeting of the Work Programme on 7 May 2015 in Bonn, Germany, "gender equal" refers to equal rights, responsibilities, and opportunities for men and women, boys and girls. "Gender balance" refers to the ratio of men to women in any given situation and does not have to be 50:50; gender parity is a 50:50 balance specifically. "Gender mainstreaming" is the integration of gender considerations into every stage of policy processes. "Gender sensitive" refers to programs in which gender norms, roles, and inequalities have been considered and awareness of the issues has been raised, though appropriate actions may not have been taken. "Gender responsive" goes a step further: it considers gender norms, roles, and responsibilities and takes appropriate actions. This explanation is from my personal observation at the meeting of the Work Programme.
34 Saleemul Huq, IIED, interview with author, 2014.
35 Developed country delegate, interview, 9 June 2015. This delegate was in a key position during negotiations and was present for all the negotiations on gender and climate in Lima.
36 See draft of the Paris Agreement, 5 December 2015.
37 The Population and Climate Change Alliance later changed its name to the Population and Sustainable Development Network to focus more broadly on sustainable development issues, particularly the Sustainable Development Goals and the resulting 2030 Action Agenda for Sustainable Development.
38 For 2005–8, WEDO had 73 connections, IUCN 112, and WECF 34. For 2009–15, WEDO had 274, IUCN 266, and WECF 215.
39 Anonymous developing country delegate, interview with author, 2014; Gotelind Aber, Gender CC, interview with author, 2014.
40 Eva Quistorp, former member of the EU Parliament and early anti-nuclear and women's ecology movement activist. She founded the first parallel event at COP 1 to discuss gender issues at the UNFCCC, called Solidarity of Women in the Greenhouse.

41 Sabine Bock, WECF, interview with author, 2014.

42 Cate Owren. interview with author, 2014.

43 Ulrike Röhr, Life e.V., interview with author, 2014.

44 Ulrike Röhr, Life e.V., interview with author, 2014. Cate Owren, interview with author, 2014. Finland's Sixth National Communications to the UNFCCC reports that the Government of Finland provided €6 million to the Global Gender and Climate Alliance for 2008–14. Available at: http://stat.fi/tup/khkinv/fi_nc6.pdf (see page 22).

45 Anabella Rosemberg, ITUC, interview, 3 March 2014

46 Anabella Rosemberg, ITUC, interview, 3 March 2014.

47 Peggy Nash, MP, interview, 2014; Brian Kohler, IndustriALL, interview, 2014.

48 Irene Dankelman, WEDO, interview with author, 2014. Several other respondents discussed the relevance of the IPCC's focus on the impacts of climate change in the fourth Assessment Report: Ulrike Röhr, Life e.V., interview with author, 2014; Roger-Mark DeSouza, formerly Population Action International, interview with author, 2014. Cate Owren, interview with author, 2014.

49 Cate Owren, interview with author, 2014.

50 Anabella Rosemberg, ITUC; Brian Kohler, IndustriALL; Philip Pearson, TUC. All were involved in the early mobilization of labour unions in the climate change regime. Ms Rosemberg is currently responsible for training ITUC members on climate change issues. All these actors cited the IPCC as a turning point in their thinking and desire to engage in climate change as a labour movement.

51 Lucien Royer, Canadian Labour Congress, interview with author, 2015. Irene Dankelman, interview with author, 2014.

52 Lucien Royer, Canadian Labour Congress, interview with author, 2015. Mr Royer was with the ICFTU in the mid-2000s.

53 For example, see ITUC's statement "ISO Is Failing the Standard Test" regarding the work of the organization to establish a standard for occupational health and safety systems. Available at http://www.ituc-csi.org/iso-is-failing-the-standard-test?lang=en.

54 Lucien Royer, Canadian Labour Congress, interview with author, 2014.

55 Irene Dankelman, interview with author, 2014.

56 The framework is available at https://knowledge.unccd.int/sites/default/files/inline-files/Decision23_COP11_0.pdf.

57 Bridget Burns, interview with author, 2014.

58 Irene Dankelman, WEDO, interview with author, 2014.

59 Bridget Burns. Ms Burns is the current focal point for the Women and Gender Constituency in the UNFCCC and has worked on gender and environmental issues since the mid-2000s. Interview with author, 2014.

60 Cate Owren, interview with author, 2014.
61 Anabella Rosemberg, ITUC, interview, 2014; Lucien Royer, Canadian Labour Congress, interview with author, 2015.
62 Anonymous labour delegate, interview with author, 2014. This delegate has written and advocated for consideration of climate change issues in his union's work, and for technological solutions since 1992. His union has been engaged sporadically in the UNFCCC since the adoption of the Kyoto Protocol in 1997.
63 Anonymous, interview with author, 2014.
64 Philip Pearson, TUC, interview with author, 2014; Peter Colley, interview with author, 2014; Ashley Haugo, interview with author, 2014.
65 "Ban urges leaders at Davos to forge 'Green New Deal' to fight world recession." UN News Centre; with breaking news from the UN News Service. UN News Centre, 29 January 2009. http://www.un.org/apps /news/story.asp?NewsID=29712#.Vvm4IkeYH74.
66 Anonymous labour delegate, interview with author, 2014.
67 Labour union delegate who asked that these comments be anonymous, interview with author, 2014.
68 Ashley Haugo, interview with author, 2014; Philip Pearson, TUC, interview with author, 2014. Mr Pearson was a central figure in the early engagement in climate change by the labour movement. He chaired several coordination meetings of the nascent trade union NGO constituency in the UNFCCC from 2007 to 2009.
69 Anonymous labour advocate, interview with author, 2014.
70 See, for example, a WEDO publication in 2007 titled "Changing the Climate: Why Women's Perspectives Matter in Climate Change." It has two main sections: "Climate Change Ampifies Inequality" and "Women as Untapped Resources." Available at http://www.wedo.org/wp-content/uploads /changing-the-climate-why-womens-perspectives-matter-2008.pdf.
71 There is potentially a case to be made linking violence against women with climate change. According to a 2010 Report to the 16th session of the Human Rights Council by Margaret Sekaggya, women environmental defenders are more at risk than male environmental defenders and experience gender-specific forms of violence such as sexual harassment, sexual violence, and rape. Many of these women environmental defenders work on land, agriculture, forest, or mining-related issues. All of these issues are also implicated in various aspects of the climate change regime.
72 Anabella Rosemberg, ITUC, interview with author, 2014.
73 Anabella Rosemberg, ITUC, interview with author, 2014.
74 Philip Pearson, TUC, interview with author, 2014.
75 Anabella Rosemberg, ITUC, interview with author, 2014.
76 Philip Pearson, TUC, interview with author, 2014.

77 Anonymous American union delegate, interview with author, 2014.
78 Anonymous American union delegate, interview with author, 2014. This delegate was at the 2010 World Congress.
79 Anonymous American union delegate, interview with author, 2014.
80 Anonymous American union delegate, interview with author, 2014.
81 Benjamin Denis, ETUC, interview with author, 2014.
82 That NGOs reach consensus on a statement is a norm shared and practised by most constituencies at the UNFCCC. The Environmental NGO Constituency is an exception to this. Climate Action Network represents roughly 14 per cent of environmental NGOs, and the Climate Justice Now! network represents around 4 per cent (anonymous UN Secretariat, interview with author, 2014). Both groups give statements on behalf of their networks, as the major groups of environmental NGOs. It is unusual, however, for non-NGOs to be invited to attend the constituency meetings. The Women and Gender Constituency has an open door policy as a way to acknowledge that gender is a cross-cutting issue and to build a network of women interested in advancing gender issues.
83 Sabine Bock, WECF, interview with author, 2014.
84 Gotelind Alber, Gender CC, interview with author, 2015.
85 Sabine Bock, WECF, interview with author, 2014. Bridget Burns of WEDO makes a similar statement – that the network has become more cohesive by using constituency status as a forum. Interview with author, 2014.
86 Kathleen Mogelgaard, interview with author, 2014.
87 Kathleen Mogelgaard, interview with author, 2014.
88 Kathleen Mogelgaard, interview with author, 2014.
89 The NGO is now called Population Matters and continues to campaign on this idea.
90 This delegate asked that this comment be anonymous; interview with author, 2014.
91 Kathleen Mogelgaard, interview with author, 2014.
92 Kathleen Mogelgaard, interview with author, 2014.
93 This delegate asked that this comment be anonymous, interview with author, 2014.
94 This delegate asked that this comment be anonymous, interview with author, 2014.
95 Anabella Rosemberg, ITUC, interview with author, 2014.
96 Anabella Rosemberg, ITUC, interview with author, 2014.
97 As noted in chapter 3, indigenous peoples, local governments, and municipalities were established as UNFCCC constituencies before 2007 (when labour applied). These groups are also Agenda 21 Major Groups.
98 Anabella Rosemberg, ITUC, interview with author, 2014; Philip Pearson, TUC, interview with author, 2014.
99 Gotelind Aber, Gender CC, interview with author, 2015.

100 Of the thirty-four labour and gender activists interviewed, twenty mentioned the constituency and twelve of those used the term recognition.

101 Anabella Rosemberg, ITUC, interview with author, 2014.

102 Camille Risler, Asia Pacific Forum for Women, Law, and Environment.

103 Anabella Rosemberg, ITUC, interview with author, 2014.

104 Philip Pearson, TUC, interview, 28 May 2014.

105 Gotelind Alber, Gender CC, interview with author, 2015.

106 Decision 1/CP.21 (the Paris outcome) tasks several UNFCCC subsidiary and constituted bodies with work to develop a common set of rules for the provisions of the Paris Agreement. For example, the SBSTA is to develop common rules and modalities for the accounting of the provision and mobilization of financial resources to developing countries.

107 Internal email to the Constituency in May 2016.

108 Anonymous labour advocate, interview with author, 2014; Ashley Haugo, interview with author, 2014; Philip Pearson, TUC interview with author, 2014.

109 Philip Pearson, TUC, who attended the 2006 UNFCCC conference, and the round table held by Kenyan unions, interview with author, 2014.

110 Philip Pearson, TUC, interview with author, 2014.

111 Anabella Rosemberg, ITUC, interview with author, 2014.

112 Anonymous delegate of an environmental NGO, interview with author, 2015.

113 Bridget Burns, WEDO, interview with author, 2014.

114 Cate Owren, interview with author, 2014.

115 Irene Dankelman, interview with author, 2014.

116 Cate Owren, interview with author, 2014; Bridget Burns, WEDO, interview with author, 2014.

117 Anabella Rosemberg, ITUC, interview with author, 2014.

118 Philip Pearson, TUC, interview with author, 2014

119 The labour delegate interviewed asked that this comment be kept anonymous; interview with author, 2014.

120 Developed country delegate, interview with author, 2015.

121 Philip Pearson, TUC, interview with author, 2014.

122 Peter Colley, interview, 2 February 2014.

123 Developed country delegate, interview with author, 2015.

124 Bridget Burns, WEDO, interview with author, 2014.

125 Developed country delegate, interview with author, 2015.

126 Brian Kohler, IndustriALL, interview with author, 2014. Mr Kohler was one of the first architects of the term "just transition."

127 Philip Pearson, TUC, interview with author, 2014; Anabella Rosemberg, ITUC, interview with author, 2014; Lucien Royer, Canadian Labour Congress, interview with author, 2015; anonymous labour delegate, interview with author, 2015; Cate Owren, interview with author, 2014; Bridget Burns, WEDO, interview with author, 2014.

128 Primarily these were the ICFTU, the World Confederation of Labour (WCL), the Trade Union Advisory Committee to the OECD (TUAC), and the SustainLabour Foundation.
129 Internal ICFTU briefing on the conference.
130 Philip Pearson, interview with author, 2014.
131 Lucien Royer, interview with author, 2015; Philip Pearson, TUC, interview with author, 2014; Anonymous labour delegate, interview with author, 2014.
132 Cate Owren, interview with author, 2014.
133 The UNFCCC archive of side events is available at: https://seors.unfccc.int/seors/reports/archive.html. Often, side event organizers do not upload their programs to the archive.
134 Anonymous former UNFCCC Secretariat member, interview with author, 2014.
135 Anonymous UNDP staff member, interview with author, 2014.
136 Anonymous American union delegate, interview with author, 2014.

5. The Radical Challengers: Climate Justice Now!

1 Dorothy Guerrero, Focus on the Global South, interview with author, 2015; Nicola Bullard, Focus on the Global South, interview with author, 2014; Sam Lund, World Development Movement, interview with author, 2014.
2 See, for example, Tom Mertes and Walden Bello, *A Movement of Movements: Is Another World Really Possible?* (London: Verso, 2004).
3 Anonymous, interview with author, 2014. This interviewee was present in the early years of CJN!.
4 The Indigenous Environmental Network states its mission as follows: "The Indigenous Peoples of the Americas have lived for over 500 years in confrontation with an immigrant society that holds an opposing world view. As a result we are now facing an environmental crisis which threatens the survival of all natural life." See http://www.ienearth.org/about.
5 Gerak Lewan later organized the protests around the Nineteenth Ministerial of the WTO in Bali in November 2014.
6 Nicola Bullard, Focus on the Global South, interview with author, 2014.
7 Nicola Bullard, Focus on the Global South, interview with author, 2014; Dorothy Guerrero, Focus on the Global South, interview with author, 2015.
8 Wally Menne, TimberWatch, interview with author, 2014; Nicola Bullard, Focus on the Global South, interview with author, 2014.
9 Wally Menne, TimberWatch, interview with author, 2014; Anne Petermann, Global Justice Ecology Project, interview with author, 2014.
10 Eight interviewees relayed this story, most of whom used the term "walked down the hall." This group includes founding members of CJN! such as Anne Petermann, Global Justice Ecology Project, interview with author, 2014; Tamra Gilbertson, Carbon Trade Watch, interview with author, 2014;

and Sam Lund-Harket, World Development Movement, interview with author, 2014. Others highlighting this event include Michael Dorsey, Joint Center for Political and Economic Studies, interview with author, 2014; and an anonymous climate justice activist, interview with author, 2014.

11 Anonymous climate justice activist who was present at the 2007 Bali Conference and worked with the key founding members of CJN!, interview with author, 2014.

12 Anonymous CJN! organizer, interview with author, 2014; Anne Petermann, Global Justice Ecology Project, interview with author, 2014.

13 Anne Petermann, Global Justice Ecology Project, interview with author, 2014.

14 Nicola Bullard, Focus on the Global South, interview with author, 2014.

15 CJN! internal meeting minutes from June 2010. Shared with author from a CJN! member.

16 CJN! organizer, interview with author, 2014.

17 CJN! organizer, interview with author, 2014.

18 Dorothy Guererro, Focus on the Global South, interview with author,, 2015.

19 Anonymous climate justice activist, interview with author, 2014.

20 Anonymous CJN! organizer, interview with author, 2014.

21 Anonymous CJN! organizer, interview with author, 2014.

22 Michael Dorsey, Joint Center for Political and Economic Studies, interview with author, 2014.

23 A founding CJN! member who asked to be anonymous for some comments, interview with author, 2014.

24 Nicola Bullard, Focus on the Global South, interview with author, 2014.

25 Anonymous CJN! organizer, interview with author, 2014.

26 Anne Petermann, Global Justice Ecology Project, interview with author, 2014; Anonymous CJN! organizer, interview with author, 2014.

27 ETC group is an NGO with this self-stated mission: "ETC Group works to address the socioeconomic and ecological issues surrounding new technologies that could have an impact on the world's poorest and most vulnerable people." It has six current focal areas: climate and geoengineering; biodiversity; sustainable development; corporate monopolies; synthetic biology; and technology assessment. See http://www.etcgroup.org/mission.

28 Mooney was referencing the People's Climate March in New York in September 2014.

29 Personal observation from participation in the 2015 Paris Climate Conference.

30 Analysis of World Social Forum agendas, 2007–16.

31 For the 2005–8 period, Transnational Institute had 117 connections, Friends of the Earth 104, World Rainforest Movement, 80, and Focus on the Global South, 72.

32 Wally Menne, TimberWatch, interview with author, 2014.

33 Dorothy Guerrero, Focus on the Global South, interview with author, 2015.
34 In the 2009–15 time frame, Jubilee South had 222 connections, Friends of the Earth 216, and Focus on the Global South 201. The Indigenous Environment Network, World Rainforest Movement, and La Via Campesina followed with 166, 167, and 168 respectively.
35 Notes from a planning meeting June 2011 shared by a CJN! organizer.
36 The Appendix discusses how the social network analysis indicators varied slightly for the climate justice movement because of this difference. Because there was no formal alliance or list of members, the press releases of the Durban Group for Climate Justice, CJN!, and the Global Campaign to Demand Climate Justice were used as evidence of shared membership in the group.
37 Interview with author, 2014.
38 Nicola Bullard, Focus on the Global South, interview with author, 2014; Wally Menne, TImberWatch, interview with author, 2014.
39 Nicola Bullard, Focus on the Global South, interview with author, 2014.
40 Anonymous CJN! organizer, interview with author, 2014.
41 Meena Raman, Third World Network, interview with author, 2014.
42 Timberwatch is an environmental NGO focused on forest conservation and management that is part of the Durban Group for Climate Justice and later Climate Justice Now! Interview with author, 2014.
43 Nicola Bullard, Focus on the Global South, interview with author, 2014.
44 Simone Lovera, Global Forest Coalition, interview with author, 2014.
45 Anonymous CJN! organizer, interview with author, 2014; Anne Petermann, Global Justice Ecology Project, interview with author, 2014.
46 Anonymous delegate from an environmental NGO, interview with author, 2015.
47 Larry Lohmann, the Corner House, personal communication with author, 2014.
48 Dorothy Guerrero, Focus on the Global South, interview with author, 2015.
49 Nicola Bullard, Focus on the Global South, interview with author, 2014; Dorothy Guerrero, Focus on the Global South, interview with author, 2015.
50 Nicola Bullard, Focus on the Global South, interview with author, 2014.
51 Anonymous CJN! organizer, interview with author, 20134.
52 See for example, CorpWatch's statement that climate justice means "challenging [fossil fuel] companies at every level – from the production and marketing of fossil fuels themselves, to their underhanded political influence, to their PR prowess, to the unjust "solutions" they propose, to the fossil fuel based globalization they are driving."
53 Wally Menne, TimberWatch, interview with author, 2014.
54 Anne Petermann, Global Justice Ecology Project, interview with author, 2014; Dorothy Guerrero, Focus on the Global South, interview with author, 2014; Larry Lohmann, the Corner House, interview with author, 2014.

55 The Mary Robinson Foundation – Climate Justice states that "climate justice links human rights and development to achieve a human-centred approach, safeguarding the rights of the most vulnerable and sharing the burdens and benefits of climate change and its resolution equitably and fairly."

56 Pascoe Sabido, Corporate Europe Observatory, interview with author, 2014.

57 Anne Petermann, Global Justice Ecology Project, a founding member of the Durban Group for Climate Justice and CJN!, interview with author, 2014.

58 Focus on the Global South, interview with author, 2014; Anonymous CJN! organizer, interview with author, 2014.

59 Dorothy Guerrero, Focus on the Global South, interview with author, 2014; Anne Petermann, Global Justice Ecology Project, interview with author, 2014; Larry Lohmann, The Corner House, interview with author, 2014.

60 CJN! internal meeting minutes from June 2010, shared with author.

61 An environmental NGO representative who was part of CJN! and asked that these comments be anonymous, interview with author, 2014.

62 Anne Petermann, Global Justice Ecology Project, interview with author, 2014.

63 Meena Raman, Third World Network, personal communication with author, 2014; Dorothy Guerrero, Focus on the Global South, interview with author, 2015.

64 Meena Raman, Third World Network, interview with author, 2014.

65 Anne Petermann, Global Justice Ecology Project, interview with author, 2014; Wally Menne, TimberWatch, interview with author, 2014.

66 Dorothy Guerrero, Focus on the Global South, interview with author, 2015.

67 Anne Petermann, Global Justice Ecology Project, interview with author, 2014; Teresa Andersen, interview with author, 2014.

68 Teresa Andersen, Gaia Foundation, interview with author, 2014.

69 Chris Lang, REDD Monitor, interview with author, 2014.

70 Nicola Bullard, Focus on the Global South, interview with author, 2014.

71 Michael Dorsey, Joint Centre for Political and Economic Studies, interview with author, 2014.

72 The Climate Action Network puts a mark on the badges of its members, either a sticker or a hole punch in the badge. In this way, they can identify their members and can make sure that their members are the only ones in their strategy meetings.

73 Michael Dorsey, Joint Centre for Political and Economic Studies, interview with author, 2014.

74 Anonymous UNFCCC Secretariat member, interview with author, 2014.

75 Anonymous UNFCCC Secretariat member, interview with author, 2014.

76 A principal theme across all of the interviews with justice advocates is that CJN! stands in opposition to many of the Climate Action Network's positions on market mechanisms and forests. Furthermore, many highlighted the northern domination of the Climate Action Network. This

group included Pasco Sibido, CEO, interview with author, 2014; Dorothy Guerrero, Focus on the Global South, interview with author, 2015; Michael Dorsey, Joint Centre for Political and Economic Studies, interview with author, 2014; Wally Menne, Timberwatch, interview with author, 2014; and anonymous CJN! organizer, interview with author, 2014.

77 Personal observations from twelve UNFCCC meetings, each of which included several statements from CJN! and Climate Action Network. Anonymous Secretariat office, interview with author, 2015.

78 Several CJN! members describe CJN! as a response to the Climate Action Network, including Michael Dorsey, Joint Center for Political and Economic Studies, interview with author, 2014; anonymous CJN! organizer, interview with author, 2014; and Simone Lovera, Global Forest Coalition, interview with author, 2014.

79 Anonymous CJN! organizer, interview with author, 2014.

80 Anonymous environmental NGO, interview with author, 2015.

81 Wally Menne, TimberWatch, interview with author, 2014.

82 Anonymous CJN! organizer, interview with author, 2014.

83 Anne Petermann, Global Justice Ecology Project, interview with author, 2014.

84 Anonymous climate justice activist, interview with author, 2014.

85 Anonymous climate justice activist, interview with author, 2014.

86 Anonymous climate justice activist, interview with author, 2014.

87 Anonymous CJN! organizer, interview with author, 2014.

88 Simone Lovera, Global Forest Coalition, interview with author, 2014.

89 Anonymous climate justice advocate, interview with author, 2014.

90 Anonymous climate justice advocate, interview with author, 2014.

91 Nicola Bullard, Focus on the Global South, interview with author, 2014.

92 Dorothy Guerreo, Focus on the Global South, interview with author, 2015.

93 Nicola Bullard, Focus on the Global South, interview with author ,2014.

94 Nicola Bullard, Focus on the Global South, interview with author, 2014.

6. The Uninterested and Impeded: Health and Human Rights

1 Nick Watts, Climate and Health Council and Global Climate and Health Alliance, interview with author, 2014.

2 According to the official UNFCCC Participation list for COP 13, pt II.

3 See the Global Call to Climate Actions' 2009 *tcktcktck* Call to Action here: http://tcktcktck.org/partners/partner-call-to-action.

4 A delegate who was with a major human rights NGO in the late 2000s and who asked that these comments be anonymous; interview with author, 2014.

5 A delegate who was with a major human rights NGO in the late 2000s and who asked that these comments be anonymous, interview with author, 2014.

6 A delegate who was with a major human rights NGO in the late 2000s and who asked that these comments be anonymous, interview with author, 2014.

7 Lynn Wilson, Seatrust Institute, interview with author, 2014. Ms Wilson was at this early meeting and continues working with Nurses Across the Borders on climate change and health issues.

8 Lynn Wilson, Seatrust Institute, interview with author, 2014.

9 Health co-benefits means the beneficial effects of (in this case) climate policies. Generally, the term refers to the health benefits of mitigation policy. For example, reducing the use of coal would reduce the release of air pollutants that contribute to asthma and other respiratory and cardiovascular diseases.

10 The membership of the GCHA can be found at http://www.climateand-healthalliance.org/members. The public health members are the Inches Network, European Respiratory Society, and Public Health Institute.

11 Nick Watts, Climate and Health Council and Global Health and Climate Alliance, interview with author, 2014.

12 The World Medical Association has sixty-three connections, the IFMSA seventy.

13 Charlotte Holm-Hansen, IFMSA, interview with author, 2014.

14 Anonymous health advocate, interview with author, 2014. The WHO staff working on climate change met the IFMSA delegates at the UNFCCC in 2009.

15 Personal observation.

16 Izobel Braithwaite, Healthy Planet UK, interview with author, 2014.

17 All these activities are listed on the World Medical Association website: http://www.wma.net/en/20activities/index.html.

18 Cathey Falvo, President, International Society of Doctors for the Environment, interview with author, 2015.

19 Clarisse Delorme, World Medical Association, interview with author, 2014.

20 Participant observation from attending the conference, 27–9 August 2014.

21 Clarisse Delorme, World Medical Association, interview with author, 2014.

22 This health and climate advocate asked that these comments be anonymous; interview with author, 2014.

23 Joe Amon, Human Rights Watch, interview with the author, 2014.

24 Stephen Humphreys, formerly with the International Council on Human Rights Policy, and currently at the London School of Economics, interview with author, 2014.

25 This was raised by four respondents, most explicitly by Isobel Braithwaite, Healthy Planet UK, interview with author, 2014; Cathey Falvo, International Society of Doctors for the Environment, interview with author, 2014.

26 Cathey Falvo, International Society of Doctors for the Environment, interview with author, 2014.

27 Clarisse Delorme, World Medical Association, interview with author, 2014.
28 Isobel Braithwaite, Healthy Planet UK, interview with author, 2014.
29 Joe Amon, Human Rights Watch, interview with author, 2014.
30 Joe Amon, Human Rights Watch, interview with author, 2014.
31 Stephen Humphreys, International Council of Human Rights Policy, interview with author, 2014.
32 Claudel P-Desrosiers, IFMSA Coordinator, interview with author, 2014.
33 For a few, Cathey Falvo, International Society of Doctors for the Environment, interview with author, 2015; Nick Watts, Climate and Health Council and GCHA, interview with author, 2014; Isobel Braithwaite, Healthy Planet UK, interview with author, 2014. Participant observation in the WHO Conference on Health and Climate Change, 27–9 August 2014.
34 Cathey Falvo, International Society of Doctors for the Environment, interview with author, 2014.
35 Participant observation of the WHO Conference on Health and Climate Change, 27–9 August 2014.
36 Nick Watts, Climate and Health Council and GCHA, interview with author, 2014.
37 See the World Medical Association's webpage devoted to its work on human rights and health: http://www.wma.net/en/20activities/20humanrights.
38 Clarisse Delorme, World Medical Association, interview with author, 2014.
39 Clarisse Delorme, World Medical Association, interview with author, 2014.
40 Several participants spoke about the Clean Development Mechanism, Global Environment Facility, and other climate finance mechanisms as possible sources of funding. No representatives of these institutions were present to explain that these mechanisms are not designed to support such initiatives. Conference participants asked for WHO to produce a primer on climate finance, which the WHO later suggested would require external expertise.
41 Nick Watts, GCHA, interview with author, 2014.
42 Charlotte Holm-Hansen, IFMSA, interview with author, 2014.
43 Charlotte Holm-Hansen, IFMSA, interview with author, 2014.
44 Nick Watts, GCHA, interview with author, 2014.
45 Claudel P-Desrosiers, IFMSA, interview with author, 2014.
46 Nick Watts, GCHA, interview with author, 2014.
47 Lynn Wilson, Seatrust Institute, interview with author, 2015.
48 Nick Watts, GCHA, interview with author, 2014.
49 In the lead-up to the Paris conference, the IFMSA did seek to add mention of health co-benefits to a very early draft of the agreement (UNFCCC 2014). The suggestions were detailed textual amendments to the text, which was at the time largely a conceptual outline of the elements of a draft agreement. Delegates had yet to agree on major aspects of

the agreement. These amendments were not discussed or taken up by parties.

50 Anonymous labour advocate, interview with author, 2014; Anonymous UN employee, interview with author, 2014.

51 Personal observation at the June meeting of the subsidiary bodies in June 2014, held in Bonn, Germany. A health advocate who asked that these comments be kept anonymous was also present at this meeting and shared the same anecdote and interpretation of the reception that the health advocate and presentation received in the meeting of the forum.

52 Nick Watts, Climate and Health Council and GCHA, interview with author, 2014. In the quote, "streams" refers to the two workstreams of the *ad hoc* Working Group for the Advancement of the Durban Platform, the negotiation group tasked with developing the post-2015 agreement (workstream one) and enhancing pre-2020 action (workstream two).

53 Nick Watts, Climate and Health Council and GCHA, interview with author, 2014. He was likely referring to the CDM Methodology ACM0013, which was approved in 2007.

54 Nick Watts, Climate and Health Council and GCHA, interview with author, 2014.

55 National adaptation plans of action were established in 2001 to assist Least Developed Countries only. There is an eight-step process that helps the country identify projects that will help them adapt to climate change. National adaptation plans were a process agreed to in 2010 and established in 2011. The negotiations and implementation focus on a flexible process to help developing countries develop medium- and long-term plans, rather than projects.

56 Nick Watts, Climate and Health Council and GCHA, interview with author, 2014.

57 Claudel P-Desrosiers, IFMSA, interview with author, 2014.

58 Isobel Braithwaite, Healthy Planet UK, interview with author, 2014.

59 Lynn Wilson, the Seatrust Institute, interview with author,, 2015.

60 Anonymous health advocate, interview with author, 2014.

61 Anonymous health advocate, interview with author, 2014.

62 A member of the health network who asked that this comment be anonymous; interview with author, 2014.

63 Anonymous health advocate, interview with author, 2014.

64 Anonymous health advocate, interview with author, 2014; Nick Watts, Climate and Health Council and GCHA, interview with author, 2014.

65 A summary of these reports can be found at http://www.ucsusa.org /global_warming/science_and_impacts/impacts/climate-change-and -your-health.html#.WGxLzfkrLIU.

66 The WHO Congress passed a resolution on health and climate change in 2008, which recognizes that climate change is a new issue for WHO.

67 Anonymous UN employee, interview with author, 2014. The twenty members of the task group on the social dimensions of climate change are: Food and Agriculture Organization of the United Nations; International Labour Organization; International Organization for Migration; International Telecommunication Union; Office of the High Commissioner for Human Rights; Joint United Nations Programme on HIV/AIDS; UN Department of Economic and Social Affairs; UNDP; UN Educational, Scientific and Cultural Organization; UN Population Fund; UN Human Settlements Programme; UN Children's Fund; UN Institute for Training and Research; UN International Strategy for Disaster Reduction; UN Research Institute for Social Development; United Nations University; UN Women World Bank; UN World Food Programme; and WHO.

68 An environmental NGO, health-climate NGO representative, and a human rights NGO representative expressed this concern, but all asked for this comment to be anonymous. Interviews were all in 2014.

69 A health/climate NGO delegate who asked that these comments be anonymous; interview with author, 2014.

70 Anonymous health advocate, interview with author, 2014.

71 Nick Watts, Climate and Health Council and GCHA, interview with author, 2014.

72 Anonymous health advocate, interview with author, 2014.

7. The New Climate Activists' Future

1 There are four staff working in the climate change unit at the WHO.

2 Several respondents I spoke with suggested Guy Ryder as someone knowledgeable about how and why labour took on climate change.

3 UN OPCW outlined the agreement among member-states to undertake work related to the Sustainable Development Goals: https://www.opcw .org/media-centre/news/2018/10/opcw-further-enhance-contributions -united-nations-sustainable-development.

4 UN OPCW outcomes of the 2018 meeting, including member-states' call for mainstreaming gender considerations: https://www.armscontrol.org /print/10067.

5 There are four characteristics of POPs (persistence, toxicity, long-range environmental transport, and bioaccumulation). If chemicals are found to meet these criteria, they may be added to the Convention by parties.

6 The NAZCA portal is available at: http://climateaction.unfccc.int. Entries are catalogued by theme, region, and actor type, among other search options. The portal highlights the greenhouse gas emissions, gases included, and change in emissions resulting from an action. For adaptation-related entries, these data, as of April 2019, were labelled "coming soon."

Appendix: Multimethod Approach to Studying NGO Forum Multiplying

1   The other approach identified by Laumann and colleagues is the nominalist approach, which imposes a conceptual framework to serve analytical purposes.

2   The other approach is the event-based approach, which uses common participation in an event as evidence of a connection between actors. While this approach has been used to study NGOs operating in different organizations by Orsini (2013) and offers several benefits, it potentially conflates participatory longevity with network centrality (an actor's relative number of connections). Greater institutional participation will appear as a greater number of network connections, even though it is possible to attend every meeting and not interact with other NGOs. Furthermore, in climate change COPs there are often more than 3,000 people, up to 40,000 people at the Paris conference. This is too large a group for us to infer that NGOs interacted because they attended the same meeting.

Bibliography

Acharya, A. (2004). How ideas spread: Whose norms matter? Norm localization and institutional change in Asian regionalism. *International Organization, 58*, 239–275. https://doi.org/10.1017/S0020818304582024

AFL-CIO. (2007). *AFL-CIO energy task force: Jobs and energy for the 21st century.* Retrieved May 23, 2014, from: www.workingforamerica.org/documents /PDF/1agexecutivealert.pdf.

Aguilar, L., et al. (2009). *Training manual on gender and climate change.* Published by IUCN, UNDP, and GGCA. San Jose, Costa Rica.

Alcock, F. (2008). Conflict and coalitions within and across the ENGO community. *Global Environmental Politics 8*(4), 66–91. https://doi.org/10.1162 /glep.2008.8.4.66

Allan, J. I. (2018). Seeking entry: Discursive hooks and NGOs in global climate Politics. *Global Policy, 9*(4), 560–569. https://doi.org/10.1111/1758-5899.12586

– (2019). Dangerous incrementalism of the Paris Agreement. *Global Environmental Politics, 19*(1), 4–11. https://doi.org/10.1162/glep_a_00488

Allan, J. I., & Dauvergne, P. (2013). The global south in environmental negotiations: The politics of coalitions in REDD+. *Third World Quarterly, 34*(8), 1307–1322. https://doi.org/10.1080/01436597.2013.831536

Allan, J. I., & Hadden, J. (2017). Exploring the framing power of NGOs in global climate politics. *Environmental Politics 26*(4), 600–620. https://doi.org /10.1080/09644016.2017.1319017

Alter, K., & Meunier, S. (2009). The politics of international regime complexity. *Perspectives on Politics, 7*(1), 13–24. https://doi.org/10.1017/S1537592709090033

Andresen, S., & Skodvin, T. (2008). Non-state influence in the International Whaling Commission, 1970 to 2006. *NGO diplomacy: The influence of nongovernmental organizations in international environmental negotiations,* 119–148.

Arts, B. (1998). *The political influence of global NGOs: Case studies of climate and biodiversity conventions.* International Books.

Arts, B., & Mack, S. (2003). Environmental NGOs and the biosafety protocol: A case study on political influence. *Environmental Policy and Governance*, 13(1), 19–33. https://doi.org/10.1002/eet.309

Avant, D. D., Finnemore, M., & Sell, S. K. (Eds.). (2010). *Who governs the globe?* Cambridge: Cambridge University Press.

Bäckstrand, K., & Lövbrand, E. (2016). The road to Paris: Contending climate governance discourses in the post-Copenhagen era." *Journal of Environmental Policy and Planning*, 21(5), 519–532. https://doi.org/10.1080/1523908X.2016.1150777

Baumgartner, F. R., & Jones, B. D. (1991). Agenda dynamics and policy subsystems. *The Journal of Politics*, 53(4), 1044–1074. https://doi.org/10.2307/2131866

– (1993). *Agendas and instability in American politics*. University of Chicago Press.

Benford, R. D., & Snow, D.A. (2000). Framing processes and social movements: An overview and assessment. *Annual Review of Sociology*, 26, 611–639. https://doi.org/10.1146/annurev.soc.26.1.611

Bernauer, T., & Gampfer, R. (2013). Effects of civil society involvement on popular legitimacy of global governance. *Global Environmental Change*, 23(2), 439–449. https://doi.org/10.1016/j.gloenvcha.2013.01.001

Betsill, M. M. (2002). "Environmental NGOs meet the sovereign state: The Kyoto Protocol negotiations on global climate change." *Colorado Journal of Environmental Law and Policy*, 13, 49–64.

– (2008). Environmental NGOs and the Kyoto Protocol negotiations: 1995 to 1997. *NGO diplomacy: The influence of nongovernmental organizations in international environmental negotiations*, 43–66.

– (2015). NGOs. In K. Bäckstrand & E. Lövbrand (Eds.), *Research handbook on climate governance*. Edward Elgar.

Betsill, M. M., & Corell, E. (Eds). (2008). *NGO diplomacy: The influence of nongovernmental organizations in international environmental negotiations*. MIT Press.

Biermann, F., et al. (2009). The fragmentation of global governance architectures: A framework for analysis. *Global Environmental Politics*, 9(4), 14–40. https://doi.org/10.1162/glep.2009.9.4.14

Bob, C. (2005). *The marketing of rebellion*. Cambridge University Press.

Böhmelt, T., Koubi, V., & Bernauer, R. (2014). Civil society participation in global governance: Insights from climate politics. *European Journal of Political Research*, 53(1), 18–36. https://doi.org/10.1111/1475-6765.12016

Bond, P. (2012). *Politics of climate justice: Paralysis above, movement below*. University of Kwa Zulu Natal Press.

– (2015, September). Challenges for the climate justice movement: Connecting dots, linking Blockadia, and jumping scale. Ejolt report No. 23, 17–33. http://www.ejolt.org/wordpress/wp-content/uploads/2015/09/EJOLT-6.17-33.pdf

Bond, P., & Dorsey, M. (2010). Anatomies of environmental knowledge and resistance: Diverse climate justice movements and waning eco-neoliberalism. *Journal of Australian Political Economy, 66,* 286–310.

Borgatti, S. P., Everett, M. G. & Freeman, L. C. (2002). *Ucinet 6 for Windows: Software for social network analysis.* Analytic Technologies.

Boyd, D. R. (2011). *The environmental rights revolution: A global study of constitutions, human rights, and the environment.* UBC Press.

Brady, H. E., & Collier, D.C. (Eds.). (2004). *Rethinking social inquiry: Diverse tools, shared standards.* Rowman and Littlefield.

Brown Thompson, K. (2002). Women's rights are human rights. In S. Khagram, J. V. Riker, & K. Sikkink (Eds.), *Restructuring World Politics: Transnational Social Movements, Networks, and Norms.* Minneapolis: University of Minnesota Press.

Bullard, N., & Müller, T. (2012). Beyond the "green economy": System change, not climate change? *Development, 55,* 54–62. https://doi.org/10.1057/dev.2011.100

– (n.d.). Beyond the "green economy": System change, not climate change?" Draft paper prepared for UNRISD.

Burgiel, S. W. (2008). Non-state actors and the Cartagena Protocol on biosafety. *NGO diplomacy: The influence of nongovernmental organizations in international environmental negotiations,* 67–100.

Burt, R. S. (2004). Structural holes and good ideas. *American Journal of Sociology, 110*(2), 349–399. https://doi.org/10.1086/421787

Busby, J. W., & Hadden, J. (2014). Nonstate actors in the climate arena. Stanley Foundation Report. http://www.stanleyfoundation.org/publications/working_papers/StanleyNonState_BusbyHadden.pdf.

Busby, J. W., & Ochs, A. (2004). From Mars to Venus down to Earth: Understanding the transatlantic climate divide. In D. Michel (Ed.), *Climate policy for the 21st century: Meeting the long-term challenge of global warming.* Center for Transatlantic Relations.

Busch, M. (2007). Overlapping institutions, forum shopping, and dispute settlement international trade. *International Organization, 61*(4), 735–761. https://doi.org/10.1017/S0020818307070257

Carbon Trade Watch. (2009). Carbon trading – What it is and why it fails. *Critical Currents, 7.* http://www.carbontradewatch.org/publications/carbon-trading-how-it-works-and-why-it-fails.html.

Carpenter, R. C. (2007). Setting the advocacy agenda: Theorizing issue emergence and nonemergence in transnational advocacy networks. *International Studies Quarterly, 51*(1), 99–120. https://doi.org/10.1111/j.1468-2478.2007.00441.x

– (2011). Vetting the advocacy agenda: Networks, centrality, and the paradox of weapons norms. *International Organization, 65*(1), 69–102. https://doi.org/10.1017/S0020818310000329

– (2014). *"Lost" causes: Agenda vetting in global issue networks and the shaping of human security*. Cornell University Press

Casula Vifell, A. (2010). WTO and the environmental movements: On the path to participatory governance? In C. Jönsson & J. Tallberg (Eds.), *Transnational actors in global governance: Patterns, explanations, and implications* (pp. 110–123). Palgrave Macmillan.

Chasek, P. S. (2001). NGOs and state capacity in international environmental negotiations: The experience of the Earth Negotiations Bulletin and developing countries in multilateral negotiations. *RECIEL, 10*(2), 168–176. https://doi.org/10.1111/1467-9388.00273

Chatterton, P., Featherstone, D., & Routledge, P. (2012). Articulating climate justice in Copenhagen: Antagonism, the commons, and solidarity. *Antipode, 45*(3), 602–620. https://doi.org/10.1111/j.1467-8330.2012.01025.x

Ciplet, D. (2014). Contesting climate injustice: Transnational advocacy network struggles for rights in UN climate politics. *Global Environmental Politics, 14*(4), 75–96. https://doi.org/10.1162/GLEP_a_00258

CJN! – Climate Justice Now! (2007, December 14). What's missing from the climate talks? Justice! [Press release]. http://www.climate-justice-now.org/cjn-founding-press-release

– (2009). Corrupt Copenhagen "accord" exposes gulf between peoples' demands and elite political interests. http://links.org.au/node/1427

– (2010). A short history of Climate Justice Now! http://www.climate-justice-now.org/about-cjn/history

Clark, A. M., Friedman, E. J., & Hochstetler, K. (1998). The sovereign limits of global civil society: A comparison of NGO participation in UN world conferences on the environment, human rights, and women. *World Politics, 51*(1), 1–35. https://doi.org/10.1017/S0043887100007772

Climate Action Network. (2006). Views on the participation of observers in the Kyoto Protocol process. Submission to the UNFCCC Subsidiary Body for Implementation.

Coleman, K.P. (2013). Locating norm diplomacy: Venue change in international norm negotiations. *European Journal of International Relations, 19*(1), 163–186. https://doi.org/10.1177/1354066111411209

Colgan, J. D., Keohane, R. O., & Van de Graaf, T. (2012). Punctuated equilibrium in the energy regime complex. *The Review of International Organizations, 7*, 117–143. https://doi.org/10.1007/s11558-011-9130-9

Cooley, A., and James, R. (2002). The NGO scramble. *International Security, 27*(1), 5–39. https://doi.org/10.1162/016228802320231217

Cooper, S. (1999, December 2). Teamsters and turtles: They're together at last. *Los Angeles Times*.

Corell, E. (2008). NGO influence in the negotiations of the desertification convention. *NGO diplomacy: The influence of nongovernmental organizations in international environmental negotiations*, 101–118.

Costello, A., et al. (2009). Managing the health effects of climate change. *The Lancet 373*(9676), 1693–1733. https://doi.org/10.1016/S0140-6736(09)60935-1

Cox, R. W., & Schechter, M. G. (2002). *The political economy of a plural world: Critical reflections on power, morals, and civilization.* Psychology Press.

Dankelman, I. (2010). *Gender and climate change: An introduction.* Routledge.

Dauvergne, P., & LeBaron, G. (2014). *Protest, Inc.: The corporatization of activism.* Polity Press.

Della Porta, D., & Tarrow, S. (2005). *Transnational protest and global activism.* New York, Rowman and Littlefield.

Dellas, E., Pattberg, P., & Betsill, M. (2011). Agency in earth system governance: Refining a research agenda. *International Environmental Agreements: Politics, Law, and Economics, 11*(1), 85–98.

Diani, M., & and McAdam, D. (Eds.). (2003). *Social movements and networks: Relational approaches to collective action.* Oxford University Press.

Downie, C. (2014). Transnational actors in environmental politics: Strategies and influence in long negotiations. *Environmental Politics, 23*(3), 376–394. https://doi.org/10.1080/09644016.2013.875252

Drezner, D. W. (2009). The power and peril of international regime complexity. *Perspectives on Politics, 7*(1), 65–70. https://doi.org/10.1017/S1537592709090100

Durban Group for Climate Justice. (2004). Climate justice now! The Durban declaration on carbon trading. http://www.durbanclimatejustice.org/durban-declaration/english.html

Eisinger P. (1973). The conditions of protest behavior in American cities. *American Political Science Review, 67*(1), 11–28. https://doi.org/10.2307/1958525

ETUC. (2007). Climate change and employment. https://www.etuc.org/publications/study-climate-change-and-employment-0#.WtiVBIjwbIU

Falkner, R. (2016). The Paris Agreement and the new logic of international climate politics. *International Affairs, 92*(5), 1107–1125. https://doi.org/10.1111/1468-2346.12708

Finnemore, M., & Sikkink, K. (1998). International norm dynamics and political change. *International Organization, 52*(4), 887–917. https://doi.org/10.1162/002081898550789

Fisher, D. R. (2010). COP-15 in Copenhagen: How the merging of movements left civil society out in the cold. *Global Environmental Politics, 10*(2), 11–17. https://doi.org/10.1162/glep.2010.10.2.11

Fisher, D. R., & Galli, A. M. (2015). Civil society. In K. Bäckstrand and E. Lövbrand (Eds.), *Research handbook on climate governance.* Edward Elgar

Focus on the Global South. (2019). Growth, degrowth, and climate justice. https://www.globaljustice.org.uk/blog/2019/sep/19/degrowth-and-perspectives-about-it-south#:~:text=Deglobalisation%20means%20the%20transformation%20of,peoples%2C%20nations%2C%20and%20communities.

Gaer, F. D. (1995). Reality check: Human rights nongovernmental organisations confront governments at the United Nations. *Third World Quarterly, 16*(3), 389–404. https://doi.org/10.1080/01436599550035960

Gamson, W. A., & Meyer, D. (1996). Framing political opportunity. In D. McAdam, J. McCarthy, & M. Zald (Eds.), *Comparative perspectives on social movements* (pp. 275–290). Cambridge University Press.

GCDCJ. (n.d.). Fight for climate justice [Founding statement]. http://demandclimatejustice.org/news-2/7-fight-for-climate-justice.

GCHA. (2011). The Durban Declaration on climate and health. http://www.climateandhealthalliance.org/climate-health/climate-change-impacts-on-health

Gender CC. (n.d.). Population, gender, and climate change. Available from https://www.gendercc.net/gender-climate/population.html

– (2005). Gender and climate change research workshop: What do we know? What do we need to find out? http://gendercc.net/fileadmin/inhalte/dokumente/6_UNFCCC/G_CC_research_workshop_report.pdf

– (2007). Statement to the UNFCCC plenary. https://wrm.org.uy/articles-from-the-wrm-bulletin/section1/gender-issues-and-climate-change

– (2009). Gender into climate policy: Toolkit for climate experts and decision makers. https://www.gendercc.net/fileadmin/inhalte/dokumente/5_Gender_Climate/toolkit-gender-cc-web.pdf

– (2011). A closer look at the numbers: Gender CC discussion paper on population growth, climate change, and gender. https://gendercc.net/fileadmin/inhalte/dokumente/5_Gender_Climate/Population/GenderCC_discussion_paper_on_population_-_FINAL-2.pdf

George, A. L., & Bennett, A. (2005). *Case studies and theory development in the social sciences*. MIT Press.

GGCA. (2007). Women ministers speak out on climate change. Press release. https://www.wedo.org/wp-content/uploads/womenministerspeakoutonclimatechange.html

– (2009). Engendering REDD workshop report. http://theredddesk.org/sites/default/files/resources/pdf/engendering_redd_workshop.pdf

– (2009b). Submission to the AWG-LCA on a shared vision: WEDO on behalf of the GGCA. Available in UNFCCC Submission Portal.

– (2012). Overview of the linkages between gender and climate change. http://www.undp.org/content/dam/undp/library/gender/Gender%20and%20Environment/PB1_Africa_Overview-Gender-Climate-Change.pdf

– (2013). Overview of the linkages between gender and climate change. Policy brief https://www.undp.org/content/dam/undp/library/gender/Gender%20and%20Environment/PB1-AP-Overview-Gender-and-climate-change.pdf

Goddard, S. (2009). Brokering change: Networks and entrepreneurs in international politics. *International Framework, 1*(2), 249–281. https://doi.org/10.1017/S1752971909000128

Goffman, E. (1974). *Frame analysis: An essay on the organization of experience.* Harvard University Press.

Gómez-Mera, L. (2015). International regime complexity and regional governance: Evidence from the Americas. *Global Governance: A Review of Multilateralism and International Organizations, 21*(1), 19–42. https://doi.org/10.1163/19426720-02101004

Goodman, J. (2009). From global justice to climate justice? Justice ecologism in an era of global warming. *New Political Science, 31*(4), 499–516. https://doi.org/10.1080/07393140903322570

Gough, C., & Shackley, S. (2001). The respectable politics of climate change: The epistemic communities and NGOs. *International Affairs, 77*(2), 329–345. https://doi.org/10.1111/1468-2346.00195

Granovetter, M. (1973). The strength of weak ties. *American Journal of Sociology, 78*(6), 1360–1380. https://doi.org/10.1086/225469

Green, J. F. (2013). *Rethinking private authority: Agents and entrepreneurs in global environmental governance.* Princeton University Press.

The Guardian. (2015). Paris climate activists put under house arrest using emergency laws. https://www.theguardian.com/environment/2015/nov/27/paris-climate-activists-put-under-house-arrest-using-emergency-laws

Gupta, J. (2014). *The history of global climate governance.* Cambridge University Press.

Haas, E. B. (1980). Why collaborate? Issue-linkage and international regimes. *World Politics, 32*(3), 357–405. https://doi.org/10.2307/2010109

Hadden, J. (2014). Explaining variation in transnational climate change activism: The role of inter-movement spillover. *Global Environmental Politics, 14*(2), 7–25.

Hadden, J. (2015). *Networks in contention.* Cambridge University Press.

Hafner-Burton, E. M. (2009). The power politics of regime complexity: Human rights trade conditionality in Europe. *Perspectives on Politics, 7*(1), 33–37. https://doi.org/10.1017/S1537592709090057

Hale, T. (2016). "All hands on deck": The Paris agreement and nonstate climate action. *Global Environmental Politics, 16*(3), 12–22.

Hale, T., Held, D., & Young, K. (2013). *Gridlock: Why global cooperation is failing when we need it most.* Polity Press.

Hall, N. (2015). Money or mandate? Why international organizations engage with the climate change regime. *Global Environmental Politics, 15*(2), 79–97. https://doi.org/10.1162/GLEP_a_00299

Hall, P., & Taylor, R. C. R. (1996). Political science and the three new institutionalisms. *Political Studies, 44*(5), 936–957. https://doi.org/10.1111/j.1467-9248.1996.tb00343.x

Hampton, P. (2015). *Workers and trade unions for climate solidarity: Tackling climate change in a neoliberal world*. New York: Routledge.

Hanegraaff, M. (2015). Transnational advocacy over time: Business and NGO mobilization at UN climate summits. *Global Environmental Politics, 15*(1), 83–104. https://doi.org/10.1162/GLEP_a_00273

Hanegraaff, M., Vergauwen, J., & Beyers, J. (2019). Should I stay or should I go? Explaining variation in nonstate actor advocacy over time in global governance. *Governance 1*, 1–18. https://doi.org/10.1111/gove.12427

Helfer, L. R. (2004). Regime shifting: The TRIPs agreement and new dynamics of international intellectual property lawmaking. *Yale Journal of International Law, 29*, 1–82. https://doi.org/10.2139/ssrn.459740

Hemmati, M. (2005). *Gender and Climate Change in the North: Issues, Entry Points, and Strategies for the Post-2012 Process and Beyond*. genanet/Focal Point Gender Justice and Sustainability, Berlin.

Hemmati, M., & Röhr, U. (2009). Engendering the climate-change negotiations: Experiences, challenges, and steps forward. *Gender and Development, 17*(1), 19–32.

Hjerpe, M., & Buhr, K. (2014). Frames of climate change in side events from Kyoto to Durban. *Global Environmental Politics, 14*(2), 102–121. https://doi.org/10.1162/GLEP_a_00231

Hoffmann, M. J. (2006). Beyond regime theory: Complex adaptation in the ozone depletion regime. In N. E. Harrison (Ed.), *Complexity in world politics: Concepts and methods of a new paradigm*. SUNY Press.

Hopgood, S. (2006). *Keepers of the flame: Understanding Amnesty International*. Cornell University Press.

Humphreys, D. (2004). Redefining the issues: NGO influence on international forest negotiations. *Global Environmental Politics, 4*(2), 51–74. https://doi.org/10.1162/152638004323074192

– (2008). NGO influence on international policy on forest conservation and trade in forest products. In M. M. Betsill and E. Corell (Eds.), *NGO diplomacy: The influence of nongovernmental organizations in international environmental negotiations*, 149–176. MIT Press.

Huq, S., Roberts, E., & Fenton, A. (2013). Loss and damage. *Nature Climate Change, 3*, 947–949. https://doi.org/10.1038/nclimate2026

ICHRP. (2008). Climate change and human rights: A rough guide. ICHRP.

IISD. (2014a). Summary of the twentieth Conference of the Parties to the UN Framework Convention on Climate Change. *Earth Negotiations Bulletin 12*(619).

– (2014b). Summary of the World Health Organization (WHO) Conference on Health and Climate. *Earth Negotiations Bulletin 224*(1).

– (2015). Summary of the twenty-first Conference of the Parties to the UN Framework Convention on Climate Change. *Earth Negotiations Bulletin 12*(663).

- (2016). Summary of the Bonn climate change conference. *Earth Negotiations Bulletin 12*(676).

ILO. (2015). *Guidelines for a just transition toward environmentally sustainable economies and societies for all.*

IPCC. (1995). *Climate Change 1995: Impacts, adaptations and mitigation of climate change: Scientific-technical analyses.* R. T. Watson, M. C. Zinyowera, & R. H. Moss (Eds).

- (2007a). *Climate Change 2007: Synthesis report. Contribution of working groups I, II, and III to the Fourth Assessment Report of the Intergovernmental Panel on Climate Change.* R. K. Pachauri and A. Reisinger (Eds.).

- (2007b). *Contribution of working group II to the Fourth Assessment Report of the Intergovernmental Panel on Climate Change.* M. L. Parry, O. F. Canziani, J. P. Palutikof, P. J. van der Linden, & C. E. Hanson (Eds.).

- (2014). *Climate Change 2014: Synthesis report. Contribution of working groups I, II, and III to the Fifth Assessment Report of the Intergovernmental Panel on Climate Change* core writing team, R.K. Pachauri and L.A. Meyer (eds.). IPCC, Geneva, Switzerland.

ITUC. (2007). Trade unions at the UN Framework Convention on Climate Change – UNFCCC COP13 [Report of activities]. http://www.ituc-csi.org /IMG/pdf/No_15_IV_-_WrapUpCOP13ReportFinal.pdf

- (2008). Trade unions at the UN Framework Convention on Climate Change UNFCCC – COP14, December 7–18, 2008 – Poznan, Poland. http://www .ituc-csi.org/IMG/pdf/WrapUpCOP14ReportITUC_Final.pdf

- (2009). Trade unions at the UN Framework Convention on Climate Change UNFCCC – COP15, December 7–18, 2009 – Copenhagen, Denmark. [Report of activities]. http://climate.ituc-csi.org/IMG/pdf/ITUC_COP15_ITUC _report_final.pdf

- (2010). Resolution on combatting climate change through sustainable development and a just transition. http://www.ituc-csi.org/IMG/pdf /2CO_10_Sustainable_development_and_Climate_Change_03-10-2.pdf

- (2015). Call for dialogue: Climate action requires just transition. http:// www.ituc-csi.org/IMG/pdf/call_for_dialogue_en.pdf.

Jinnah, S. (2011). Climate change bandwagoning: The impacts of strategic linkages on regime design, maintenance and death. *Global Environmental Politics, 11*(3), 1–9. https://doi.org/10.1162/GLEP_a_00065

- (2014). *Post-treaty politics: Secretariat influence in global environmental governance.* MIT Press.

Jinnah, S., Munoz Cabre, M., & Kulovesi, K. (2009). Tripping points: Barriers and bargaining chips on the road to Copenhagen. *Environmental Research Letters, 4*(3). https://doi.org/10.1088/1748-9326/4/3/034003

Joachim, J. (2007). *Agenda setting, the UN, and NGOs: Gender violence and reproductive rights.* Georgetown University Press.

Jönsson, C., & Tallberg, J. (2010). *Transnational actors in global governance: Patterns, explanations, and implications*. New York: Palgrave and Macmillon.

Junk, W. M., & Rasmussen, A. (2019). Framing by the flock: collective issue definition and advocacy success. *Comparative Political Studies, 52*(4), 483–513. https://doi.org/10.1177/0010414018784044. PMid:30886439 PMCid: PMC6380451

Kapstein, E. B., & Busby, J. W. (2013). *AIDS drugs for all: Social movements and market transformations*. Cambridge: Cambridge University Press.

Keck, M. E. & Sikkink, K. (1998). *Activists beyond borders: Advocacy networks in transnational politics*. Cornell University Press.

Khagram, S., Riker, J. V., & Sikkink, K. (Eds). (2002). *Restructuring world politics: Transnational social movements, networks, and norms*. University of Minnesota Press.

Kingdon, J. W. (1984). *Agendas, alternatives, and public policies*. HarperCollins.

Kitschelt, H. (1986). Political opportunity structures and political protest: Anti-nuclear movements in four democracies. *British Journal of Political Science, 16*(1), 57–85. https://doi.org/10.1017/S000712340000380X

Knox, J. H. (2009). Linking human rights and climate change at the United Nations. *Harvard Environmental Law Review, 33,* 477–498.

Kohler, B. (1998). Just transition – a labour view of sustainable development. *CEP Journal 6*(2).

Krasner, S. D. (1983). Structural causes and regime consequences: Regimes as intervening variables. In S. D. Krasner, *International Regimes* (pp. 1–21). Cornell University Press.

Labor Notes. (2000). What to know about the WTO: A union activists' guide. http://www.labornotes.org/2000/02/what-know-about-wto-union-activists-guide

Lake, D. A., and Wong, W. (2009). The politics of networks: Interests, power, and human rights norms. In M. Kahler (Ed.),*Networked politics: Agency, power, and governance*. Cornell University Press.

Laumann, E. O., Marsden, P. V., & Prensky, D. (1989). The boundary specification problem in network analysis. In R. S. Burt & M. J. Minor (Eds.),*Applied network analysis* (pp.18–34). Sage.

Lecocq, F., and Capoor, K. (2005). *State and trends of the carbon market 2005 (English)*. World Bank Group. http://documents.worldbank.org/curated/en/310671468139796353/State-and-trends-of-the-carbon-market-2005

Levy, M. A., Young, O. R., & Zurn, M. (1995). The study of international regimes. *European Journal of International Relations, 1*(3), 267–330. https://doi.org/10.1177/1354066195001003001

Lisowski, M. (2005). How NGOs use their facilitative negotiating power and bargaining assets to affect international environmental negotiations.

Diplomacy and Statecraft, 16(2), 361–383. https://doi.org/10.1080
/09592290590948405

Lowder, J. B. (2014, September 8). "Queering the Climate." *Slate*. http://www
.slate.com/blogs/outward/2014/09/08/queers_for_the_climate_why
_queer_people_should_get_involved_with_climate.html

Marin, A., & Wellman, B. (2010). Social network analysis: An introduction."
In J. Scott and P. J. Carrington (Eds), *The SAGE Handbook of Social Network
Analysis*. Sage.

McAdam, D., McCarthy, J. D., Zald, M. N., & Mayer, N. Z. (Eds.). (1996).
*Comparative perspectives on social movements: Political opportunities, mobilizing
structures, and cultural framings*. Cambridge: Cambridge University Press.

Meyer, D. S. (2004). Protest and political opportunities. *Annual Review of
Sociology, 30*, 125–145. https://doi.org/10.1146/annurev.soc.30.012703.110545

Meyer, T. M., et al. (2012). A public health frame arouses hopeful emotions
about climate change. *Climatic Change, 113*, 1105–1112. https://doi.org
/10.1007/s10584-012-0513-6

Moghadam, V. M. (2005). *Globalizing women: Transnational feminist networks*.
Washington DC: Johns Hopkins University Press.

Muñoz Cabré, M. (2011). Issue-linkages to climate change measured through
NGO participation in the UNFCCC. *Global environmental politics, 11*(3), 10–22.
https://doi.org/10.1162/GLEP_a_00066

Murdie, A., & Davis, D. R. (2012). Looking in the mirror: Comparing INGO
networks across issue areas. *The Review of International Organizations, 7*,
177–202. https://doi.org/10.1007/s11558-011-9134-5

Murdie, A., & Peksen, D. (2014). The impact of human rights INGO shaming
on humanitarian intervention. *Journal of Politics, 76*(1), 215–228. https://doi
.org/10.1017/S0022381613001242

Murdie, A., & Urpelainen, J. (2014). Why pick on us? Environmental INGOs
and state shaming as strategic substitute. *Political Studies, 63*(2), 353–372.
https://doi.org/10.1111/1467-9248.12101

Nasiritousi, N., Hjerpe, M., & Bäckstrand, K. (2015). Normative arguments
for non-state actors participation in international policymaking processes:
Functionalism, neocorporativism, or democratic pluralism. *European Journal
of International Relations, 22*(4), 920–943. doi:10.1177/1354066115608926

Newell, P. J. (2006). *Climate for change: Non-state actors and the global politics of
the greenhouse*. Cambridge University Press.

– (2008). Civil society, corporate accountability, and the politics of climate
change. *Global Environmental Politics, 8*(3), 122–154. https://doi.org/10.1162
/glep.2008.8.3.122

Nicholson, S., & Chong, D. (2011). Jumping on the human rights bandwagon:
How rights-based linkages can refocus climate politics. *Global Environmental
Politics, 11*(3), 121–136.

OHCHR. (2009). Report of the office of the United Nations high commissioner for human rights on the relationship between climate change and human rights. UN Doc. A/HRC/10/61

O'Neill, K. (2012). Comparative study of social movements. In P. F. Steinberg & S. D. VanDeveer (Eds.), *Comparative environmental politics: Theory, practice, and prospects*. MIT Press.

Orr, S. K. (2006). Policy subsystems and regimes: Organized interests and climate change policy. *Policy Studies Journal, 34*(2), 147–169. https://doi.org /10.1111/j.1541-0072.2006.00164.x

– (2007). The evolution of climate policy – business and environmental organizations: Between alliance building and entrenchment. In K. Ronit (Ed.), *Global policy arrangements: Business and the countervailing powers of civil society* (pp. 154–173). Routledge.

– (2016). Institutional control and climate change activism at COP 21 in Paris. *Global Environmental Politics, 16*(3), 23–30. https://doi.org/10.1162/GLEP _a_00363

Orsini, A. (2013). Multi-forum non-state actors: Navigating the regime complexes for forestry and genetic resources. *Global Environmental Politics, 13*(3), 34–55. https://doi.org/10.1162/GLEP_a_00182

Orsini, A., Morin, J-F., & Young, O. (2013). Regime complexes: A buzz, a boom, or a boost for global governance?" *Global Governance, 19*(1), 27–39. https:// doi.org/10.1163/19426720-01901003

Paterson, M. (2019). Using negotiation sites for richer collection of network data. *Global Environmental Politics, 19*(2), 81–92. https://doi.org/10.1162 /glep_a_00504

Picard, A. (2016). Climate change a significant threat to public health, CMA members hear. *The Globe and Mail*. http://www.theglobeandmail.com /news/national/climate-change-a-significant-threat-to-public-health-cma -members-hear/article31501589/

Population Matters. (n.d.). About PopOffsets. http://www.popoffsets.org /about.php

Price, R. (1998). Reversing the gun sights: Transnational civil society targets land mines. *International Organization, 52*(3), 613–644. https://doi.org/10.1162 /002081898550671

– (2003). Transnational civil society and advocacy in world politics. *World Politics, 55*(4), 579–606. https://doi.org/10.1353/wp.2003.0024

Rahman, A., & Roncerel, A. (1994). A view from the ground up. In I. M. Mintzer and J. A. Leonard (Eds),*Negotiating climate change: The inside story of the Rio Convention* (pp. 239–273). Cambridge University Press.

Rao, K. P. R., and Bazilli, S. (2013). Gender-responsive climate change initiatives and decisionmaking global gender and climate alliance – GGCA: Evaluation Report, Volume 1. https://erc.undp.org/evaluation/evaluations /detail/7042

Räthzel, N., & Uzzell, D. (2011). Trade unions and climate change: The jobs versus environment dilemma. *Global Environmental Change, 21*(4), 1215–1223. https://doi.org/10.1016/j.gloenvcha.2011.07.010

Raustiala, K. (1997). States, NGOs, and international environmental institutions. *International Studies Quarterly, 41*(4), 719–740. https://doi.org /10.1111/1468-2478.00064

Raustiala, K., & Victor, D. G. (2004). The regime complex for plant genetic resources. *International Organization, 58*(2), 277–309. https://doi.org/10.1017 /S0020818304582036

Röhr, U. (2007). Gender, climate change, and adaptation. Introduction to the gender dimensions. In *Adapting to climate change: How local experiences can shape the debate* [Briefing paper]. http://www.unep.org/roa/amcen /Projects_Programme/climate_change/PreCop15/Proceedings/Gender -and-climate-change/Roehr_Gender_climate.pdf

Rosemberg, A. (2010). Building a just transition: The linkages between climate change and employment. *International Journal of Labour Research, 2*(2), 125–141. https://doi.org/10.5848/ILO.978-9-221254-79-9_2

– (2013). Developing global environmental union parties through the International Trade Union Confederation. In N. Räthzel & D. Uzzell (Eds.), *Trade unions in the green economy: Working for the environment* (pp. 15–28). Routledge.

Ruggie, John Gerard, ed. (1993). *Multilateralism matters: The theory and praxis of an institutional form.* Columbia University Press.

Sakaguchi, I. (2013). The roles of activist NGOs in the development and transformation of IWC regime: The interaction of norms and power. *Journal of Environmental Studies and Sciences, 3,* 194–208. https://doi.org/10.1007 /s13412-013-0114-3

Schattschneider, E. E. (1960). *The semi-sovereign people.* Holt, Rinehart and Winston.

Schipper, E. L. F. (2006). Conceptual history of adaptation in the UNFCCC process. *RECIEL: Review of European Community and International Environmental Law, 15*(1), 82–92. https://doi.org/10.1111/j.1467-9388.2006 .00501.x

Schlosberg, D., & Collins, L. B. (2014). From environmental to climate justice: Climate change and the discourse of environmental justice. *WIREs Clim Change, 5*(3), 359–374. https://doi.org/10.1002/wcc.275

Schreurs, M. A., Selin, H., & VanDeveer, S. D. (2009). *Transatlantic environment and energy politics: Comparative and international perspectives.* Surrey, UK: Ashgate.

Scott, J. (2000). *Social network analysis: A handbook* (2nd ed.). Sage.

Selin, H., & VanDeveer, S. D. (2003). Mapping institutional linkages in European air politics. *Global Environmental Politics, 3*(3), 14–46. https://doi.org/10.1162 /152638003322469268

Snell, D., & Fairbrother, P. (2012). Just transition and labour environmentalism in Australia. In N. Räthzel and D. Uzzell (Eds.), *Trade unions in the green economy: Working for the environment* (pp. 146–161). Routledge.

Snow, R. D., & Benford, R. D. (1988). Ideology, frame resonance, and participant mobilization. *International Social Movement Research, 1,* 197–217.

Smith, J. (2008). *Social movements for global democracy.* Washington DC: Johns Hopkins University Press.

Steffek, J. (2010). Explaining patterns of transnational participations: The role of policy fields. In C. Jönsson & J. Tallberg (Eds.), *Transnational actors in global governance: Patterns, explanations, and implications* (pp. 67–87). Palgrave Macmillan.

Stroup, S. S., & Wong, W. (2017). *The authority trap.* Cornell: Cornell University Press.

Sundstrom, L. M. (2005). Foreign assistance, international norms, and NGO development: Lessons from the Russian campaign. *International Organization, 59*(2), 419–449. https://doi.org/10.1017/S0020818305050149

– (2006). *Funding civil society: Foreign assistance and NGO development in Russia.* Stanford University Press.

SustainLabour. (2010). 2010: Finding reasons to persevere [Annual report]. http://www.sustainlabour.org/reportesanuales.php?lang=EN

– (2011). 2011: Toward Rio+20 [Annual report]. http://www.sustainlabour.org/reportesanuales.php?lang=EN

Sweeney, S. (2014). Unions, climate change, and the great inaction: The "green economy" illusion and the need for a programmatic shift. http://unionsforenergydemocracy.org/wp-content/uploads/2014/09/TUED-working-paper-2.pdf

Tallberg, J., et al. (2013). *The opening up of international organizations.* Cambridge: Cambridge University Press.

Tarrow, S. (1998). *Power in movement: Social movements and contentious politics.* Cambridge University Press.

– (2001). Transnational politics: Contention and institutions in international politics. *Annual Review of Political Science, 4,* 1–20. https://doi.org/10.1146/annurev.polisci.4.1.1

– (2005). *The new transnational activism.* Cambridge University Press.

Tarrow, S., & McAdam, D. (2005). Scale shift in transnational contention. In D. Della Porta and S. Tarrow (Eds.), *Transnational protest and global activism* (pp. 121–150). New York: Rowman & Littlefield.

Thelen, K., & Steinmo, S. (1992). Historical institutionalism in comparative politics. In S. Steinmo et al. (Eds), *Structuring politics: Historical institutionalism in comparative analysis* (pp. 1–32). Cambridge University Press.

Tilly, C. (1978). *From mobilization to revolution.* Addison-Wesley.

Tilly, C., and Tarrow, S. G. (2015). *Contentious politics*. Oxford: Oxford University Press.

Turbulence Collective. (2007). Are we winning? http://www.turbulence.org .uk/turbulence-1/are-we-winning/index.html

UNDP. (2012). Gender and climate change training module: Overview of linkages between gender and climate change. http://gest.unu.edu/static /files/tm1_africa_genderclimatechange_overview.pdf

UNEP. (2007). Labour and the environment: A natural synergy. https:// wedocs.unep.org/bitstream/handle/20.500.11822/7448/-Labour%20and %20the%20Environment_%20A%20Natural%20Synergy-2007739.pdf ?sequence=3&isAllowed=y

— (2008). Green jobs: Towards a decent work in a sustainable, low-carbon world. http://www.ilo.org/wcmsp5/groups/public/---ed_emp/---emp _ent/documents/publication/wcms_158727.pdf

UNFCCC. (1992). The UN Framework Convention on Climate Change.

— (2012). WHO submission on national adaptation plans. http://unfccc.int /resource/docs/2012/smsn/igo/60.pdf

— (2015). Decision 1/CP.21. The Paris Agreement on climate change.

Unmüßig, B. (2011). *NGOs and climate crisis: Fragmentation, lines of conflict, and strategic approaches*. Berlin: Ecology & Energy Heinrich Böll Foundation.

UN Secretary General. (2007). Chair summary on the high-level event on climate change as read by the secretary-general. https://www.un.org/sg /en/content/sg/statement/2007-09-24/ chair-summary-high-level-event-climate-change-read-secretary-general

UN Women. (2015). In Mali, renewable energy boosts agricultural production. http://www.unwomen.org/en/news/stories/2015/9/mali-renewable -energy

Victor, D. G. (2001). *The collapse of the Kyoto Protocol*. Princeton University Press.

— (2011). *Global warming gridlock*. Cambridge University Press.

Wamukona, N., & Skutsch, M. (2008). Is there a gender angle to the climate negotiations? UNEP. http://www.unep.org/roa/amcen/Projects _Programme/climate_change/PreCop15/Proceedings/Gender-and-climate -change/IsthereaGenderAngletotheClimateChangeNegiotiations.pdf

Wapner, P. (1996). *Environmental activism and world civic politics*. SUNY Press.

— (2002). Horizontal politics: Transnational environmental activism and global cultural change. *Global Environmental Politics*, 2(2), 37–62. https://doi.org /10.1162/15263800260047826

Watts, N., et al. (2015). Health and climate change: Policy responses to protect public health. *The Lancet*, 386(10006), 1861–1914. https://doi.org/10.1016 /S0140-6736(15)60854-6

Weible, C. M. (2007). An advocacy coalition framework approach to stakeholder analysis: Understanding the political context of California marine protected area policy. *Journal of Public Administration Research and Framework: J-PART*, *17*(1), 95–117. https://doi.org/10.1093/jopart/muj015

WHO & Health Care Without Harm. (2013). Healthy hospitals, health planet, healthy people: Addressing climate change in health care settings [Discussion draft]. https://www.who.int/globalchange/publications/healthcare_settings/en/

Williams, M. (2016). *Gender and climate change financing: Coming out of the margin.* Routledge.

Women and Gender Constituency. (n.d.). Call for a gender/woman paragraph in the shared vision. http://gendercc.net/fileadmin/inhalte/dokumente/6_UNFCCC/women_and_gender-input-shared-vision.pdf

– (2012). From research to action, leaf by leaf: Getting gender right in REDD+ SES – 1. http://www.wedo.org/wp-content/uploads/leafbyleaf_booklet1_web.pdf

World Medical Association. (2008). Delhi declaration on health and climate change. http://www.wma.net/en/30publications/10policies/c5/

Young, O. R. (2010).*Institutional dynamics: Emergent patterns in international environmental governance*. MIT Press.

Zelli, F. (2011). The fragmentation of the global climate governance architecture. *Wiley Interdisciplinary Reviews: Climate Change*, *2*(2), 255–270. https://doi.org/10.1002/wcc.104

Zelli, F., & Van Asselt, H. (2013). Introduction: The institutional fragmentation of global environmental governance: Causes, consequences, and responses. *Global environmental politics*, *13*(3), 1–13. https://doi.org/10.1162/GLEP_a_00180

Index